POPULATION FALLACIES

POPULATION FALLACIES

JACK PARSONS

ELEK/PEMBERTON
LONDON

First published in Great Britain in 1977 by
Elek Books Ltd, 54–58 Caledonian Road, London N1 9RN
for Pemberton Publishing Co. Ltd.

ISBN 0 301 74031 3 (Cloth)
ISBN 0 301 74032 1 (Paper)

Printed in Great Britain by
Unwin Brothers Limited
The Gresham Press, Old Woking, Surrey

DEDICATION

To all those workers by hand and brain whose labour produces the 'surplus' wealth which has enabled me to sit, read, think, discuss and write in comfort and such tranquillity as I am capable of.

It is not taken for granted.

CONTENTS

Preface

This book has had a somewhat chequered career. I started writing a book called *The Population Challenge* in 1965, but this grew and grew until, by about 1968, it became clear that there was already enough material for two books, perhaps even more, and the problems of determining the planes of cleavage and orders of priority became urgent. However, with the kind help of the late Hector Hawton, then Managing Director of the Pemberton Publishing Company, and not a little heartburn, these were solved. After some reworking and rounding off, the most important of my population fallacies, that of individual liberty, was published in 1971 under the title *Population Versus Liberty.*

I then set to work to collect, update, rewrite and amplify all of the material which had been laid aside, this process being greatly helped by a year's sabbatical leave from Brunel University (hence my Dedication) which was spent at our quiet Buckinghamshire home.

After twelve months of peaceful retreat had produced a longish book, the rapidly worsening economic climate constrained my publisher to plead for a shortish book instead, so that a good deal of delicate and somewhat traumatic filleting was needed before the reduced manuscript could be handed over in the spring of 1973.

By this time the Pemberton Publishing Company was in a turmoil of reorganisation, finally leading to a partnership with Elek Books, which was further complicated by staff turnover. Delays mounted, so that only in the summer of 1976 did I correct the proofs and write this Preface. During the long years of waiting, a crisis of conscience developed about whether the book should be published at all, but as there had been some opportunity for updating tables and so forth, and the arguments had been designed to be as near universally valid as possible, both my publishers and I were able to decide—with last-minute corrections—to let it stand.

With regard to the rest of the material accumulated for the original book, plus another eight years of my somewhat magpie-like researching, I hope I can truthfully say that a third book is somewhere in the pipeline. This one—a development of a theme started in the first volume to be published—ought to be called *The Ecology of Liberty*, and it is expected to contain a substantial section on migration control. Another, at some even less determinate point in the gestation process, is on the critical and much neglected topic of competitive breeding. However, the heavy demands made by my new job at the David Owen Centre for Population Studies, mean that both will be a long time in the making.

Acknowledgements

First of all, I wish to thank my wife, Barbara, who has again tapped out many tens of thousands of words on succeeding drafts, an especially onerous task when editing, and mounting delays and the necessary up-dating, involved the rewriting of a good deal of ostensibly completed material.

I also owe a debt to those of my former colleagues at Brunel University who took on the non-droppable parts of my work in the School of Social Sciences so that I was able to enjoy a year's sabbatical leave in the academic session 1972–73 and concentrate on getting the book into shape.

My thanks are also due to Dave Waterman, from the Physics Department at Brunel, who read the manuscript and checked all the figures and calculations, especially those in the never-never land of exponential economic growth which mostly turn out to be totally unacceptable until they have been checked at least twice.

I thank also the secretarial staff at the David Owen Centre—Diana Alexander, Lillian and Vivienne Lewis—who, in the frenzied final burst to get the bibliography and indexes finished and typed before the 1976 academic session began, put in many hours of hard work in the face of seemingly endless interruptions.

I am indebted to Mr George H. Brown, Director of the Bureau of Census of the US Department of Commerce, for literature and further information on the American population 'clock', and I wish to express my gratitude for substantial help in sorting out some tricky statistical problems, especially for table 2/1, given by several officials of the Office of Population Censuses and Surveys, who prefer to remain anonymous. Similarly, I thank the Inner London Education Authority's Research Group for permission to use some of their unpublished material, and to the Principal Probation Officer of Dumbartonshire, Mr W. R. McGregor, for information on family size and delinquency.

It is obvious from the references and bibliography that I owe a debt approaching the astronomical dimensions discussed in chapter 6, to the army of researchers and scholars beavering away to increase and disseminate knowledge and understanding in a wide range of fields. I hope that any of them who happen to see their material here will feel it has been put to reasonably good use. If any of them have views about this I shall be glad to learn what they are.

Finally, I want to thank all those who have helped to further the development of my views on the topics dealt with here by listening, arguing, criticising, making counter-proposals and generally being friendly and constructive, especially the members of the many scores of audiences I have been fortunate enough to encounter up and down the country, both within the groves of Academe and outside, over the last fifteen years. The rapport which developed on a surprising number of these occasions has moved and inspired me and I am very grateful to them all.

If any person who feels that he or she has made a particular contribution is omitted from these acknowledgements, I apologise.

Thanks are due to the following publishers for permission to reprint tables, figures, or both:

George Allen & Unwin Ltd, London, for the PEP extracts.
Dover Publications, New York, for the Lotka & Gause diagrams.
Victor Gollancz, London, for the William Petersen material.
Her Majesty's Stationery Office for a number of tables, all of which are also acknowledged in the text.
Macmillan & Co. London, for the table from Roy Glenday.
Random House, Inc., New York, for the Thomlinson and Wrong diagrams.

LIST OF TABLES AND FIGURES

Part I

A RECAPITULATION

CHAPTER 1

The philosophical argument: The fallacy of individual liberty

'Governments must ensure that . . . people are free to follow the mandates of their own conscience in the matter of family size.' Report of the Second World Food Congress.[1]

'The family . . . should . . . have the right to decide the number of its children.' First UN declaration on family planning.[2]

'One thing is sure; compulsion is out.' Lord Kennet, Conference of Labour Women.[3]

'The State has no business in the bedroom of the nation.' Pierre Trudeau.[4]

'Freedom of choice is the essential condition . . .' Douglas Houghton, MP.[5]

These quotations clearly express what I have called 'the fallacy of individual liberty',[6] and they could be matched by many others. But the fallacy's clearest expression, paradoxically, is not in words at all but in the conspiracy of silence on the part of Government, parties, churches, and conservation groups,[7] and the almost total lack of effective action. Population control is officially a non-subject largely because it is feared that it would be seen as an invasion of individual liberty.

The argument can be stated simply, as follows:

First premise: We now have liberty of the individual.

Second premise: Liberty must not be reduced.

Third premise: Population control would reduce individual liberty.

Conclusion: Population control must be opposed.

This mode of arguing is based on an even more fundamental

3

fallacy, that liberty and control in society are inversely related, a belief which may be expressed as follows:

First premise: All social controls reduce individual liberty.
Second premise: Population control is a form of social control.
Conclusion: Population control would reduce individual liberty.

This belief seriously misrepresents not only control and liberty, but the whole social process; it would be nearer the truth to stand it completely on its head and argue that without control there is no liberty at all. As Cicero put it: 'We are all the law's slaves that we may be free.' Liberty as we experience and value it, in other words, is not the antithesis but in part at least the *product* of social control; though of course it does not follow that the more controls we impose on ourselves the freer we are. With either too little or too much control, we miss out on liberty, and if we wish to maximise it our problem is one of optimising social control rather than minimising it.

Liberty, however, means many things to many people, and it is necessary to define what is meant here. My own formula involves looking on a person's liberty as the sum of all his *microfreedoms*, where a microfreedom is one single and indivisible freedom from something undesirable or freedom to do something which is desirable. When we get down to asking what particular individuals are actually free to enjoy or free not to have to endure, we are brought face to face with the fact that not only is it possible for A's freedom to guarantee B's slavery, but that A's minifreedom number one can conflict with his own desired minifreedom number two, and so on.

Where two or more microfreedoms conflict it becomes necessary to choose between them, and from a series of choices we can construct a pyramid of mutually compatible microfreedoms, with the most important one, at the top, resting on increasing numbers of lesser microfreedoms in the layers below. In this connection we can ask whether the microfreedom to reproduce ad lib should be at the top, or whether the microfreedoms from hunger, poverty, overcrowding, excessive competition for scarce resources—including amenities such as clean air and wild life—ought to have equal or greater weight.

4

From this analysis we can write a little equation for liberty as follows:

$$Mf = \sum_{0}^{n} mf$$

This simply means that macrofreedom—the total liberty of one individual—is equal to the sum of his microfreedoms, as follows:

1. Microfreedoms *for*: the sum of all the things he can do if he wants to, and;
2. Microfreedoms *from*: the sum of all the things he does not have to put up with against his will.

Thinking in these terms we can return to the population control and individual liberty problem and see immediately that its formulation was inadequate and misleading as it stood. Instead of asking the question, 'Would population control reduce individual liberty?', we must ask two related questions: 'Which would reduce individual liberty *most*: (1) Population control, or, (2) Unrestricted population growth?'

The effect of population growth is complex: it enhances some existing microfreedoms and creates some quite new ones, but it must also progressively diminish some existing microfreedoms and destroy others completely. As numbers continue to increase, the microfreedoms being diminished or destroyed tend more and more to be the most fundamental ones—such as freedom from overcrowding, hunger, and violence—so that, beyond a certain critical point, population control is necessary not *in spite* of the need to preserve individual liberty, but *in order* to preserve it.

The will of the people

Rousseau argued that liberty resides to some degree in the expression of the will of the people. Over this issue, the will of the people is clear—public opinion has been shown to be overwhelmingly in favour of population control. I have documented this elsewhere,[8] and will here merely repeat one example and quote two more recent pieces of evidence. The first results from a survey carried out by the South Buckinghamshire branch of the Conservation Society. In this largely

5

rural area, insulated to some degree from population pressure, the survey showed that:

(1) 88% of those responding thought that family planning should be provided free under the National Health Service;

(2) 74% thought that Great Britain was already overpopulated;

(3) $57\frac{1}{2}$% that it may become necessary for the Government to exert some influence over family size;

(4) 56% approved the use of tax incentives as a way of encouraging smaller families.[9]

These results, though interesting, are local. But there is a vast array of evidence collected on a national scale, to support them. Two recent surveys, one commissioned by the Birth Control Campaign and carried out by National Opinion Polls, and another by *New Society*—have confirmed the earlier findings.[10] The *New Society* survey, on attitudes and expectations in many fields, showed that on the question of free or cheap abortion on demand, 46% thought it desirable and likely, while a further 19% thought it desirable but unlikely in present circumstances. With respect to free contraception on the NHS, 79% thought it both desirable and likely and 16% desirable though unlikely—a staggering 95% consensus.

The survey conducted by NOP for the Birth Control Campaign, repeating in December 1972 the essentials of the NOP *Daily Mail* survey of January 1972, showed a striking increase in support for population control over the year. By

Table 1/1

Percentage Proportions thinking Britain's population presents problems—January and December, 1972

Seriousness of problem	Very Serious	Serious	A problem	No problem
January	23	34	28	12
December	36	30	21	9

6

December the proportion agreeing that the Government should take steps to slow down population growth had increased from 64% to 71%. The proportions thinking that our population growth presents problems increased as shown in Table 1/1. The most striking change here is the shift from 23% to 36% in the 'very serious' category; and we see that in toto 87% think our numbers present a problem, no less than two-thirds thinking it 'serious' or 'very serious'. In addition, 60% thought that the Government should spend money on a national education and publicity campaign for birth control.

Ross Panel on Population control and liberty

The Ross Panel Report,[11] though a very much milder and more discreet document than the Report of the Parliamentary Select Committee,[12] nevertheless did deal with the question of population control and liberty and—after an almost spirited rejection of any Governmental interference in family life— came down quite firmly in favour of an effective Government policy, including the future use of sanctions if and when the situation deteriorates appreciably.

'Sooner or later, Britain must face the fact that its population cannot go on increasing indefinitely. Society will have to adapt itself to . . . a stationary population . . . the time has come when the Government should consider whether, and if so, how to act to influence the rate of population growth' (para. 35).

'. . . Public opinion now demands and the facts of the population situation require that the Government define its attitude to questions concerning the level and rate of increase of population' (para. 36).

While arguing that 'The situation is not such as to require immediate . . . initiatives . . . to reduce dramatically the rate of increase' (para. 32), the Panel put forward part of the case argued in *Population Versus Liberty*, in the following words: '. . . a large . . . population would entail a very complex organisational system to cope with all its demands . . . in the middle of the century it would necessitate a considerably more regulated society than at present.' (para. 369).

Having accepted these facts it gently paves the way for future controls: 'Any policies designed to influence the number of children people have would involve some extension of the role of the State *as so far conceived* in this country . . . and raise very deep questions of individual freedom and the privacy of the family. . . . Any approach to population questions must recognise the importance of these issues' (para. 379; italics added).

It should be noted that controls are by no means ruled out: 'If . . . family size were to remain well above replacement level in the long term, a situation would arise where the use of persuasive techniques of more direct fiscal measures (or both) might have to be considered.' They reinforced these arguments by pointing out that parents '. . . do not take account of the implication of their own decisions about family size on the overall population situation: there is no reason why the sum of individual rational decisions should produce the rate of population growth which the community as a whole would choose' (para. 394b). They also gave a timely warning about the long delays which may be met, and urged an early start on initiating the necessary measures: 'Given the time that any measures to affect population growth might take to act, and the in-built momentum due to the age-structure of the population, any slowing down of population growth would have to start some 60 years in advance of the time of reaching a stationary population' (para. 375).

One of the first acts of the first 1974 Labour Administration, in a very difficult and unpromising economic climate, was to make the family planning service free and appoint a Minister to oversee population problems. At the uppermost levels of our political hierarchy the seeds of population control seem to have taken firm root, even if those concerned refuse to acknowledge the fact or make their policies explicit.[13]

Postscript

It is possible to derive a little comfort from the latest world population figures which show that socio-economic development and population control programmes are beginning to bite. Ray Ravenholt of the US Agency for International Development has now calculated that the annual rate of increase has dropped by mid-1974 from 2 percent to 1·63 percent and the absolute increase from around 75 to 63 millions. At that time the crude birth rate was 28·1, the death rate 11·8, and natural increase 16·3. The mid 1976 total was 4,009 millions. See his paper World Epidemiology and Potential Fertility Impact of Voluntary Sterilisation Services', presented to the Third International Conference on Voluntary Sterilisation, Tunis, 2 February 1976.

CHAPTER 2

The latest population figures in brief

Section A: World population
World population is increasing fairly precisely along the lines projected for some years now, and, barring major calamities, the 4,000 million mark will have been passed by mid-1976. The overall crude death rate is about 13 per thousand and the birth rate around 33 per thousand, giving a natural increase of 20 per thousand, equal to 2% per annum. In terms of numbers, this means a yearly increment of 80 millions, roughly equal to the combined populations of the United Kingdom, Belgium, and the Netherlands. Of course birth and death rates vary a great deal from country to country; in the case of births, from 9·1 in West Berlin up to 52 per thousand in Niger, Rwanda and Swaziland. Death rates vary from 5 per thousand in Fiji, Singapore, Hong Kong, and Taiwan[1] up to 30 in Angola and Portuguese Guinea. Infant mortality varies from 229 per thousand live births in Gabon to 11·1 in Sweden, and life expectancy at birth (male and female combined) from the lowest world figure of 34 years in Angola and Portuguese Guinea, up to 74·5 in Sweden.

Projections
Official United Nations projections for the world population are not published annually, a fact presenting a problem for those interested in population questions, but the Population Reference Bureau reported on their behalf in 1974 (for 1973) a 'medium' estimate of 6,500 millions for the year 2000, implying that the annual increase of 2% a year will continue at least until then. Virtually all commentators are agreed that in the absence of calamities on a scale never before conceived, nothing can prevent this massive increase in world population, at least one further doubling, and probably more. Although

9

population control programmes are spreading and intensifying, it is a practical impossibility for them to bring growth to a halt in less than two generations because of the high preponderance of young people[2] at the present time and the great momentum of cultural values and social institutions at present favouring high fertility.[3]

We must all face the fact that this great surge in numbers will continue, putting colossal pressure on the world's already strained resources, and we must do all we can to make the best of it by becoming as self-sufficient as possible and reducing our drain on the raw materials, sources of energy, and food so badly needed by the exploding populations of the third world.

Section B: The United Kingdom
Since *Population Versus Liberty* the situation has improved in the sense that our crude birth rate has fallen from 16·3 per

Figure 2/1.   Natural increase UK 1946–1974 inc.

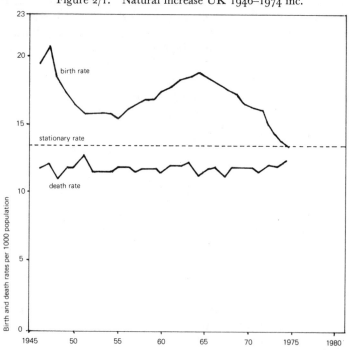

thousand (in 1970) to 14·0 in 1973. At the same time, however, things have got worse in another sense. Although the birth rate has been falling, it has still been above the replacement rate so that numbers have increased by more than half a million[4] in spite of an excess of emigrants over immigrants of about 120,000.

The changes in our population year by year since the

Table 2/1

UK population since 1945 (1,000s)§

Mid-year ending	Births		Deaths		Natural increase	Net migration	Other changes	Net increase	Increase since 1945	Mid-year population* Total/Home
	No.	rate†	No.	rate†						
1945										49,182
6	838	19·4	569	11·6	270	−235		35	35	49,217
7	1,059	20·7	606	12·1	453	−150		303	338	49,520
8	945	18·1	537	10·9	409	+85		494	832	50,014
9	878	17·0	588	11·7	290	+8		298	1,130	50,312
1950	837	16·2	580	11·7	258	−5		253	1,383	50,565
1	811	15·8	652	12·6	158		..*	−275*	1,108*	50,290
2	786	15·7	560	11·4	227		−86	141	1,249	50,431
3	800	15·9	597	11·4	203		−41	162	1,411	50,593
4	801	15·7	563	11·4	239		−67	172	1,583	50,765
5	785	15·5	603	11·7	182		−1	181	1,764	50,946
6	812	16·1	592	11·7	219		+18	237	2,001	51,184
7	835	16·6	557	11·5	278		−32	247	2,248	51,430
8	862	16·9	630	11·7	232		−10	222	2,470	51,652
9	880	16·9	615	11·7	264		+39	304	2,774	51,956
1960	890	17·5	578	11·5	311		+105	416	3,190	52,372
1	932	17·9	635	12·0	296		+138	435	3,625	52,807
2	965	18·3	636	11·9	329	+112	+26	467	4,092	53,274
3	981	18·5	657	12·2	324	−31	−14	278	4,370	53,553
4	1,000	18·8	606	11·3	393	−32	−28	333	4,703	53,885
5	1,006	18·4	616	11·6	390	−33	−24	333	5,036	54,218
6	987	18·0	648	11·8	339	−58	+2	282	5,318	54,500
7	982	17·6	609	11·3	373	−88	+15	300	5,618	54,800
8	948	17·2	658	11·9	289	−37	−4	249	5,867	55,049
9	943	16·6	646	11·9	296	−54	−28	214	6,081	55,263
1970	899	16·3	667	11·8	232	−60	−14	158	6,239	55,421
1	915	16·2	639	11·6	276	−39	−48	188	6,427	55,610
2	865	14·9	661	12·1	204	−34	+14	184	6,611	55,793
3	807	13·9	672	12·0	135	+4	+1	140	6,751	55,933
4	752	13·2	664	11·9	88	−55	−1	31	6,782	55,965
5	722	—	671	—	51	−54	—	−2	6,780	55,962

† Based on calendar year births and deaths per 1,000 mid-year population.

* The net increase of −275,000 is a result of the change in definition of population; estimates of population for the years 1945 to 1950 relate to TOTAL population and thereafter to HOME population.

§ Figures have been independently rounded; totals may not add up precisely.

Second World War are shown in Table 2/1. Births and birth rates, deaths and death rates, natural increase, net migration, net yearly change, cumulative increase, and mid-year populations are given for each year separately from 1946 to 1975 inclusive. These figures will be useful since they are not officially collected or published in this synoptic form anywhere else.[5] Gaps are left for the years 1975–1980, inclusive, for readers to fill in, if they wish, as the facts become available.

Table 2/2

United Kingdom
Population projections for AD 2000

Year projection published*	Projected total mid-yr. population in AD 2000 (1,000s)
1969	68,190
1970	66,100
1971	66,100
1972	63,088
1973	62,132
1974	59,272
1975	59,736
1980	
1985	
1990	
1995	

* The projections are based on the data of the year before. The 1974 projection is 1973-based, e.g.

Our crude birth and death rates and rate of natural increase for every year since the war are given in graphical form in Fig. 2/1. This also shows the amount by which the birth rate must fall or the death rate rise in order to reduce national increase to zero. The dotted line[6] indicates the level to which our death rate must rise as the age-structure settles down, and by the same token, the level at which the birth rate must settle down as we achieve a stationary population.

Even at the much lower rate of natural increase experienced in 1973 our population would double in five lifespans and our numbers were swelled—allowing for emigration—by about 123,000. This meant the equivalent of one new village a day (338 persons), one extra small town a week (2,365 persons). or one city for the year, with all that implies in the building of homes, schools, shops, hospitals, roads and other services.

Table 2/2 is a continuation of Table 4/13 in *Population Versus Liberty*, which gives all the official UK projections for the decade 1959–1969. It shows that estimates have continued to fall, with the birth rate, so that the number projected for the year 2000 is now around 9 million less than the figure published in 1969. However, at 59·272 millions it is still 3,178,000 above the mid-1974 figure, which will mean increased pressure[7] on our already over-extended resources and substantial further encroachments into our already inadequate agricultural land.

Table 2/3

British population projections. 1971–2051

	1971	2011	2051	Change in 2051	
	Millions			Millions	%
Model I (low)	54·1	60·7	63·6	+0·0	0·0
Model II (medium)	54·1	66·1	81·9	+0·4	0·5
Model III	54·1	74·3	116·5	+1·3	1·2

Source: Report of the Population Panel (1973) (p. 95)

The Ross Panel projections
The projections done for the Ross Panel Report, published in March 1973, are the latest to look at our likely numbers over a longish period on the basis of differing assumptions. Table 2/3 reproduces their estimates (for Great Britain only, not the UK) up to the year 2051—models I, II, and III, the 'low', 'medium', and 'high', respectively. The 'low' model would produce a population which was virtually stationary at 63·6 millions

(plus Northern Ireland) by AD 2030, a further 10 million increase in round figures; and models II and III would both produce much larger increases coupled with high continuing rates of increase. With model III, for example, the population would double in one lifespan, and at the end of that time be increasing at more than 1·25 million each year.

Reasons for the falling birth-rate

Why is the birth-rate going down now? Does anyone know? Is it because of changes inside the individual—are we becoming different sorts of people with substantially different ideas and values in the field of procreation—or are we basically the same sorts of people merely being subjected to different influences? Could changes in these external influences—possibly including even a reversion to an earlier state—lead to a significant rise in the birth-rate? If we have good reason to suppose that there has been no change in fecundity, there is no less reason to believe that a change to a socio-economic climate which parents judged to be more favourable in general terms might well be accompanied by a belief that it was more favourable for rearing children also, leading to a rise in the birth rate of the kind we have experienced more than once already.

The present situation seems to have a good deal in common with the 1930s, when the birthrate reached a level which, with the mortality rates then prevailing, would not have sufficed to replace the population in the long run, although in fact numbers continued to increase substantially over the whole period. Admittedly, we are not now raising a great hullaballoo about it, as demographers and others did then; but it is early days yet, and several prominent people have tried to restart the chorus, notably Cardinal Heenan who recently declaimed from the pulpit: 'In this country there is an organised attack on life itself. . . . We have been misled . . . If the trend continues we shall soon be a disappearing race.'[8]

Everyone must decide for himself whether this was an informed and constructive contribution to the population debate; and, by the same token, only commonsense can tell us whether there is a parallel between the 1930s and now. The low birthrate of that time was in a climate of opinion bruised by the First World War and its aftermath, slumps, mass unemployment, hunger marches, the Depression, the loud creaking of an Empire about to break up, the rise of Fascism in Italy, Nazism in Germany, the Spanish Civil War, Stalinism in the Soviet Union, Japanese militarism in the Far East, and other factors hardly likely to foster confidence and encourage potential parents to go ahead.

In the mid-1970s a comparably anomic situation faces us— the escalating arms race with its gigantic stockpiles of nuclear bombs, the new and deadly chemical and biological weapons, massive environmental pollution, a world shortage of food and raw materials, an energy crisis, inflation getting close to the runaway level, entry into the Common Market against the wishes of many people, rising crime rates, undeclared civil war in Northern Ireland, recent wars in the Middle and Far East, industrial strife, the Cod War, a widespread disenchantment with the party system, and land and house-prices creating new records month by month.

It is hardly surprising that young couples are holding back at this time. Indeed, it would be more surprising if the birth rate had *not* sagged. Can we be sure that it will not soar again if, as we all hope, the present wave of troubles loses its impetus and we enter an era of peace and reasonable sufficiency? As the Ross Committee put it: '. . . there is nothing to suggest the imminence of a sharp fall in family size, and we expect a recovery in the future number of births' (para. 140).

15

Part II

THE 'COMMONSENSE' FALLACIES

CHAPTER 3

The statistical argument: the fallacy of unreliable figures

'. . . so much nonsense has been written about population statistics . . . that one may hazard a guess that they constitute the least of our dangers . . .' Editor of *The Listener*.[1]

'. . . we do not seem to be faced with any . . . problems arising from the disproportion between the increase of population and the supply of food. Arguments to this effect are based on such unreliable and controversial data that they can only be of very uncertain validity.' Pope John XXIII.[2]

'To count is a modern practice. The ancient method was to imagine and conjecture. But then, how . . . avoid exaggeration?' Samuel Johnson.[3]

'Oh, don't bother *me*', said the Duchess. 'I never could abide figures!' Lewis Carroll.[4]

When Disraeli coined the phrase 'There are lies, damned lies, and statistics', he gave voice to a feeling, still widely prevalent, that statistics can be made to prove anything and therefore prove nothing. This feeling is reinforced by the fact that numbers and algebraic signs form the bulk of statistical expressions, making them doubly suspicious. Most people seem to suspect statistics, the terminology of statistics, statisticians themselves, and anybody who uses statistics to argue a case. Thus we ignore them, especially when they look awkward. The (statistical) evidence about smoking causing bronchitis, lung cancer and heart disease, appears overwhelming, but millions totally ignore it and hundreds of thousands die painful and premature deaths because of their folly. The vast majority of motorists similarly ignore the evidence that safety belts save lives.

Statistics and the population problem
Comprehensive statements about births, marriages, deaths, life-expectancies, migration, and so forth, can be expressed only in statistical form: but the population problem cannot be simply because people tend to find statistics in general or population statistics in particular suspicious. The alleged facts and their apparent implications must be studied, and re-jected—if they *are* to be rejected—only on the basis of better facts, that is to say facts which are more accurate, more rele-vant, more plentiful, or all three: and this means *better statistics.* It is especially important to make this point in relation to the population question because errors in 'projections' into the future made by demographers, whose basic tool is statistics, are often used to denigrate demography *as a whole*; with the impli-cation that everything emanating from demographers—includ-ing a vast body of sound historical fact and unchallengeable contemporary data—may be regarded as wrong, or at least suspicious, and therefore be safely ignored.

Let us examine some of the ways in which statistics are abused in our society.

The ostrich ploy
To fail to acknowledge that statistics exist in some disturbing field or to refuse to acknowledge their validity is itself of course to emulate the ostrich. But an even more ostrich-like policy is sometimes followed by the responsible authorities when they refuse to collect, collate, and publish statistics in some sensitive field.

A good example is to be found in Britain's land use policy. Much official self-congratulation accompanies the designation of green belt land and national parks to which we have re-cently seen some substantial additions. These are very welcome, of course, but merely *retitling* a piece of land is only a beginning —it must at least be protected, if not enhanced, and here we are failing lamentably. Annual statistics are published on the numbers of planning permissions in the country as a whole and inside green belts and national parks. These show that the proportions of permissions granted for development of one sort or another are almost as high in the 'protected' areas as outside. In 1972 for example a typical year, the figures for permissions granted were: 83·6% in non-protected land; 72·6% inside the green belts; and 80·4% inside the national parks.[5]

The questions which immediately spring to mind are:

1. What are the populations inside the protected areas and what is the application rate per head?
2. How much protected land is lost each year through the permissions granted?

On these two key questions officialdom is mute; it is claimed that the figures simply do not exist. Yet every application must state exactly what is intended and it would be a simple matter to tot up the loss of open land.

The pontifical ploy, outright rejection

The Roman Catholic establishment has got itself into such a frame of mind over population issues that, if hundreds of millions were not suffering and dying unnecessarily, it would be charitable to avert the gaze from the spectacle. Intelligent educated men prostitute fact, science, logic, and commonsense in attempts to evade the simple facts of population and resources in order to justify the unjustifiable—the stand taken by the Roman Catholic hierarchy on the issue of birth-control. Non-Catholics naturally find it difficult to feel sympathy for a belief in the Dogma of Infallibility; but it must be hard for even the most devout to find justification for Papal pronouncements which flatly contradict themselves in adjacent paragraphs.

In *Mater et Magistra*, an Encyclical written in 1961, Pope John XXIII said on the one hand:

> It is . . . impossible for wealthy nations to look with indifference upon the hunger, poverty and misery of other nations whose citizens are unable to enjoy even elementary human rights. . . . It will not be possible to preserve a lasting peace so long as these glaring economic and social inequalities persist (para. 157). . . . We are sick at heart . . . when we observe the fearful spectre of want and misery which threatens to extinguish human life . . . (para. 198).

And, on the other hand:

Truth to tell, we do not seem to be faced with any immediate or imminent world problem arising from the disproportion between the increase of population and the supply of food. *Arguments to this effect are based on such unreliable and controversial data that they can only be of very uncertain validity* (para. 188: italics added).

Here again we have a patent attempt at evading obvious and painful facts by means of an attack on statistics. The Holy Father, by all accounts a kind and gentle man, seems to have granted himself a dispensation—perhaps a self-indulgence would not be too unkind a way of putting it—to obtain release not only from plain dealing with facts and logic but also from the most elementary tenets of commonsense.

The side-step
A more sophisticated way of evading hard statistical data than that adopted by Pope John is to side-step the statistical approach, avoiding open condemnation. This course was adopted by Lord Longford, when Leader of the House of Lords, in a speech to his fellow peers in a debate on World Population and Family Planning: 'I am not quite so gloomy, even on the statistical side . . . as the noble Lord [Lord McCorquodale] who . . . introduced this debate . . . and, *so far as I remember, I am not going to introduce a single figure*' (italics added).[6]
He went on: 'The Royal Commission on Population was set up in this country in 1941 because they thought the population was vanishing; but by the time it had finished, the trouble seemed to be the other way. *Then down went the population from 1947.* . . . But then quite unexpectedly, it swung round, and from 1955–56 it started to go up and it has been going up— ever since' (italics added).
After the bland disclaimer that he was 'not going to introduce a single figure', Lord Longford was able to give an air of respectability to his highly tendentious speech (he admitted he was defending the Roman Catholic position on birth control) by making it seem that he was resting his arguments on a valid quantitative basis without specifying that basis in any way. And in fact some of his statements were quite false. The population no more 'went down' from 1947 onwards than it did

from 1930 onwards, during the alleged population crisis of that period; and since it never went down it is hard to see how it could have 'swung round' about 1955 and 'started to go up'.

Blinding with science

Another way of abusing statistics is to use them as a smoke screen—to imbed the more doubtful points you want to make in such a variety and profusion of tables and figures, preferably valid ones, that the bulk of your audience will go away with the conviction that anything in such a manifestly scholarly piece of work must be true. For example, Colin Clark's book, *Population Growth and Land Use* (1967), is packed with statistics on a great variety of topics. Yet not one of the author's central contentions is documented at all. The great mass of figures, interesting and useful though they often are, relate to relatively peripheral topics.

The central message of the book, as of most of Dr Clark's writing and lecturing, can be summarised as follows: 'I am a dogmatic Roman Catholic of the old school. My concern is to protect the declared and unchangeable truth of the Roman Church on birth control by proving that there is no such thing as a population problem, as it is ordinarily understood.' Of course it would be a bit difficult for him to state such a position openly, so what he in fact says in his preface is: 'The principal problems created by population growth are not those of poverty but of exceptionally rapid increase of wealth in certain favoured regions. . . .'

This astounding contention flies in the face of all the evidence, of expert opinion and the judgement of world leaders, including recent Popes, from the President of the World Bank downwards. But there is not a scrap of evidence in the whole of this weighty tome, said to have taken twenty years to prepare, to justify it. There *is* a problem of a world 'wealth gap', but it is in part produced by population growth. Of course it may be that Colin Clark is right and that virtually everybody else has got it wrong. He could be the Galileo of demography; but if he is he must produce his telescope and let us to have a look for ourselves.

23

The Noble Lie

I almost called this the 'Goebbels ploy', but decided that the Platonic description was more appropriate because people adopt this technique only for what they regard as worthy ends, as Plato advocated. The noble lie technique involves issuing authoritative-sounding statistics couched in seemingly precise scientific terminology, which have the drawback only of being totally false. The 'error' is of course slanted in magnitude and/or direction so as to bolster the case being argued.

John Maddox has adopted this ploy on a number of occasions while defending his thesis that Britain has no population problem. In the BBC series, 'It's Your Line', for instance, Mr Maddox discussed this question with Dr John Loraine of the Conservation Society and asserted that our annual rate of growth was '0·16% per annum',[7] which hundreds of thousands of viewers must have thought reflected the ultimate in scientific precision.

In fact the figure was then nearly 0·5% per annum, more than 200% larger than the Maddox figure and giving a doubling-time of about two lifespans, an increase which is anything but 'minuscule', as Mr Maddox claimed.

Pseudo-statistics

Many people try to get the best of both worlds, by rejecting or even ridiculing valid statistics while bolstering their own arguments with pseudo-statistics. Advertisers often imply a valid statistical basis for their claims: 'Doctors say that Bloggs's Beautiful Bunion Cream is the finest on the market.' Leaving aside the possibility that their claim is completely false, that no doctor ever said anything favourable about their bunion cream, it may be true that two doctors did say something of the sort. However, the meaning hinted at is not that two, three, or even fifty of Great Britain's 60,000 doctors, but that a significant proportion or even the majority of the medical profession has paid homage to the House of Bloggs.

Arguments about coloured immigrants in Britain are often well laced with pseudo-statistics. The country is said to be overrun with them, whereas they and their children number around $2\frac{1}{2}$% of the population.[8] They are said to be 'draining' our National Health and Social Security funds, whereas in fact they absorb a tiny amount in absolute terms and less than their share in relative terms, as well as making a proportionately greater contribution to the funds because a bigger proportion of them are in the younger age-groups and consequently are both healthy and working. Pseudo-statistics are difficult to pin down because they are implied rather than stated.

This is not to say that a rational case for, say, restricting immigration cannot be made out, but to insist that most discussion of restriction is vitiated by invalid 'statistics'.

Plumbing the depths
There is one audacious strategy of evasion based on the statistics of non-statistics. This involves assessing the frequency and significance of events which have not been processed as conventional statistics, either because the figures are not available or because they are not amenable to that process.

Capital punishment is a fertile field for this strategy, and one of my favourite examples occurred in *The Times* when the House of Commons first voted to abolish capital punishment.[9] In an extraordinarily irrational editorial outburst, the statistics showing that 'abolition of the death penalty has not been followed by any increase in violent crime' were dismissed as 'foreign', then attacked by the argument that even if they had been true-blue 'the moderate defender of capital punishment . . . would reply . . . *statistics are not enough*' (italics added). Finally, having rejected all statistics, *The Times* went on to 'plumb the depths': '. . . Capital punishment . . . is not to be judged by the murderers convicted *but by the potential murderers who for fear of the gallows never run the risk*' (italics added).

The basis of this passionate advocacy of capital punishment was therefore the number of a certain class of events—not of events which had occurred but of events which *would* have occurred if the situation had been different.

If this example is thought to be rather dated, here is Henry Fairlie a decade later on the same topic: '. . . There is one single point which . . . knocks the bottom out of the Home Office Research Unit's statistics. . . . No penalty is a deterrent in the case of crimes which have already been committed and *it is only with crimes which have already been committed that statistics can be concerned*' (italics added).[10]

The 'silent majority'

The 'silent majority' is a pseudo-statistical concept used very frequently these days to bolster arguments, often of a reactionary kind. Let us consider one example from the field of religion. Pope Paul, speaking on the need to preserve priestly celibacy and to oppose movement towards change in the Roman Church, said that he did not have any 'bureaucratic statistics . . . to cite of the number of those . . . understanding and silent ones who pray, who hope and who suffer with their bishops and with us—but they are very many and they are scattered throughout the world'.[11]

On one of the issues on which the Pope and the hierarchy are tenaciously opposing change, the legitimation of effective means of birth control, all the published evidence is that the vast (and 'silent') majority[12] of Roman Catholics simply ignore the official position and practise the allegedly illicit forms of birth control with a more or less clear conscience.

Statistics and measurement

Statistics is a kind of measurement—the assignment of numbers or quantities to variables which seem important for one purpose or another. This is quite obvious in formal tables of births and deaths, stock exchange prices, football results, and the like. However, the idea and practice of measurement is very often present in some form even where the tables are absent. People who reject statistics at the conscious level know perfectly well at the intuitive level that numbers can be used to measure things and base their everyday lives on this elementary fact. No one would dream of taking on a new job on the strength of the prospective employer's assurance that the wages would be 'adequate', 'normal', or even 'excellent'. We want to *know*, in pounds and pence, what our labour will earn for us, and, by the same token a shopper wants to know not that an article is 'cheap' or 'reasonable', but *how much* it costs.

Every time someone uses an argument containing expressions such as 'everybody knows such and such', 'nobody does this or that any more', or 'the great majority would agree with me on this', he is attempting to bolster his position with a quantitative—a statistical prop, which can be either provable or disprovable and therefore at least potentially valid, or neither provable nor disprovable and therefore necessarily invalid— i.e. pseudo-statistics.

In other words, we accept statistics, probability, their mathematical basis, and the whole notion of applying measurement to our social life not only as a normal, but as an *essential* part of everyday life. We tend to reject statistics, in fact, only when they present a threat to comfortable habits of thought.

Perhaps the most fundamental fact is that statistics is a language which can be used to speak various kinds and qualities of truth, or to tell a variety of lies in a variety of ways just like any other language. If someone tells you a whopper, whether in English, Hottentot, or Linear B, the normal and perfectly appropriate response is not to reject the language the liar happened to choose—still less to reject language itself— but to subject the statement containing the whopper to analysis and verification in that same language. If a judge were to say to a witness, 'you have just told a lie in English, the court cannot accept any further submission in that language', we would think him barmy, but this is just what many people do with the language of statistics.

Every meaningful consideration of the population problem, as of very many others, must start from the position that good statistics, properly used, cannot hinder but can only help. Good statistics are those which are relevant to the particular topic under consideration and reasonably complete and accurate—only rarely do they have to be exact. What is 'reasonable' can be determined only by judgement and with reference to a particular purpose—statistics which are 'good' for one job may be 'bad' for another. As George Polanyi puts it, when pointing out the flaws in the National Plan on the manpower situation, 'Inaccurate statistics (where the inaccuracy is unavoidable) are not in themselves to be condemned. What is objectionable is the failure to point out clearly the margin of error and to qualify all deductions accordingly'.[13]

Having overcome this irrational and mistaken suspicion, even fear, of statistics as such, the prudent citizen must hasten to gird his cerebral loins, as it were, with rational and informed scepticism about people using statistics to prove a case—the author of this book being no exception. The more extreme the argument and the more passionate the tone, the beadier must be the eye cast upon the facts, figures, and all other methods used to support it.

We must also view with a healthy scepticism the works of apologists in subjects amenable to statistical treatment who carefully avoid any statistical framework.

CHAPTER 4

The crystal ball argument: the fallacy of the unfathomable future

'You can never plan the future by the past.' Edmund Burke.[1]

'Time present and time past
Are both perhaps present in time future,
And time future contained in time past.' T. S. Eliot.[2]

This book contains a good many statements about the future, and these are by no means unusual. But many people try to argue their way out of the population problem on the grounds that we haven't got one yet, and that we are not in a position to say anything meaningful about the future. The logic of the argument goes as follows:

First premise: The future is unknown.
Second premise: Arguments based on the unknown are invalid.
Third premise: Warnings about population problems are based on arguments involving the future.
Deduction: Therefore warnings about population problems are invalid.

If we take the strongest possible connotation of the verb 'to know', meaning something of which we are fully informed and absolutely certain, then the argument seems watertight. We must ask, however, how often we *are* fully informed and absolutely certain: further, we must ask how often, when we *are* sure that both of these criteria are satisfied, we turn out to be wrong on one or both counts.

We do not order our affairs in a state of godlike certitude— our nearest approach to it is to be found in what philosophers call 'analytical' statements such as those found in mathematics. When we write $2 + 2 = 4$ this is certain, because we made up the rules and because it contains no information about the world of experience. Although it is true that 2 beans and 2 beans make 4 beans, it is not true that 2 raindrops and 2 raindrops on your window make 4 raindrops. The answer here is one trickle or smear, and the way we find out whether or how far arithmetic applies to the real world is by looking.

Although we sometimes feel certitude and sometimes turn out to be right, our normal activities are based on habits, reasonable expectations, hopes, fears, doubts, setbacks, surprises, and a continuous flow of new information which makes us relearn or reorientate ourselves to some degree, if only in the weak sense of adapting the defence of old prejudices to meet new challenges. We are not *absolutely* certain even that the sun will rise tomorrow or that the earth's atmosphere will continue to support life, so arguments rejecting reasonable and qualified forecasts about the immediate future on the grounds that they lack certitude are at the least disingenuous.

Statements about the future in this book

Statements about the future are all conditional, that is to say they are made on the assumption that certain conditions will obtain, in all really fundamental respects, on much the same basis as they do now. This is not to say that we shall not have great changes in the future, or to deny that we can expect some of them to be totally unexpected. However, we do feel it is unlikely that, say, the earth will get so much bigger as to make room for appreciably more people, or that human food requirements will suddenly drop by 75%. Even if both these

29

improbable events did come about, they would merely post-pone the day of reckoning and do nothing to cure it in the long run.

Statements made here about the future are therefore of the form: 'such and such is likely to happen *if no major new factors enter the situation*'. If new factors *do* appear they will clearly make a difference, and their future interaction with trends continuing from the present cannot be predicted.

Possible new factors
Factors which might enter future situations could be divided into two major groups, the expected and the unexpected. Hermann Kahn of America's leading 'think-tank', the Hudson Institute, has coined the expression 'surprise-free' futures, with the obvious corollary that some futures *would* surprise us. Let us examine some of these;

(1) *Hydrogen bomb warfare*
Among the most painfully obvious of the possible surprise-free futures is one involving hydrogen bomb warfare. By 1969 the nuclear powers had stock-piled missiles adding up to about 320,000 megatons, equivalent to about 100 tons of high explosive for every man, woman, and child on earth.[3] The use of only a fraction of this terrible potential would transform the situation in ways we cannot foresee. However, contrary to some rather cynical opinion, it is very unlikely that this would solve the population problem, since these bombs, as well as destroying people, would also destroy stocks of food and the means of growing and transporting more. It follows that, although the population after a nuclear war might be very much smaller, it could easily be worse off because large areas of the earth's surface could be rendered unproductive and uninhabitable for centuries, perhaps millennia.

(2) *Chemical and biological warfare (CBW)*
Another non-surprising possibility is chemical and/or biological warfare, which again could easily ravage the human race. In this case the factories and transport systems would not be destroyed so that—provided the earth's fertility were not

impaired (as it might very well be by techniques like those adopted by the USA in Vietnam)—the survivors might be better off on a crude materialistic basis.

Ehrlich and Ehrlich have summarised this possibility very well, pointing out that a C/B calamity could occur simply by accident, through the escape of deadly substances from the research establishments which are being introduced by more and more governments. These weapons are particularly dangerous because almost any country can afford to set up a few well-trained chemists or microbiologists in a small laboratory and immediately be in business. With ever-increasing numbers and movement, and with so many tens of millions with lowered resistance because of malnutrition and natural disease, casualties could be numbered in billions, and it is not impossible that our species could be made extinct.

(3) Famine

Massive famines could hardly surprise us, since they have been one of the most persistent of man's misfortunes throughout the ages. Cornelius Walford listed over 200 famines between the year AD1 and 1850 in the territories now comprising Great Britain alone. Over the same period there were getting on for 2,000 famines in China, almost one a year. It has been estimated that between 5 and 10 millions have died during famines in Russia in the twentieth century. There were possibly 3 million deaths in West Bengal in 1943, a large number in Biafra, Ethiopia, and the South West Sahara even more recently. It will be surprising if major calamities do not overtake the hard pressed population of Bangladesh in the near future, and some observers think that famine will be commonplace well before the end of this century.[4] A review of the population-food situation is attempted in Chapter 14.

(4) New plagues

The emergence of new diseases, or of new uncontrollable strains of viruses causing already familiar diseases, is another possibility, leading to epidemics on a scale grander than that of the great European wave of 'Spanish Flu' after the First World War, said to have carried off 200,000 in Great Britain alone, a

31

loss greater than any since the Black Death. There was a cholera scare in 1970, a smallpox scare in 1973, two more in 1972, and there could easily be pandemics engulfing whole continents.

With our incredibly thoughtless use of pesticides, antibiotics (in man and animals) and other forms of chemical manipulation of living organisms, we are breeding resistant strains of germs which are becoming harder and harder to control. The distinguished biologist, John Maynard Smith, said in a discussion on the Third Programme[5] recently that it is becoming positively dangerous to go into hospital because of the concentrations of resistant strains of bacteria created there by our present medical techniques.

(5) *Earth movements*

We know that our earthly home is in a continuous state of change. The continents float about and collide with each other from time to time: Australia is due to crash into Japan at some not too distant point in the future, geologically speaking, as India once crunched into Tibet and threw up the Himalayas, Land masses rise, tilt, fall and erode, the level of the sea rises and falls through hundreds of feet, and many other changes will certainly affect the earth's carrying capacity and therefore the size and nature of human society.

In the case of Britain, the land mass on which we stand is tilting fairly rapidly[6] so that the South-East is disappearing beneath the waves—hence the danger of serious flooding in London and the need for the great tidal barrage which at a capital cost of many hundreds of millions will, it is hoped, give protection for about one lifespan into the future.

Sudden fluctuations of this kind would surprise us; but the long-term prospects can only be of great change profoundly important to man.

(6) *Ecocatastrophe from pollution*

The ecologically informed, at least, would not be surprised if we maltreated our environment in such a way as to make the continuance of human life difficult or even impossible. The UN Secretary General reported in 1969:

Increasing populations bring increasing demands upon agri-

THE CRYSTAL BALL ARGUMENT

cultural lands . . . fertilisers and new pesticides . . . have side effects . . . that we are only now beginning to comprehend. . . . atmospheric oxygen and the production of marine environments depend upon photosynthesis by marine plants, mostly the floating algae of microscopic size. Minute amounts of such pesticides as DDT have been found to inhibit photosynthesis in these algae by 75%. Nevertheless, we have dumped an estimated billion pounds of DDT into our environment and are adding an estimated hundred million pounds per year . . . these compounds . . . have been of serious consequence in many areas . . .[7]

His report showed that not only could our activities poison the environment, they might more or less wreck it:

. . . at the 23rd session of the General Assembly it was pointed out that . . . reliance . . . upon . . . fossil fuels has brought a 10% increase in atmospheric carbon dioxide over the past century . . . this could rise to 25% by 2000 AD. The consequences . . . upon world climate are uncertain, but could . . . be catastrophic.[8]

Increases in atmospheric carbon dioxide cause the earth to absorb more of the sun's energy, thereby tending to raise the earth's temperature and gradually melt the polar ice-caps. If this happened it would lead to a rise in sea level which could drown large areas of land and many of the world's major cities.

Another source of potential danger, reinforcing this trend, is that of man's rapidly increasing use of inanimate energy. In Britain our consumption increased by 45 per cent between 1950 and 1970, the United States increased two and a half times over the period 1940 to 1970, and world energy consumption is doubling every fifteen years or so. All of this finds its way in a degraded form into the environment so that it tends to warm up the earth.

Perhaps fortunately—no one can really tell—there are countervailing tendencies. We are also putting hundreds of millions of tons of dirt into the atmosphere, and this tends—by scattering the sun's energy back into space—to have the opposite effect to that just described, so that the earth could become cooler and possibly enter a new ice-age.

In the case of Britain, unexplained changes in the climate

increased the length of the growing season by as much as two
or three weeks in the early part of this century, consequently
changing the pattern of farming behaviour and increasing
food production by a substantial amount. In the period since
1940 the trend has been reversed, again for unknown reasons,
and this is a somewhat disturbing omen with our increasing
numbers and heavy dependence on overseas food supplies.
The work of Professor J. H. Lamb has shown that even more
recent trends give cause for disquiet. The frequency of westerly
winds is markedly diminishing, so that we are getting rain
much less frequently and in larger and more destructive bursts.
In 1974 a number of crops had to be ploughed in because of
drought.[9]

For the earth as a whole, the average temperature appears
to have been going down for a generation; but nobody knows
whether this is a short-term fluctuation or the start of a trend,
or whether or by how much it is due to man's activities as a
polluter.

In addition to the possibility that we might disrupt the world
climate accidentally, there is the further danger that we might
purposely initiate changes which then get out of hand. The
great pressure on scientist and governments to do everything
possible to produce more food for the burgeoning billions of
the immediate future is a major factor making hasty, ill-
considered forays into the control of the environment more
likely. We are now being urged to farm the sea and even control
the climate to make agriculture more productive. Clumsy
attempts to modify the performance of this huge and subtle
engine we call the weather could lead to catastrophic results.

Amidst this fog of ignorance the two beacons of certitude
are: (1) that we do not understand these enormously complex
mechanisms or the scale of possible repercussions; and (2) in
a situation so fraught with danger we ought surely to err on
the side of caution.[10]

Possible surprises

(1) *Astro-catastrophe*

Let us consider first an astronomical calamity. Ignoring the
grand but somewhat imperfectly documented theories of

Velikovsky,[11] let us examine a few lesser events. The asteroid Icarus only just missed the earth on June 15 1968—by about 4 million miles: that is, a near miss by astronomical standards. Icarus is about a kilometre in diameter and shoots past us every nineteen years with a relative velocity of 100,000 miles per hour. Fred Hoyle has said that it is inevitable that it will strike the earth one of these years. The asteroid Apollo missed us by only 2 million miles in 1952, Adonis by one million miles in 1936, Hermes by half a million miles in 1937, and so on. None of these asteroids would by any means wreck the earth, but much more formidable objects are hurtling through space. If one of these hit us it would introduce a very large and unpredictable variable into man's future.

(2) *Spontaneous climatic change*
Even if we manage not to produce major climatic changes accidentally, these could quite easily occur naturally. It is not long since the last Ice Age, and nobody knows whether there will be another, whether the mechanisms leading to a recurrence are already in operation, or whether we would have enough knowledge and power to reverse such a trend. There have already been twenty ice-ages, four of them very recent by geological time-scales. Indeed, they were comparatively recent even by human standards, taking place within the past 600,000 years, during the last quarter or so of man's span on earth. The last one ended less than 10,000 years ago, and no one knows whether we are now merely passing through the 'fifth' interglacial period.[12]

(3) *Evolutionary progress*
A new species of living creature could evolve, more intelligent and powerful and/or less scrupulous than ourselves, and *homo sapiens* could go down one or two pegs in the food-chain, which would be *very* surprising

(4) *Invasion from outer space*
Hardly less surprising would be invasion from outer space. Great squadrons of those flying saucers really could appear one day and some sort of living entity could hop, creep, or trickle

out and take control—possibly simply devouring or vaporising us all, and curing our population problem that way.

(5) *Spontaneous control*

For the last surprise let us consider whether some kind of spontaneous innate mechanism for the control of human population could emerge. Many other species have these control mechanisms built in, as it were, showing themselves in instinctive behaviour. Birds, for example, often control their populations through the instinct of territory; many species cannot mate and reproduce unless they have first established a breeding site. The amount of space available automatically fixes the number of territories, which in turn determines the number of birds which can pair off and reproduce, and so controls the size of the population. It could be that at a certain density, a certain state of population growth, standard of living, stress, tension, conflict—or whatever the symptoms might be—such a mechanism will manifest itself in human beings.

A milder form of 'spontaneity' could be a general intuitive recognition of an optimum or overpopulation situation which led to the prevention of further growth by means of individual parental action through birth control and/or abortion. This is the sort of mechanism required by the theory of the demographic transition, dealt with in Chapter 9, which may have started to operate in a few societies such as Sweden. It is at a higher level than an instinctive evolutionary mechanism but, arguably, at a lower level than rational conscious choice.

An unclassifiable possibility: the use of foresight and rational planning

A final possibility—hard to classify as surprise or non-surprise —would be imaginative and intelligent control of human destiny, including the regulation of numbers and a respect for the ecological balance.

Man's intelligence creates a problem here. If it is the nature of intelligence to solve problems, one of the more important of which is survival, are we not 'bound' to use ours to correct our population and environmental excesses before it is too late? If we are by nature problem-solving-creatures, will this not provide a 'spontaneous' mechanism for the solution of this

36

problem? This probably boils down to a question of preference and definition, but a useful guide is probably the lateness of the hour and the consequent seriousness of our problems. If we leave it until we are nearly overwhelmed and really have no option we may choose to call it a spontaneous mechanism, whereas if we use foresight, imagination, and intelligence to change course long before disaster is upon us we could fairly label it rational planning. Time is slipping past so quickly, however, that it is already getting rather late to apply this label to our conduct.

If any of these things were to happen, or important things not yet thought of, then our predictions about the future would be wrong. However, the fact that new things *might* happen is no excuse for not thinking about the future, or for rejecting reasoned predictions about it. We have to make plans in the light of the best information we have now, and of our experience and knowledge about the way the system has behaved in the past. By and large the basic relationships between societies and their environments do not change all that much, all that quickly, or all that often.

Population and the future: Problems of demographic forecasting
In one of the early debates on population problems in the House of Lords referred to in the last chapter, Lord McCorquodale made the somewhat injudicious statement: 'It is certain that by the year 2000 the world population will be well over 6,250 million'.

This provided an admirable opening for Lord Longford who made a meal of it and thereby avoided the real issue: 'I did not take down the noble lord's words but I think he said that something very frightening was certain to happen. . . . I do not think certainty exists in this field; far from it. . . . I do not take the view that these colossal figures . . . are bound to happen'.[12]

What Lord McCorquodale should have said is that it is *virtually* certain or *very highly probable* that the world population will be approaching 7 thousand million by the end of the century, in which case his statement would have been unexceptionable, especially since—barring great calamities—a substantial proportion of the people who will be alive then are

37

already alive now. The substantive issue is not whether the world population will be 6,250 million in the year 2000 but whether the current rate of increase is large and whether very big increases are probable on the best evidence we have. In attacking the spurious precision suggested by a single figure the apologists are enabled to evade the real question entirely.

An entirely opposite judgement to that of Lord Longford was made by Winston Churchill, who said: 'There is no branch of human knowledge in which we can pierce the mysteries of the future so clearly as in the trend of population. . . . Here the searchlight of statistics ranges with accuracy for 30 or 40 years ahead'.

What is the truth of the matter? How is it possible to strike a balance between these two extreme positions?

Some technical problems and methods
Population projections are based partly on facts and partly on assumptions; and—though there is no absolute dividing line between the two—we should be constantly attempting to improve the accuracy and immediacy of the facts, to state clearly the assumptions and to clarify the distinction between them. The two main methods of projecting population growth are, firstly, by means of extrapolation, either by rule of thumb —simply extending the curve on the graph as far as is thought justified. The second is by means of the 'component' or 'analytic' method.

(1) *The method of extrapolation*
The *mathematical* type of extrapolation has a longish history but a shrinking reputation, partly because some of its earlier exponents carried it to quite ridiculous lengths. and tried to forecast population centuries ahead. A professor of mathematics, H. S. Pritchett, was so wedded to the theory of the 3rd degree parabola that with its aid he forecast the population of the United States 1,000 years later: 41 thousand million by 2900. To the best of my knowledge the mathematical technique has not been tried recently for limited projections, of say five to twenty years, but I suspect that if it were it might give quite useful results; it certainly is worth doing for a comparison with

the more complicated analytical method. It could be partially combined with this method, mortality and migration being treated as separate components, and a formula worked out to extrapolate the fertility trends. All could be recombined at the end of this process and projections then made.

The *graphical* method of extrapolation is based on the same basic judgement as the mathematical—that the forces giving the curve its shape will not change all that much or all that quickly—and therefore has about the same validity. It can be a useful guide for a limited period if nothing better is forthcoming.

(2) *The 'component' or 'analytic' method*
This may be called the standard demographic projection technique, and it rests on an attempt to isolate, measure, understand, relate to each other, and forecast all the facts relating to the 'components' of population dynamics—births, deaths, and migration. These are then incorporated into a mathematical 'model' of reality, which in turn must rest on a valid theory, and which can then be used to extrapolate future events, *if present trends continue*. The almost insuperable difficulty here lies in isolating and quantifying the relevant factors; for it seems likely that a complete explanation of reproductive behaviour would approximate to an explanation of a total society, as Bagehot observed some time ago.

This is in no sense intended to cast doubt on—much less to ridicule—the activities of mathematically inclined students of population, the problem is worthy of their greatest endeavours and every further increase in sophistication takes us a step away from ignorance and guesswork towards knowledge. The trouble is that the problem is *inherently* intractable and until we get better knowledge about what parents-to-be *intend* to do we cannot be more definite or precise about the demographic outcome. Sample surveys of parental intentions, dealt with later, can help in this field.

Indicators of likely population growth
There are a number of more or less technical ways of measuring and indicating rates of population growth or decline,

none of them completely satisfactory. To simplify as far as possible let us rule out migration, leaving births and deaths only.

(i) *Natural increase*

This is obtained by comparing birth and death rates (normally so many per 1,000 head of population per year and called the 'crude' rates) when the difference will give the rate of growth, or decline, as the case might be. If there are 20 births and 10 deaths per 1,000 per annum, then the natural increase is 10 ($= 20 - 10$) per thousand per annum. It is easy to convert this to a percentage; 10 per 1,000 equals 1 per 100 equals 1 per cent per annum increase. (The 1972 figure for the UK was 2·8 per 1,000 giving a doubling time of about three and a half lifespans.

This is all very well for a population with a normal age structure, that is to say with stable and persisting proportions in the various age groups, but if there are more people than usual in the reproductive age group the natural increase is misleading, perhaps very seriously. For example, let us imagine that an 'artificial' society is set up at an Antarctic research station or, a few decades hence, on the moon, consisting of 1,000 selected persons. Let this be comprised of 500 couples, all young, fecund, and fairly newly married, who start to have children up to the nominal replacement rate of 2 per family, a total of 1,000 children. The death rate will of course be virtually zero for many years so that all births will increase the population. If childbearing is spread over, say, five years, this would mean that 200 children would be born each year (1,000 children divided by 5 years) and give a natural increase of 200 per annum. This means an increase of 20 per cent of the original 1,000 each year and a doubling-time of five years, a rate which is both unprecedented and impossible to sustain. (Normally the annual percentage increase is compound, of course; 20 per cent compound interest gives a doubling-time a little under four years.)

From this we see that a population which is barely maintaining itself in the short run and failing to maintain itself in the long run (because in future generations some must die without having replaced themselves) appears to be breaking all records for growth.

In a greatly exaggerated way this explains what was happening in Britain's great population scare in the 1930s. Although our numbers never failed to rise by at least 0·25 per cent a year (ignoring immigration), demographers feared we were not replacing ourselves in the long run. A small proportion of our growth in 1973 is due to the same cause.

It follows from this that natural increase by itself is useless as an indicator of the long-term future of a population, although of course it has great significance in the short run.

(2) General fertility rate

This measure ignores the overall population size and all adult males. It works on the basis of the number of women in the reproductive age group only, generally taken to be fifteen up to fifty years, and their children. The rate is then taken to be the number of births per 1,000 women in that age group, and it is of course four or five times as large as the crude birth rate because all the births are related to the 'mothers' only and this group normally forms only 20 to 25 per cent of the total population. Very often the general fertility rate will remain in step with the crude birth and death rates; but if there are fairly rapid changes in reproductive behaviour, as in the timing of births, they can diverge significantly, so that a more precise measure is needed.

(3) The total fertility rate

In the case of the general fertility rate, the results may be distorted by an unusual distribution of mothers within the fifteen to fifty year group: there may be too many in their twenties, for example. For this reason the refinement was introduced of age-specific birth rates—described by two demographers as 'the most important basic refinement in the measurement of natality that has ever been made'. [13]

With this indicator, birth rates are referred not to the total population, or even to the total 'mother' group, but separately to each age group within the group of 'mothers' as a whole. Every age from fifteen to forty-nine could be considered singly, but for convenience they are normally clustered in five-year intervals—15–19; 20–24; and so on up to 45–49 years—so that we end up with seven separate birth rates, each of which is 'specific' to an age group. 'Total' fertility is obtained by adding all the age-specific birth rates and multiplying by five (because there are five one-year groups in each five-year group), which automatically bypasses and therefore compensates for the actual distribution of mothers by age at that time. This measure is slightly better than the GFR, as it corrects for age imbalance; but it still leaves a lot to be desired.

(4) *The reproduction rate*
This is a further refinement over the TFR, worked out in two ways, leading to slightly different results which are given separate labels to make it clear which is which.

The *gross-reproduction rate* (GRR) simply means the relationship between mothers and daughters instead of between mothers and all children, as in the use of the total fertility rate. If we start with a group—sometimes called a cohort—of 1,000 mothers, who produce 1,000 daughters then they have replaced themselves and the population will not decline. (Bear in mind that nature ensures that about 1,050 sons will be born with the 1,000 daughters, so that the fathers will be more than replaced. However, in the real world some of the 1,000 mothers must die before they can replace themselves, so the population *would* decline if the other women did not produce a few extra daughters to compensate for premature deaths. Also in the real world some of the 1,000 daughters produced would also die before they replaced themselves so—and here we are beginning to repeat ourselves, since the daughters of one generation are the mothers of the next.

The *net reproduction rate* (NRR) is used to allow for deaths and is calculated by a roundabout (though simple) arithmetical route to allow for premature deaths. The long and the short of it is that if we wind up with a ratio (daughters divided by mothers) of 1·0, then the population is replacing itself exactly. *Less* than one means that it is not replacing itself in the long run (it may be rising meanwhile) and *more* than one means that it is more than replacing itself.

Both GRR and NRR are calculated on the assumption, that the age-specific birth rates remain constant throughout the reproductive period; but of course this is rarely the case, and though these basic calculations can be refined in all sorts of ways—by applying a 'marriage-standardised' correction, for example, which allows for the proportion of daughters failing to marry—the fact is that no amount of juggling can make the NRR an accurate forecaster of later population size. The Report of the Royal Commission on Population concluded: 'The Net Reproduction Rate cannot be relied upon to show the underlying trend of the population in any significant sense' (paragraph 15, appendix 3).

(5) *Completed fertility*
This simply refers to the average number of children born to a group of women who have passed out of the reproductive period and therefore cannot have any more children. One of its advantages is that it can be done for several successive age-groups simultaneously, including groups long dead, so that any changes in completed family size can be spotted immediately.

Table 4/1 shows the decline in average completed family size for UK, marriages from 1861 to 1951.

Table 4/1

Decline in completed family size, UK 1861–1951.

Year of marriage	Average completed family size
1861–69	6·16
1871	5·94
1881	5·27
1890–99	4·13
1900–09	3·30
1911	2·83
1921	2·38
1931	2·08
1941	2·10
1951	(2·24)*

* up to 1971 only.

The great drawback of this method is that we have to wait thirty-five years to be sure that a woman has finished having children (although most families are complete after fifteen years and 98 per cent are complete after twenty years). The great delay means that the behaviour even of living groups studied over the past thirty-five to seventy-five years may have little bearing on what young mothers are doing now and will do in the future. .

(6) *Cohort analysis*

We have already seen the basic idea of cohort analysis used in the last section. A cohort is simply a group of women married in a particular year whose fertility is studied separately, as before, the difference being that the study starts from a recent year and is carried on as the cohort passes through the reproductive years—attempts being made to record the spacing of births, as well as their number—so that a profile of reproductive behaviour is gradually built up which is about as up to date as one can get. Modern projection procedures rest very heavily on this type of analysis, but even this is not good enough, since the future behaviour of prospective parents is involved. If women are marrying younger and having more children in the early years, does it mean that they are intending to go on and have large families, or merely to complete their families earlier and perhaps go on to a career? The demographer can only wait and see.

The irony of it all is that the component method can work only if trends continue, but if they *do*, elaborate mathematical analysis becomes almost redundant since rule of thumb forecasts can be made—from these same trends—which are as good as and sometimes better than those statisticians can give us.

Contribution of sample surveys

Myra Woolf makes the claim, and gives some good evidence, that population forecasting will be greatly improved if we can cut down our uncertainty about completed family size, caused mainly by the extremely long potentially fertile period of a human female.[14] We can do this if we sample the *intentions* of potential mothers and use these to build on the foundation of reproductive behaviour up to the point at which the intentions were measured. In other words, total fertility equals past fertility plus intended fertility, *provided* that intentions are realised in fact. On this last point she feels that, although there are many individual lapses in insight, judgement, and contraceptive behaviour on the part of the parents-to-be who are sampled, the errors tend to cancel out, as evidenced by her own research and other work in the United States, so that we can have a fair degree of confidence that 'mean expected family size [is] a valid measure of mean ultimate family size' (6·6).

Even if this turned out not to be so in the long run, it seems unlikely that the discrepancy would be completely random, so that the calculation of a standard weighting factor is possible: we could add or subtract four or five 'centichildren' (one 'centichild' = one hundredth of a child) from the expected completed family size and wind up with very much more accurate forecasts than we now produce.

Unfortunately Myra Woolf does not submit herself to the test and go on to project the UK population on the basis of her findings, so that her evidence is somewhat unsettling on this point. At marriage the average expected family size was 2·7 and, although this was reduced to 2·5 after marriage, the figure is still very much too large to give us a stationary population. Even worse, the 'ideal' family size for people with 'no particular worries about money or anything like that' (page 33) was 3·4, which, if adopted as the norm and lived up to, would give us an astronomical rate of increase.

If we relate this to the theory of the population cycle (dealt with in detail in Chapter 9), which rests on the assumption that, as societies become wealthier through industrialisation, so family-size goes down and their populations automatically stabilise, we see that beyond a certain point wealth may trigger off a second population explosion. Fortunately wealth and poverty are relative concepts. It seems likely that the people asserting that 3·4 is the ideal average number of children if they had 'no particular worries about money or anything like that', implying a level of income which would obviate these worries, would increase their material expectations if and when that level was reached, so that they would still feel their financial resources were inadequate to support the 'ideal' number of children. The more rapidly the rise in income came about, the less time they would have for adopting higher material standards, so the subjective feeling of affluence would be greater, giving an increased likelihood of higher fertility—if the correlation is valid, that is. Conversely, one might expect reduced fertility from families subjected to fairly rapidly falling incomes, in absolute or relative terms, and this seems a fruitful area for research.

The population 'flywheel'

In his 'Essay on the art of conjecture', Bertrand de Jouvenal referred to what he called 'structural certainties' which enable predictions to be made because of the semi-permanent structure of social institutions which continue to *make* things happen in certain ways. There is a parallel of a kind in demography, the fact that population may be predicted with confidence in some respects because of its present structure, resulting, in turn, from what had happened in the past. A growing population is like a heavy rotating flywheel, insofar as it has a lot of 'momentum' and requires a substantial amount of effort and/or time to slow it down.

In 1972 37 per cent of the world's population was under fifteen years (against 23 per cent in the UK), and unless there is a calamitous increase in mortality these young people are virtually all going to grow up and have children. Even if they restrict themselves to replacement-size families, world population must swell appreciably before it becomes stationary because only small numbers of their parents will be dying off as their children appear. The only ways to prevent this would be to persuade people to have much smaller than replacement size families for a time, a most unlikely prospect; or to bring about a great increase in mortality, an unthinkable prospect unless there are many great calamities.

Several studies have been made of the effects of the attainment of replacement size families at different times and one of these was done by the Population Council.[15] From their composite graph, reproduced in Fig. 4/1, we see the repercussions of the attainment of the average two-child family by

1980, 2000, 2020, or 2040, leading to ultimate population sizes of about $6\frac{1}{4}$, 8, $11\frac{1}{4}$, and $15\frac{3}{4}$ thousand million, respectively, the last involving more than two doublings of the present size. As they point out, the lowest estimate ($6\frac{1}{4}$ billions) is virtually out of the question, 'because that would require a fertility

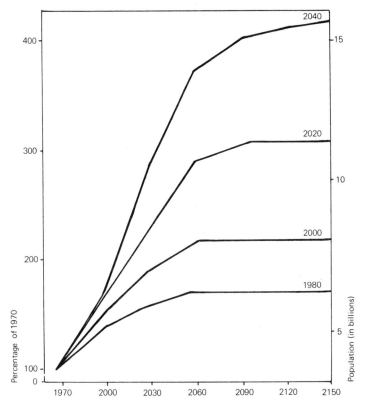

Figure 4/1.   The population flywheel—world population
AD 1970–2150

decline so rapid that within 10 to 15 years the average family size over the whole world would . . . be approximately two.'

From this we see that, although he ought not to have put it like that, Lord McCorquodale was right, practically speaking, about the 'certainty' of there being 6 thousand million by 2000.

47

Table 4/2 contains three projections of the UK population based on the years 1968, 1971, and 1973 and shows the 'structural' element in terms of generations.

Table 4/2

Composition of UK population by generations in AD 2000

Generations	Base Year		
	1968 base	1971 base	1973 base
Survivors of those alive in base year	33·6m	35·3m	36·6m
Children of those alive in base year	26·8m	23·7m	21·0m
Children of those children	7·8m	3·8m	1·7m
Totals	68·2m	62·8m	59·3m

1968 base reproduced from *Population Versus Liberty* (p. 60)

1971 base kindly computed by the Office of Population Censuses and Surveys.

The self-negating prophecy

The idea of the self-fulfilling prophecy—a prophecy which becomes true because it stimulates the behaviour required to make it come true—is now fairly widely accepted. Perhaps less widely known is the concept of the self-*negating* prophecy, a prophecy which tends to be falsified because it stimulates unwelcoming attitudes which in turn lead to action tending to prevent the prophecy's becoming true.

Population projections, though not strictly prophecies at all, tend to bring about this second type of reaction. As the Government Actuary's staff says, 'any projection can carry within it the seeds of its own destruction'.[16] If the projections warn us of the possibility of a declining population we set up a Royal Commission, introduce a Welfare State, and so forth. If we are later told of the possibility of large and continued increases, we set up powerful pressure groups campaigning for education on these issues, and free and universal birth-control. In both cases the *action* of setting up a demographic Aunt Sally provokes the *reaction* of behaviour tending to knock it down again. Apologists who dispute the possibility of Britain or the world ever becoming overpopulated will seize on each and every downward flip in the birth-rate, however temporary, and use this as an argument to prove there was no problem in the first place, quite ignoring the fact that these changes do not take place in a vacuum but in a social climate vitally affected by population projections and the reactions they stimulate.

In the final analysis the only way to project population trends with sufficient accuracy is to plan them and bring them to fruition by deliberate and effective social policy.

Further reading on population projection

Benjamin, B. (a) 'Are population projections any good?' Family Planning, *21*, No. 4. Jan. 1973.

Benjamin, B. (b) 'Is there a population problem?', *Family Planning*, *23*, No. 2, July, 1974.

Boreham, J. The Pressure of Population. New Society, 3 March 1966.

Dorn, H. F. Pitfalls in Population Forecasts and Projections. J. Amer. Statistical Association, Sept. 1950.

Frejka, T. United States: The Implications of Zero Population Growth. Studies in Family Planning, No. 60, Dec. 1970.

Glass, D. V. Demographic Prediction. Proc. Royal Society, Series 'B', *168*, 6 June 1967.

Hajnal, J. The Prospects for Population Forecasts. J. Amer. Statistical Association, March 1955.

Hawthorne, G. 'The Birth rate, and what lies behind it', *New Society*, July 4 1974.

HMSO. Office of Population Censuses and Surveys (1971 and annually) Population Projections.

HMSO. Projecting the population of the UK. Economic Trends, Nol 139, May 1965.

Keyfitz, N. On the Momentum of Population Growth. Demography. *8*, No. 1, Feb. 1971.

Royal Commission on Population (1949) Report.

Stewart, C. The hazards of population forecasts. New Society, 23 Sept. 1971.

Thompson, E. Birth Trends. *Family Planning*, *23*, No. 2, July 1974.

Thompson, J. Population. Social Trends, 1971.

CHAPTER 5

The military argument: the fallacy of population and power

'Britain would be far stronger militarily if it could maintain a population not of 50 but of 70 or 80 millions. It might become dangerously weak—if its population fell to 40 or 45 millions. British population policy should be directed, . . . to favouring natural increase, *and* . . . a steady stream of European immigration.' Professor Ian Bowen.[1]

'The most useful woman is she who can produce the greatest supply of "cannon fodder".' Napoleon.[2]

'Number in itself in armies importeth not much, where the people are of weak courage: for, as Virgil saith, *it never troubles the wolf how many the sheep be.* Francis Bacon.[3]

This is more of a sketch for a chapter than a chapter proper, because official and other information on this topic is scarce and widely scattered. What our defence departments know they are keeping to themselves, so that what follows is food for thought rather than a knockdown case.

The fallacy here is equating mere numbers with military power, and Bacon saw through it clearly, illustrating his case with numerous instances. For example;

When Tigranes, the Armenian, with four hundred thousand men, discovered the army of the Romans, being not above fourteen thousand marching towards him, he made himself merry with it, and said, *yonder men are too many for an ambassage and too few for a fight.* But, before the sun set, he found them enow to give him the chase with infinite slaughter. This which I speak of, hath been nowhere better seen, than by comparing of England and France; whereof England, though farr less in territory and population, hath been (nevertheless) an overmatch, in regard the middle people of England make good souldiers, which the peasants of France do not.

Structure of the military fallacy

Again, the elements of the argument are simple.

First premise: Our military power must never be allowed to fall below its present level relative to that of our potential enemies.

Second premise: Military power depends on the size of the population.

Third premise: Our potential enemies are not restricting their population growth.

Conclusion: We must not restrict our population growth.

The whole argument could be made to take a slightly stronger tone by rewording the first premise to state: 'We must always strive for superior military power'. The second and third premises could also be modified, but the essence of the argument would remain and its conclusion would be valid, provided that the premises were correct. It is towards this last issue that critical analysis must be directed.

The first premise

This premise, that our military power must increase, or at least not slip back in relative terms, is neither true nor false; it is a value judgement which can be assessed only as sound or unsound, good or bad. As regards the 'strong' formulation—that military power must constantly increase—we may reject it out of hand. Most of us seem to feel that we should maintain a 'reasonable' amount of military strength of our own, ensuring national security and, if possible, world peace, by means of peaceful policies, diplomacy, and defensive alliances.

It is instructive to try to sort out who are the potential enemies against whom we must 'breed for victory'. The UK ties with Nigeria for ninth place in the population league

51

(1971 figures), at the head of which is China with perhaps 800 millions; followed by India, 570; the Soviet Union, 245; the United States, 207; Pakistan, (as it then was) 142; Indonesia, 125; Japan, 105; Brazil, 96; and West Germany, 59 millions. All of these except one are so large that we could never hope to compete, and most are so remote from us that we hardly interact with them enough to start a war, now that our imperialist phase is over and done with. The only one within competing distance is West Germany, a firm ally now and a country which is, in any case, hemmed in by the Soviet Union and the NATO alliance. True, the French, Mexicans, and Italians are coming up close behind us in numbers, but it is hard to see a threat from any of these quarters.

A further point is that two of the smallest of the industrialised countries have been the only ones to avoid war for centuries. Sweden (8·1 millions) since 1814, Switzerland (6·4 millions) since 1815, to which we can add Eire (3 millions) since the partition of Ireland, which managed to miss the Second World War. Would any of these countries have been more secure with increments of population of any feasible size? Can a country *have* more security than that implied by centuries of peace in a world of violence?

The second premise

It is manifestly false to imply that population size is the main or even the sole determinant of military power, though of course the two cannot be entirely dissociated. It is hard to imagine a situation in which, say, Lichtenstein had so compensated for its minute size that it was a match for the United States or the Soviet Union, no matter how superior its technology and wealth per capita. Population size is clearly not irrelevant, but is it the major factor determining military power?

When large numbers prevailed

There are of course some examples in military history when sheer numbers were perhaps the decisive factor. This may have been true of the Barbarian invasions of the Roman Empire; it is thought to have been a factor in the steam-roller tactics adopted by Russia to drive out the Germans towards the end of the Second World War; and the Chinese scored some successes with 'human-wave' tactics in Korea. However, for every case like these just mentioned, one can think of a score where small numbers prevailed against larger.

When small numbers prevailed

The Romans made most of their conquests with very small numbers, certainly in Britain. Small bands of Northmen gave us a terrible pounding later, and the Normans took over our country with a relatively small force. The Spanish acquisition of most of Central and South America was accomplished with microscopic numbers, as were many British conquests in our imperialist phase. Latterly there has been the struggles of Finland against the Soviet Union, of Britain against the 'Axis' powers and, latterly, of Israel against the Arab world in the Six Day War and the Yom Kippur war, and of half of Vietnam against the United States. Iceland, with a population of 220,000, has been doing just about what it likes in the cod war, against 120 million or more Europeans—and the International Court of Justice; and the tiny White minority in Rhodesia was going its own way, more or less, in spite of Britain and the United Nations, until the shift of power in Portugal and Mozambique.

The opposite case

There is something to be said for the very obverse of this 'military' argument: that is, that within limits, the smaller the population the *more* powerful is the nation. The reason for this is that a smaller nation is one which has either stopped growing, or continues to grow at a lower rate than it might have done, thus releasing wealth from the demographic investment (see page 150ff) which may—if this is desired—be invested in military technology. This could raise the fire-power of the nation by a much greater amount than if population had increased to produce more soldiers but less wealth per head to equip them. It doesn't require such thought to decide which would be the better bargain if one were offered a choice of armies to command in the field: 10,000 men equipped with swords, 5,000 with rifles, 2,500 with machine-guns, 1,250 with tanks, 625 with remotely controlled rockets, or 300-odd with lasers, chemical and biological weapons, atomic bombs and vehicles for space travel.

Again, within limits, we can say that the slower the *growth* of population the more powerful a nation will be.

View of the Royal Commission on Population

The Royal Commission considered the question of numbers power and argued:

> In the past the manpower at the disposal of a country has been a basic element in its military strength. The radical change in the relative numbers of the French and German peoples, which developed slowly but persistently over the last hundred years, exerted a profoundly important influence on the European balance of power and on wider international affairs.

They concluded: 'For the present, numbers must be regarded as an important military factor'.

It is important to note that they felt numbers are 'an' important factor not *the* main reason for military power, and even this is heavily qualified:

> Power and military strength have never depended on numbers alone; they have never been attributes of densely populated poverty-stricken countries, deficient in . . . 'industrial potential' and their importance as compared with pre-eminence in science and technology, has probably been declining in modern times; . . . it may prove to have been radically diminished by . . . the atomic bomb. (all from para. 353).

When we reflect, first, on the fact that this thinking was done a quarter of a century ago, and, second, on the speed and range of development of military technology since then, the Commission's finding gains much extra weight. Even at that juncture they thought that 'a purely national approach is unappropriate and indeed unreal. . . . No variations in our future numbers that are at all likely to occur could materially alter our position vis-a-vis the two great continental powers the United States and the Soviet Union. It went on:

For strategic purposes, Great Britain should, of course, be considered, not in isolation, but as the centre of a Commonwealth spread far and wide throughout the world. But this too is an unduly narrow approach to modern problems of power politics. It is in association or alliance with other States that the strength of the British Commonwealth is most likely to be important, not only in the eventuality of war, but in maintaining a balance of strength by which war may be averted. (para. 354.)

Perhaps by 1975 we are a little off'-centre' but the point still holds; there is even less need now to keep the maternity wards pulsating with potential cannon-fodder.

Population pressure and militarism
Hobbes said in his *Leviathan* that 'unless for the sake of room, the population growing, there would be no need of war', and those arguing for continuous increases in population in order to ensure increasing military power can easily find themselves on the slippery slope leading to militarism and aggressive warfare, without any guarantee that they can win the wars they land themselves in, as the Germans have twice found out this century.

Population and Militarism in Germany
The US Committee on Public Information published at Washington in 1918 a pamphlet with the title *Conquest and Kultur*: Aims of the Germans in their own words. This illustrated the relationship between demographic pressure and warlike trends, by quoting influential German writers. For example Arthur Dix:

> Because the German people nowadays increase at the rate of 800,000 inhabitants a year they need both room and nourishment for the surplus. . . . As a world power in the world market we must assert our place and make it secure in order that the younger hands may find room and opportunity for employment.

Another German writer, Albrecht Wirth, published a book in which he said: 'In order to live and to lead a healthy and joyous life we need a vast extent of fresh arable land. This is

55

what imperialism must give us.' Even more pointed is an authoritative statement by von Bernhardi.

> Strong, healthy and flourishing nations increase in numbers. From a given moment they require a continual expansion of their frontiers, they require new territory for the accommodation of their surplus population. Since almost every part of the globe is inhabited, new territory must, as a rule, be obtained at the cost of its possessors—that is to say by conquest, which thus becomes a law of necessity.

The cry for *Lebensraum* was taken up again by the Nazis, and this policy was intended to support not merely the existing population but a deliberately enlarged population of the future. It was accompanied by a pro-natalist policy designed to increase the 'Aryan' birthrate as high as possible to produce more and better sons and daughters of the Fatherland.

Population and Japanese Militarism

One year before Pearl Harbor the Japanese Government said in an official bulletin; 'If one thinks of the distant future of mutual prosperity in Asia, and if we give heed to the glorious mission of the Japanese race, the one thing of which we can never have enough is the number of superior people belonging to the Imperial Nation'.

To dispel the thought that only foreigners entertained these expansionist, not to say megalomaniac, dreams, we can quote our own Walter Long, President of the Local Government Board in 1916, who 'agreed that they must do everything in their power to recover the birth-rate, as it was never more essential that our great race should expand and cover the globe'.

Again, as Hobbes remarked 'When all the world is overcharged with inhabitants then the last remedy of all is war, which provideth for every man, by victory or death'.

China

Amateur strategists sometimes argue that China's policy is based on fostering a population so huge—probably already over 800 million—that defeat by another nation, however well armed, would be impossible. Even if the Chinese countryside could be sprayed with H bombs as with DDT, it is said, there would still be a hundred million or more survivors. However, the fact is that China is endeavouring to forego this demographic megalomania—her policy of population control is the most rigorous in the world. Even if there could be some lunatic sort of merit in this chamber of horrors strategy for a huge nation like China, it is hard to see its relevance to countries such as the United Kingdom, about one-fortieth China's size in terms of area, if one-fourteenth in terms of population.

Population pressure and revolution

Eric Wolf has argued that population pressure is one of the main factors producing revolutions. He gives as examples Mexico in 1910, Russia in 1917, China in the 1930s, Cuba in 1953, Vietnam in 1962, and Algeria in 1963, and states that there are typically three crises: the demographic, then the ecological, followed by the crisis of authority. He argues that 'the population increases alone . . . would have placed a serious strain on inherited cultural arrangements', and that the ecological crisis, though related to the sheer increase in numbers, is in part independent of it.

> . . . land and other resources were increasingly converted into commodities in the capitalist sense— . . . and subjected to a market which bore only a very indirect relation to the needs of the rural populations . . . peasant resources alienated directly through . . . seizure and coercive purchase or increasing capitalisation of rent. . . .
>
> Finally, both the demographic and ecological crises converged in the *crisis of authority* . . . development of the market produced a rapid circulation of the elite manipulators of the new free-floating resources . . . challenged the inherited power of the controllers of fixed social resources . . . Undisputed . . . stable claims [to power and wealth]. . . . yielded to disputed . . . unstable claims . . .[4]

Wolf's theory will be touched on again in the discussion of social change in Chapter 10, but here we need merely note that the increase in military manpower can lead not to national security but to national disaster. It seems as likely as not that continuing increase of population will lead to tensions and competition for space and raw materials which will make wars, revolutions, and civil unrest more and more likely while giving little or no likelihood of victory for those nations proving most prolific. Indeed, stockpiling cannon-fodder would almost certainly turn out to be counterproductive.

If population were the dynamo generating military power then India would be more powerful than the United States and the Soviet Union combined, and China would be almost as powerful as these two plus most of Europe. I don't think much is needed in the way of documentation to demonstrate the absurdity of such a thesis. In the case of Britain, we can surely agree with the Royal Commission that 'it is in association . . . with other States that the strength of the British Commonwealth is most likely to be important . . . in the eventuality of war, [and] in maintaining a balance of strength by which war may be averted' (para. 334).

The final attack on the argument, however, must once again be for its parochialism. Even if it were the case that population size is the main determinant of military power and that military power must be increased wherever possible, there would come a time when a halt must be called because the support system for the population and its armed forces is overloaded to breaking point.

War as population control

Here we may dispose of the argument often put forward, that war controls numbers and is therefore a necessary evil. Apart from its cruelty and cynicism, this argument falls to the ground because population continues to explode despite the fact that wars tend to get larger and more lethal. Military deaths for the whole British Commonwealth in six years of the Second World War totalled 354,000, about one year's natural increase for the UK alone in the mid-1960s. Those for Europe as a whole—the grisly total of 30 millions—still amounted to only about 1 per cent a year, less than the natural increase. Although future wars could be much more devastating, they would destroy the environment as well as human beings, so that the surviving population, however small, could be even worse off.

CHAPTER 6

The mobility argument: the fallacy of migration

It is clear . . . that with any view of making room for an unrestricted increase of population, emigration is perfectly inadequate; but as a partial and temporary expedient, and with a view to the more general cultivation of the earth, and the wider extensions of civilisation, it seems to be both useful and proper; . . .' Malthus[1]

'. . . In the very distant future, if our descendants outrun the food-producing capacity of the Earth, and of the sea, they will by that time be sufficiently skilled and wealthy to build themselves artificial satellites to live on.' Colin Clark[2]

'. . . the whole universe is about to be opened up, providing space to accommodate a million million times our present squalid little human family, . . .' Malcolm Muggeridge.[3]

The fallacy here is that population problems can be cured by the general solution of migration, by migration of surplus people into under-populated areas. Colin Clark speaking in public[4] and on television has argued that the less populated areas of the world have a moral duty to accept migration from the few definitely over-populated areas—notably islands such as Mauritius and the West Indies and that failure to adopt this policy is disguised racialism (because the coloured races are 'exploding' most).

Structure of the argument
We can again state the fallacy in the form of the syllogism.
First premise: There are some densely populated areas.
Second premise: There are some sparsely populated areas.
Third premise: The greatest population growth is in those areas already most densely populated.
Deduction: Surplus populations from densely populated areas

59

can (and should?) be accommodated in sparsely populated areas.

Of course this would normally be taken to refer to migration on the earth's surface—any other interpretation may at first sound a bit strange. Nevertheless Clark and other writers have argued a stage beyond this, as the opening quotations showed —that when the earth as a whole becomes over-populated the necessary migration will be from the earth to artificial space satellites or other planets.

(1) Terrestrial migration

It is obviously true that the population problem could, theoretically, at least, be ameliorated for a time by moving people out of over-populated areas, as Clark has suggested. But, even if this were to prove a practical possibility—and the problems are enormous—it could not be effective for more than a short time because of the finite area of the earth.

Even this amelioration cannot be brought about without finding practicable solutions to the colossal logistic problems of directed mass migrations. Assisted or sponsored migrations have been few—certainly none of the great historical migrations have been of this kind. Spontaneous migrations often take, from the demographic point of view, directions opposite to those required—that is, people often move out of sparsely populated into densely populated areas. The great migration from the country into urban areas of industrialised countries over the past two centuries is perhaps the best illustration of this.

Of course by no means all migration is in the 'wrong' direction. The great exodus from Europe into the United States in the nineteenth and early twentieth centuries is a good example of a demographic levelling out, as was (and is) emigration from Britain into Canada and Australia.

Today there are complicating factors of all sorts, some stimulating migration and others impeding it. For example, some countries have social policies which have the effect of making many of their subjects want to escape—such as East Germany, or the United States over Vietnam—and many try to compensate for this with rigorous controls to prevent their subjects from getting out. The Berlin Wall and the Soviet policy of physically preventing, or hindering by taxation, Russian Jews from emigrating to Israel, are especially striking examples of this. However, all states now have policies for controlling the movement of peoples, their own and others, sometimes to encourage a net inward flow as we saw until recently in the assisted passage scheme into Australia—and sometimes to guarantee an outward flow such as brought about by President Amin's expropriation and expulsion of Ugandan Asians. It is hard to avoid the conclusion that these will be widely extended and strengthened under the joint pressures of nationalism and overpopulation so that migration will in future be less rather than more effective.

Recent British migration

If we look at our own country over the past century or so, the balance of migration is definitely on the 'right' side (if the goal is to even out population densities). Between 1871 and 1931 we lost about four millions on balance; between 1931 and 1951 we gained 465,000; and from 1951 to 1974 the score was about even—so that on the whole the migration process has aided demographic balance.

If, however, the UK is already overpopulated, as many of us think, then the only migration rationally acceptable is outward. If we look at the composition of the migration into Britain in recent years, we see that all of it is in the wrong direction, demographically speaking. Most of the immigrants have settled in England—which has a population density of about 920 to the square mile—comes from, for example, Pakistan (392), Jamaica (450), Kenya (50), and Uganda (93 to the square mile).

Even inside the British Isles most of the migration is in the wrong direction if we are trying to even out population densities. For example, out of Eire (density 109 to the square mile) into Britain. Inside the UK, it tends to be out of Northern Ireland (280); Scotland (170); and Wales (340); all into England. Even within England itself, the pattern is the same —out of the relatively sparsely populated North and West into the densely populated South and East.

Although much of this area is under the same government, and all the governments concerned are on reasonably good terms, what sort of social, economic and political measures would be required to reverse this flow and send it at an even faster rate in the opposite direction?

The morality of the migration solution

If some regions are already overpopulated and most spontaneous migration is in the wrong direction, then we have to look not only at the practical problems but to ask some moral questions. Let us examine first of all some of the tricky and almost universally overlooked questions of morality and human rights raised by migration and by geographical mobility in general.

(1) How can 'surplus' people be made to go in the 'right' direction?
(2) How can the existing inhabitants be made to accept them?
(3) How are the newcomers to be fed and supplied, even if problems (1) and (2) are solved?
(4) How long could this remedy be applied, even if problems (1), (2) and (3) could all be solved?

Workable solutions must be found to all of these really severe problems before migration could be considered as even a partial solution. We get some inkling of the power of racial, cultural, economic, and political barriers to massive migrations of the type envisaged, in the reactions of British society in the past few decades to the relatively small number of coloured immigrants.

We tend to take it for granted that anyone with the desire to travel and the wealth to realise it is entitled, in the absence of legal barriers, to go anywhere. Where legal or economic barriers *do* exist we often think they are immoral. I argued in *Population Versus Liberty* that living creatures have a basic need for a certain amount of space to move about in, and developed the notion of an 'ecology of liberty'. Confining ourselves to the human animal we might formulate a general principle as follows:

(1) Everyone is entitled to the microfreedom to go anywhere

at any time, *provided that in exercising it he does not interfere with the microfreedom of others not to be unduly disturbed by his departure, passage, arrival and/or stay.*

The sting in the tail is deliberate, necessary, and onerous. It means we need to formulate a second principle of ecological liberty:

(2) Everyone is entitled to the microfreedom to enjoy undisturbed the pleasures and amenities of his dwelling or working place, *provided that he does not thereby interfere unduly with the microfreedom of others to move about.*

Once both principles are clearly stated, it is clear that fundamental clashes of individual liberty are to be expected, that they frequently take place, that they have important implications for travel and tourism, let alone migration, and that our society has given very little thought to resolving them equitably. It seems clear to me that inflicting untold misery on hundreds of thousands living beside roads, railways and airports so that millions may travel a little further, faster, or cheaper is an unwholesome application of the divide and rule ethos. It also seems that, as more and more holiday resorts and amenity areas reach saturation point, we shall have to switch from a policy of promoting tourism to one of containing it and, eventually, to one of rationing it.

However, we have to find some way of deciding on its rights and wrongs for practical, everyday affairs. Colin Clark has argued that wealthier and less densely populated countries have a moral duty to accept people from poorer and overpopulated regions; but this high principle stands little chance of being adopted generally, and it may also be ecologically unsound. If all populations which overrun their home territory are provided with a ready escape route, then the incentive to control their growth is weakened, or even removed altogether. And then, when the whole world is uniformly overpopulated, those societies which had restricted their native numbers—by conscious policy or by independent parental action—are not only as overcrowded as all the others but may also have lost much of their national identity and cultural heritage because the immigrants outnumber the natives.

63

The Clark imperative seems too onerous to carry out, and a more equitable arrangement would be migration by invitation and/or reciprocity. If Australia, Canada, or the United States wish to stimulate immigration from Europe, West Germany from Southern Italy or Britain from Jamaica, that seems fair enough; but very different criteria should surely apply if hundreds of thousands or even millions of citizens of one country demanded on their own account the right to move into another country without regard to the needs or wishes of the existing inhabitants. The other case, in which one country is exhorted or pressured by another country to take immigrants from a third country is even less likely to be justifiable.

Australia provides a lesson in the difficulties of solving population problems through compulsory migration. What sorts of action would be required, and who would take them, to get the huge empty areas of Australia first made habitable to men and then filled with 'surplus' Asians? Would anything short of a war waged by the United Nations against Australia —or at the very least an international blockade—bring about the desired result? Even if this proved practicable, which is extremely unlikely, how could it possibly be justified in moral and political terms?

Havens for the oppressed
A further moral point concerns the general desirability of havens, such as Britain has provided over many centuries, for the politically or socially oppressed, and the likelihood that overpopulation from natural increase plus 'routine' immigration on economic grounds, will erode this valuable liberal tradition. Had we in Britain not deliberately imported hundreds of thousands of coloured workers to correct the so-called 'labour shortage' (dealt with in Chapter 11) we could have absorbed the few thousand Asians expelled from Uganda with scarcely a ripple—certainly without any public outcry. It is a sad state of affairs when the great debate on Britain's carrying capacity for people, both in toto and in respect of ethnic and racial minorities, is carried on mainly in terms of inaccurate political abuse.

The practicality of the migration solution

Quite apart from its doubtful morality, exponents of the migration solution rarely give any hint that they have studied its logistics, the details of which turn out to be daunting. Ehrlich and Ehrlich argue[5] that if, for example the United States were to agree to help solve the Indian population problem by accepting immigrants, the entire American long-range jet transport system could transport only three-quarters of the annual *increase*, let alone the numbers required to relieve the cumulative pressure from the build-up of the past. 600 jets, each carrying 150 people and making two round trips a week could carry only 9 million per year, whereas the annual increase is 12 million. Surface transport would make only a small extra dent in the problem. Ehrlich and Ehrlich conclude that even if there were to be a place on earth where the extra millions could go, we could not muster the transport effort to get them there.

The basic flaw

However, even if every one of these problems could be solved quickly, we should soon be back once more with the basic flaw in nearly all of these arguments—parochialism. Given perfect organisation and cooperation and unlimited resources, the remedy of migration could be applied only for a mere instant, historically speaking, because the earth is finite. There must rapidly come a time when all possible receiving areas are as full as the sending areas. At present rates of growth, given perfect distribution through migration, in less than a thousand years—a small fraction of our known history—there would be less than one square yard of the earth's land surface for each person. Even given ideal conditions, it is quite impossible in both theory and practice for the migration 'solution' to do more than ameliorate the problem in the short run.

Emigration into space, an essay in astrodemography

At first sight it seems likely that here at last is a population argument which—whatever else may be wrong with it—at least is not open to the charge of parochialism; but the trouble is that 'space' means many things to many people. Before

65

July 1969, 'space travel' meant two or three men spending a few hours—a few days at most—in orbit less than 200 miles above the earth, the costs being as spectacular as the journeys. 'Space' means something radically different to the astronomer —and this argument could be put forward only by someone lacking in scientific knowledge and even commonsense.

Structure of the space migration fallacy
The meanings implied in the two quotations advocating space migration at the head of the chapter can be made explicit in logical form as follows:

First premise: Space is infinite.

Second premise: Man is conquering space.

Deduction: Infinite numbers of human beings can go and live in space.

In this case the logic is correct but the premises are shaky. Although the first one is near enough true for all practical purposes, the second is substantially false. Demonstrating that this is so requires a fairly detailed examination of what the word 'space' means.

The meaning of 'space'
Skirting the earth's atmosphere for a short time, or even visiting the moon as a few American and Russian missions have done, is very different from exploring other planets—even within our own solar system, let alone beyond it into our galaxy. Travel outside the galaxy would be still more distant, yet we still use exactly the same term, 'space', to describe the unimaginably remote realm at the theoretical limit of scientific observation. This range, a distance of 10 thousand million light years away from us, is where the velocity of the recession of the galaxies approaches the speed of light so that no energy or information about it can reach us. And of course we still use the term for regions beyond even that, the edge of the theoretically knowable universe. Quick flips round our 'space' backyard—including even the voyages to the moon, less than half a million miles there and back—simply are not in the same league.

To explore the practicalities of ameliorating or even curing the population problem by shipping off substantial numbers of people into space, let us take a look at our neighbours.

The Solar System
The earth is a member of the family of planets belonging to our sun, about 93 million miles from us. The whole group has a diameter of about 7 thousand million miles. These sound very large distances but in fact they are quite insignificant when compared with the distances within our own galaxy, let alone those of the universe as a whole.
The *Larousse Encyclopaedia of Astronomy* says:

> Let us imagine ourselves making a map of the Solar System and the nearest stars to scale. Even if we used a sheet of paper many hundreds of feet wide, the stars would still have to be marked out round the edges whilst the whole Solar System would be nothing more than a tiny dot lost in the centre of the sheet.

Planets of the solar system
Astronomers divide the planets of the solar system into two main groups—the 'terrestrial' planets: Earth, Mercury, Venus, Mars, and Pluto: and the 'gaseous giants': Jupiter, Saturn, Uranus, and Neptune.

Table 6/1 lists the terrestrial planets—excluding the Earth —giving very brief details about their distance, atmosphere, temperature, water, surface, and so forth, with a few general remarks in the right hand column. There is little point in adding to this catalogue, except to remark that Mars is the only one on which human beings could survive, but even here extensive life support systems would be required. We could live only in space suits, space capsules or houses built on the same principles, and colonists would not be able to move freely about on the surface of the planet. Clearly, there isn't going to be much room here for surplus human beings from Earth.

The Gaseous Giants
In addition to the four solid planets, there are four 'gaseous giants'. There is not much point in examining them beyond

Table 6/1

The 'terrestrial' planets (Earth excluded).

Planet	Mean distance	Atmosphere	Day temperature	Water	Surface	Remarks
Mercury	36m	hardly any	410°C	none	like moon	'temperature sufficient to melt tin'.
Venus	67m	abundant carbon-dioxide*	427°C	none	dusty desert	'. . . a very hostile world . . . animal life in any form appears to be out of the question.,,
Mars	142m	1/20th of Earth's	0/30°C	All frost and ice, less than 1/500 of Earths	dusty with very large sandstorms	Polar ice-caps but 'very advanced state of dehydration" possibly some sort of vegetation. Humans could survive with space flight equipment.
Pluto	3,670m	?	'must be very cold'	?	?	400 times further than the sun. Would take 14 years to reach (@ 30,000 m.p.h. in a straight line).

*The pressure is now thought to be 40 times that of Earth's atmosphere.
Data from 'Larousse Encyclopaedia of Astronomy', (1966).

explaining that Jupiter, for instance, has no surface in the ordinary sense of the word; there is no division as we understand it between the atmosphere and the planet itself. Even if there *were* something to stand on, it wouldn't be much use because—on account of the great gravitational force from such a huge planet—the weight of a human being would be $2\frac{3}{4}$ times what it is on earth, almost enough to crush him.

The others become progressively less hospitable as the distance from the earth increases. The surface of Saturn is described as 'unstable . . . a sort of fluid' and the planet as a whole as being 'utterly unlike anything . . . on earth . . . impossible to conceive'. Neptune is nearly 3 billion miles away and has a temperature not much above absolute zero ($-273°$C).

The Sun
The Sun, with a surface temperature of 6,000 degrees centigrade, looks an even less likely prospect, and it is clear that if we are going to move out into space we shall have to look for more suitable destinations.

The galaxy
The Solar System forms a small part of our 'galaxy', an enormous disc of stars about 100,000 light years in diameter. The sun is about 33,000 light years away from its centre (near Sagittarius). It contains over 100 billion stars adding up to a total mass about 200 billion times that of our Sun, so there is plenty of it.

The Local Group
Our nearest galactic neighbours are in the 'Local Group' (of galaxies) which has 17 members, including our own. The volume the local group occupies is a flattened ellipsoid with a major axis of 2 million light years, a minor axis of 1 million light years, and a thickness of between 400,000 and 600,000 light years. The centre is in the region of the Andromeda nebula, about a million light years away from our own galaxy which is at one extremity of the 'local group'. Our nearest galactic neighbour is called the 'Magellanic Cloud' which is 160,000 light years away and receding from us at a velocity of

at least 20,000 miles an hour. The furthest away in the local group is M33 which is 2·4 million light years away and has a speed of recession of some 300,000 miles an hour. A spaceship going there from earth would have to achieve 300,001 m.p.h. before it started making any headway.

It must be stressed that these stars are our *near* neighbours, but, as the furthest are already 2½ million light years away and receding at an enormous velocity, there isn't much point in looking beyond them.

Extra-terrestrial migration

Let us switch back to our immediate neighbours now and take the nearest possible point of call outside our Solar System but within the galaxy. The nearest star to us outside the Solar System is Alpha Centauri which is about 4¼ light years away— around 25,000 thousand million miles. At the speeds achieved by present space technology—say a maximum of 17,000 miles an hour ('escape velocity')—it would take about 170,000 years to get to this star: possibly longer than the entire existence of our species. Picture this in terms of the history of past civilisations, and imagine what would be required of social, civil, political, and scientific organisation for handling the navigation and scientific records in order to prevent the whole venture simply passing completely beyond human ken.

However, let us assume that all of these problems of navigation, range, and life-support for our space ships—each one insuperable for the foreseeable future—have been solved completely, and go on to look at what would be required at the rocket launching bases on earth from which the 'surplus' human beings would start their great collective odysseys.

The departure timetable

Let us assume that the world population reached its optimum level of about 4·0 billions by mid-1976, (at all dates later than this the situation gets more difficult, of course). Population increase in that year (at 2 per cent per annum) would be about 80 millions, so to maintain stability that is the number we would have to ship off into space. Let us further assume that we have improved our space ships to the point at which they have virtually infinite duration for both rocket and life support systems, and have given them means of safe landing on other stars and of taking off again as many times as might turn out to be necessary if the landing place turns out to be unsatisfactory. Finally, we have managed to put in enough equipment for starting off a new and self-sustaining colony at the other end, while at the same time increasing their passenger capacity to 2 or 3 families, say 10 people, about three times the present human load. The number of rockets and take-offs that would be required during the year would therefore be 8 millions—equivalent to 21,918 every day, 913 every hour, and 15·2 every minute—roughly one every four seconds.

Materials and propellants

The big rockets now taking off for relatively short and simple trips to the moon weigh about 3,100 tons on take-off, including fuel. Even if our migrant space-ships weighed no more, we would have to despatch, say 25 thousand million tons of rocketry per annum, and of course little or none of this would be salvageable.

Manpower

If we look at the manpower involved for the Mercury project —which cost only $400 million by the end of 1961—we see it involved 4,000 companies and over 200,000 persons, though not all of these were full time. According to official American figures, if the annual space budget got to 10 billion dollars there would be more than a million workers directly involved in space work, compared with only 70,000 in the whole of the American steel industry.

Man as a space animal

There are a number of problems worrying the medical men who supervise our existing space travellers. In the first place, only very highly stable, reliable and fit persons are chosen, and these would have to be rather introverted as well for long journeys. These psychological characteristics would have to be backed up by Draconian social controls during a voyage, for there would be little scope for behavioural deviance.

There are many unsolved physiological problems too: the absence of gravity leads to changes in the musculature, nervous system and bone marrow, and a substantial proportion of blood is lost even in short voyages. Artificial gravity from constant acceleration or centrifugal force may help with some of these problems but the coup de grace to our aspirations heavenwards could still be given by a phenomenon as trivial as a cold in the head. In making plans to ship untold millions of humans off the earth, it would be prudent to entertain at least the possibility that our species simply is not adapted to extended space journeys.

Ecological imperatives

Space migrants would be subject to the same basic ecological imperatives as the people they leave behind on the earth, but their impact in space would be much more immediate. Crews would have to subject themselves with extreme rigour to the very two things which our failure to practise on earth had driven them away—population control, and conservation of resources.

It would be essential to have rigid control of numbers in the spaceship, and this would mean limiting the passengers in the first place to those prepared to accept it without question, and rigorous instilling and monitoring of this value in subsequent generations born during the long space odysseys.

All excreta would have to be recycled, and even the bodies of the dead would be valuable because, if they were jettisoned in space the loss of organic matter over long periods would be very serious. Assuming that bodies were dehydrated before 'burial', and the moisture conserved, this would still leave a dry weight of about 70 lbs of material to be jettisoned at each death, so that on long journeys the loss would be insupportable. There would have to be complete recycling of human tissues on a cosmic compost heap.

Effective breeding communities

I have argued as though the ten person 'population' of these spaceships would be biologically viable; but of course they would not, for inbreeding would have to be the norm, with consequent deterioration of the stock. 500 or 600 is about the minimum viable size for a population, so the space craft would have to go off in convoys of fifty or sixty and keep close for regular commuting between them to spread the genes about a bit. This would present further difficulties in navigation and organisation, and greatly increase collision hazards.

Hostile neighbours?

The number of stars in the universe has been estimated at about 100 million million millions, of which about one in every ten thousand are single stars with planetary systems, of which about 100 million may have life already. Dr von Hoerna of the US National Radio Astronomy Laboratory has estimated that as many as 1 per cent of all stars have habitable planets, and, assuming that technical civilisations last about 100,000 years, the average distance between them is 500 light years. Fred Hoyle has said he is sure that somewhere there is a cricket eleven to beat the Australians.

This calculation still leaves quite a number of planets hospitable to life and not yet inhabited; but it also suggests that mass embassies from planet Earth might not always find a welcome. Serious research is now under way to establish communication with any other civilisations within reasonable range.

The point of the exercise

Even assuming that none of the foregoing problems existed, what would be the point of working our fingers to the bone and consuming our limited resources and wealth in order to produce and equip vast armies for shipment into space? Even if we could see the point, and managed to put the whole vast machine into operation, it would have to stop within 5,000 years, because by that time, at the present rate of world population growth, the whole mass of the known universe would have been converted into human flesh.

The basic flaw

The most perfunctory examination of the logistic problems involved in shipping off the world's population increase shows that as a practical solution—even at the 1975 level—the space migration argument is not substantial enough to qualify even as a pipe-dream. Even here, in the unlikely context of grandiose space odysseys, there is a strong strand of parochialism. The term 'space' travel—meaning handfuls of men and women pottering about in the terrestrial backyard—is taken to have the same significance when it is used to refer to the transportation of millions of people and their equipment into the unimaginable magnitude and remoteness of the universe as a whole.

Wouldn't it be wiser to get used to the idea of population control and conservation on the larger and more comfortable (so far) spaceship Earth?

CHAPTER 7

The socialisation argument: the fallacy of the large family

Members of large families are usually more stable . . . mature . . . responsible and . . . realistic'. Letter to *The Times*.[1]

'Within a large family there is a feeling of security which is usually lacking in a small family'. Eustace Chesser.[2]

'I am a great believer in the value of the family. Three or four is in itself a good number.' D. E. C. Eversley.[3]

The popular belief about large families
The belief that large families are good in themselves is part of the folklore of our society. I myself accepted it more or less unquestionably until, some years ago, I set to answer the following question: If we have to reduce the average family size in order to stabilize our population what benefits would have to be foregone and how might we compensate for them?

No definition of the 'large' family has been agreed, nor are there any definitive criteria by which we can settle the issue. One or two children would normally be thought of as small family, whereas three probably would not, though few would

74

think it large. A family of four would be thought large by most people, though not by all, and five or more would be thought large by almost everybody. I will work on the assumption that four or more constitute a large family.

Incidence and significance of large families
The 1971 census showed that there were 14,452,000 families in Great Britain. The distribution by completed family size in 1951 was as follows: no children, 13 per cent; one, 23 per cent; two, 30 per cent; three, 17 per cent; four, 9 per cent; while 8 per cent had five or more.[4] Only 17 per cent, about one-sixth of all families, were 'large'. However much people theorise about the value of the large family, not many are prepared to practise what they preach. Making an allowance for large families resulting from unplanned pregnancies and arising by mistake rather than choice would make the proportion even smaller.

In view of these figures, is it worthwhile attacking the large family syndrome? Table 7/1 shows that they contribute a substantial proportion of total fertility, nearly one third. The 'extra' children converting small families into large ones form a much smaller proportion but their numbers—at about one-sixth of all births—are enough to convert a potentially declining population into one which is expanding fairly rapidly.

Table 7/1

Proportions of large families

17% of all recent families* are large ones.

31% of all recent children are born into large families.

14% of all recent children consist of large family 'extras'.†

*1951 marriage cohort. Mean family size after 20 years, 2·24.
†Simply, in this case, those converting small families into large ones. This proportion is diminishing rapidly.

A further and perhaps more important point is that those extolling the large family ideal seem to exercise a quite disproportionate influence on the major political parties, and on government. So far they have managed to block any serious top-level debate. When Douglas Houghton made his famous 'large families are a form of social irresponsibility'[5] speech, the howls of anguish and abuse from a raucuos minority brought an abject apology from the Prime Minister, Mr Harold Wilson, and all sensible discussion to an abrupt halt.

In sum, a sane population policy seems a good deal less likely while even a significant minority subscribe unthinkingly to the large family ideal.

Structure of the large family argument

The large family syndrome can be analysed into at least two and possibly as many as five components, depending where the benefits are said to lie. These by no means watertight categories are exemplified to some degree in the following quotations; I wish to stress that my label for the *view* is not intended to categorise the *person* putting it forward—the 'egocentric' view is often put forward by people who could at most be criticised as being unthinking.

The egocentric view

This stresses the benefits conferred by a large family *on the parents*, as exemplified in an article in the *Guardian*:

'I loathe the hothouse atmosphere . . . of the two child family . . . the most neurotic society on earth . . .' (Ann Hales Took, 13 February 1963).

A letter to the *Guardian* expressed sincere concern about the population problem but went on: 'The . . . pleasure, richness . . . and solid compensations of a large family far outweigh the formidable problems. My husband and I feel slightly sorry for the parents of ones and twos who are missing the happiness we have.' (Althea Robbins, 28 June 1967.)

Another letter, to *The Times*, widens the frame of reference to include benefits to the *children*, also: 'The joy of creating and rearing a large family should be unrestrained for all who are able and willing to accept the responsibilities involved and who desire this kind of enrichment for themselves and their children' (D. R. Hughes, 20 April 1964).

The essence of the egocentric view may be expressed in the form of the syllogism:

First premise: Parents are entitled to do whatever makes them happiest.

Second premise: (Some/all) parents are made happiest by having large families.

Conclusion: (Some/all) parents are entitled to have large families.

This can be softened by laying the main emphasis on the offspring. Parents who wish their *children* to be happy may have a large family to realise this aim, and this can, of course, involve altruism—or even self-abasement—if it is believed that a large family means a heavy burden on the parents. Yet another variant involves at least an element of altruism, having a large brood at some sacrifice in order to prevent one's own social group from being inundated by another; middle-class by working class, Protestant by Catholic, caucasoid by negroid, or whatever. The most forceful statement of this point of view I have yet come across was by Dick Gregory, the American exponent of Black power: 'My answer to genocide, quite simply, is eight black kids—and another baby on the way.'[6]

The fact that this view is often put forward by people who in addition to being economically viable, are kind, generous, warm, expansive, and loving doesn't alter in the slightest the fact that no weight whatever is given to *social* considerations, which means, when you come down to it, the needs and rights of one's fellow citizens.

The sociocentric view

This is intended to describe views emphasising the benefits to society, such as the claim in a letter to *The Times* that

> members of large families are usually more 'stable . . . mature, responsible and . . . realistic' than their fellows. . . . their enforced independence requires them to take a more active part in their own advancement, and teaches them psychology early and painlessly through competitive and protective contact with their own kind. They learn to distinguish between real and false emotion and motives. Faults are amicably tolerated in others

77

though definitely armed against . . . there would be no danger of a member of a large family agreeing to the illusion of . . . mutual disarmament; he knows his fellow man too well (A. P. Munn, 13 April, 1964).

Another aspect of alleged social benefit lies in the economic sphere, as we see in this excerpt from the old *Catholic Encyclopaedia* (1907): 'The small family fosters a degree of egotism and enervating self-indulgence which in turn diminishes the incentive to labour and reduces industrial production.'

Here is the essence of this belief in polysyllogistic form.

First premise: Children reared in large families make better adults than children reared in small families.

Second premise: Better adults make better citizens.

Third premise: The nation needs the best citizens it can get.

Conclusion: The nation needs its families to be large ones.

I think we could all agree with the second and third premises, but the conclusion is false. In fact it is doubly false because, as I hope to show, the first premise is false and because the logical structure of the argument is invalid.

First refutation: the logical fallacy

The conclusion that 'The nation needs large families' does not follow logically from the premises. There is an elementary logical flaw and the correct deduction is: 'The nation needs *citizens reared* in large families'. The difference between the two conclusions is crucial, for the first is an argument in favour of an ever-increasing population as much as for the production of better citizens. If, however, it is true that large families produce the best adults and that the best adults make the best citizens this logically implies not that everybody should have as large a family as possible, but that *such citizens as are needed* should be reared in large families.

This raises two fundamental questions, both of which are begged by the earlier formulation:

(1) *How many citizens are needed,* and *when?*
(2) *Which families are to produce them?*

These questions could easily be related to eugenic policies

or elitist arguments linked to programmes restricting reproduction to a chosen few. More democratic—though possibly dysgenic—policies could work through some sort of rationing system—possibly based on chance—permitting just enough people to have large families to secure the production of the citizens required. No matter what the mechanism, however, the programme could work only at the expense of a substantial body of citizens who, for the greater good of society, would have to forego the right to reproduce.

Second refutation: the factual fallacy
There is also a factual fallacy, because several years of investigation have shown that in virtually all the areas in which one can make some kind of measurement members of a large family are not better but worse off than members of a small family. The larger the family, the worse it is as an environment for a developing individual. This appears to be a true environmental effect, not a genetic effect caused by parents of low intelligence or other generally unwelcomed characteristics having the largest families.

The case for the large family
There is no smoke on the family-size issue without a little fire. Support for the beliefs expressed in the quotations at the head of this chapter is by no means totally lacking, although I hope to show that:

(1) The overwhelming weight of evidence is negative;
(2) It doesn't really matter whether the evidence is negative or positive because there are other and quite insuperable barriers to the widespread production of large families;
(3) Just as point (2) prevents the realisation of the large family ideal, so point (1) will convince the rational parent and citizen that neither he nor the nation are missing much.

Reducing incidence of obesity
5 per cent of all our children are overweight (defined as 20 per cent or more above the average), and since more children in large families are underfed it is hardly surprising that they

79

suffer less from obesity. A survey published in *New Society* in 1972 concluded that there was 'a higher proportion of over-weight children in smaller families'.[7]

Decreasing incidence of pyloric stenosis

Pyloric stenosis is a congenital disease of the muscle controlling the opening between the stomach and the intestine, and research done in Birmingham showed that it decreases in frequency as the number of children born to a mother increases. With first-born children there are 4·3 cases per 1,000 births; second 2·8; third, 2·5; and fourth and later, 1·4.[8]

Reducing incidence of suicide

Emile Durkheim's great work *Suicide* showed a striking inverse correlation between family size and suicide. He demonstrated three basic facts that:

(1) Marriage itself was a partial 'cure' for suicidal tendencies, although only for men;
(2) Going on to have children is an even better preventive for both men and women;
(3) Living in a large family group is the most potent preventive of all.

Durkheim's studies were done mainly on late nineteenth-century statistics, and he found many complications, having household size instead of family size, for instance, so the proof is to some extent unsound. However, figures from 86 French departments showed that the suicide rate dropped from 430–380 per million inhabitants where the average household consisted of 3·47 persons to 70–30 per million where the average household was 4·34 persons. This he found to be striking confirmation of his basic argument that 'suicides diminish as family density increases . . . far from dense families being a sort of . . . luxury . . . they are actually an indispensable staff of daily life . . . however poor one is' (p. 201).

'Intangible' Qualities

It could be argued that it is of questionable value to measure intelligence, educational performance, height, and so forth, and to show, as in the rest of this chapter, that the children born into large families suffer in these respects. What really matters, it might be said, are the intangible—or at least less tangible—human qualities such as kindness, sympathy, tolerance, maturity and co-operativeness. It can still be argued that large families tend to produce effects such as these, hard if not impossible to measure.

One source of evidence on this topic of 'intangibles' lies in the subjective experience of members of large families, though this is rather hard to assess on a comparative basis for the obvious reason that most people growing up in a family of a particular size have no experience of others. However, one subjective view follows, which must be taken on its merits.

In an article called 'Happy Families' Polly Devlin, one of seven children, said:

> The stock response to the discovery that one is one of many . . . goes, . . . 'How lucky you were; All that Companionship; Love; Security; Ability to Face the World, Take Knocks and Influence People. (The last I suppose by the sheer force of numbers.) Those who say this usually exude that complacency which can only be acquired by having been an only child and the centre of their own tiny world for years. And, since an only child is seldom contradicted there is no point in me trying . . . I lurch off muttering.
>
> Leaving out the economics of the thing and the seriousness of the population explosion, there isn't much to be said from the practical point of view for big families. Though there is an extreme richness in being able to love a great number of people . . . that richness is depleted by a lack of . . . other essential endowments. . . .
>
> That asset of big families, the companionship, can wear a little thin. One could never enter a room without finding a piece of companionship already installed, usually with a scowl on its face, and there was never a vacant lavatory in the house. . . .
>
> When there are that many people about one doesn't achieve cosy security; no one has time to notice you or reassure you. Life becomes one long pluck at an adult elbow to make it twitch to prove you're there. My parents used to call us by reeling off our names in hideous composite which went 'Annmarie polvalbarriecareanelen', whoever . . . answered was smacked since we were

THE 'COMMONSENSE' FALLACIES

only called when depredation had been discovered. This was often. They said it worked, the blows averaged out. . . .

Large families engender rivalry; the acid of it seeps through every activity and everyone becomes a contender for the prize whether it is the kiss at night or the marmalade in the morning. . . . The child of a smaller family learns early to expect her due. . . . One child of many learns to grasp without looking. Selectivity is an unknown concept . . . actually being listened to is so disconcerting that I begin to babble like an idiot brook to get it all in before the listener turns the record player higher. Large families learn generosity . . . I'd rather be a happy mean.[9]

Increasing incidence of neighbourliness

However, there is one objective indicator, even in this sphere of 'intangibles'. Many of us have come to feel that neighbourliness is rapidly disappearing from our large, wealthy, urban societies and that this is a very great loss. We read about old people who died so alone that nobody knew or cared enough to make enquiries until months afterwards. In the United States the situation has deteriorated to the point at which

Table 7/2

Increase in neighbourliness with increase in number of brothers and sisters USA. 1940s

No. of children in family of origin	% of 'good neighbours' coming from that family size.
1	6·6%
2	9·6%
3	13·3%
4	15·9%
5	8·8%
6 and over	45·8%
Total	100·0%

Adapted from Sorokin, P. (1950). A Study of American Good Neighbours and Christian Saints. Altruistic Love.

people can be methodically robbed and assaulted—even murdered—in a busy street as pedestrians hustle past intent on their own affairs.

In societies developing in this direction neighbourliness is to be highly prized—indeed unless we can somehow revivify, foster and extend this quality we are more or less doomed—and anything tending to produce it could be very valuable. Some research in America showed that people classified as 'good neighbours' tended to come from large families, as we see in Table 7/2, very nearly half of them coming from families of six or more.

I have been looking out for further evidence in favour of large families for perhaps eight years now, and have found no more. No doubt there are other points to be made, but the overwhelming weight of what I have discovered must go into the other scale pan.

The case against the large family

(1) *Increasing overcrowding.*
One would expect there to be more overcrowding as family size increases, and this was borne out by the evidence put before the Royal Commission on Population, as we see in Table 7/3. Overcrowding is measured in terms not of 'persons' but of 'equivalent persons'—i.e. children under 1 year don't count at all, whilst those between 1 and 10 count as half a person only, which of course makes the situation appear better than it is in real life. Be this as it may, we see that overcrowding went up from 0·2 per cent in the smallest household group—1 to 1½ persons—to 8 per cent for families of 5 to 5½ persons, and 56 per cent for families of 9 'equivalent persons' and over.

It should be noted that overcrowding was defined here not just as an inconvenience but as 'an urgent social problem threatening the health of the victims', and that the proportion of *individuals* overcrowded was 'much larger than the proportion of *families* overcrowded'.

(2) *Increasing persistence of overcrowding*
One survey followed up a group of families from 1948 to 1950 and measured the improvement in overcrowding, any families

83

Table 7/3

Increase in overcrowding with increase in family size. UK, 1940s.

Size of family (equivalent persons)	Proportion of families overcrowded in each size group.
1–1½	0·2%
2–2½	0·6%
3–3½	2·0%
4–4½	4·0%
5–5½	8·0%
6–6½	18·0%
7–7½	27·0%
8–8½	45·0%
9 and over	56·0%

Adapted from HMSO (1949) 'Royal Commission on Population.[4]

which changed their composition over the period being dropped. The one-child families improved by 62 per cent, those with two children by 25%, those with three by 26%, while those with four or more (originally five times worse off than the one-child families) had improved by only 11 per cent.[10]

(3) *Decreasing housing amentiies*
Table 7/4 shows another aspect of living accommodation,

Table 7/4

Decrease in housing amenities with increase in family size.

Disamenity	Number of dependent children in family			
	One	Two	Three	Four or more
house in bad repair	29%	29%	38%	53%
no bathroom	42%	41%	43%	52%
no hot water	47%	47%	50%	59%

Adapted from Douglas and Blomfield (1958) 'Children under Five'.

'housing amenities', and how they decreased with increase in family size. The disparity here was not quite so striking or so uniform, but the children in the larger families were nevertheless worse off.

(4) *Increasing foetal death rate*

A 1960 study examined foetal death rates in a White American community, and showed from the second child onwards—that is, after the barrier of the first pregnancy is surmounted—a pronounced increase in foetal deaths for every increase in family size. Beyond five pregnancies the death rate is very high indeed. From 10 deaths per 1,000 births for the second child, the graph rose to 22·5 deaths at the sixth.

(5) *Increasing incidence of infant mortality*

The authors of *Britain, an Official Handbook* (1968) point out that 'the causes of the decline in mortality include . . . the smaller size of the family which has reduced the strain on mothers and enabled them to take greater care of their children'.[11]

Bernard Benjamin in *Health and Vital Statistics* (1968) agrees: 'Babies of young mothers with large families for their age have a high risk of death in the post neonatal period'. Table 7/5 shows this broken down by family size from one child up to 11 plus children.

Table 7/5

Increase in infant mortality with increase of family size (after 1st child) England and Wales, 1949–50.

	Order of birth						
	1st	2nd	3rd	4th	5th	6–10th	11th plus
Infant mortality (per 1000)	31·0	25	31	35	40	44	53

(6) *Increasing maternal mortality*
Maternal mortality also rises quite sharply after the fourth pregnancy. With 9 or more pregnancies maternal mortality is twice the average.

(7) *Increasing frequency of mongolism.*
A further risk in having large families is the increased incidence of mongolism. This results from the fact that a woman having a large family must bear children at progressively greater ages at which there is an increasing risk of a mongol birth. Table 7/6 shows this. Taking the 20–29 year group as the ideal for bearing children, and counting their incidence of mongol births as the norm, we see that in the 30–34 year group the risk is $4\frac{1}{4}$ times higher, and so on. At 45 years plus it is more than 51 times greater. We must remember, of course, that this is not a direct correlation with family size.

Table 7/6
Increase in mongolism with increase in mother's age.

	20–29	30–34	35–39	40–44	45+
Mongols per 1000 births	0·4	1·7	3·6	13·6	21·1

(8) *Decreasing quality of nutrition*
A recent report shows that in the UK in 1950 families with three or more children received 6 per cent below requirements on total protein and 8 per cent below requirements on calcium. By 1964 the larger families received 10 per cent and 13 per cent below the norm, respectively, showing that the situation had deteriorated in the intervening fourteen years. The report shows that larger families were substantially worse off in all respects than the smaller families, although in all categories except those of total protein and calcium they received on average above minimal requirements.[12]

(9) *Decreasing physical stature*
The difference in diet referred to may be one of the reasons why the children in larger families are appreciably shorter

than those from small families. Table 7/7 shows that the average difference between two large groups of children, at the age of 5½ and 14½ years, was 1·0 inches and 2·1 inches, respectively.

Table 7/7

Decline in children's height with increase in family size. UK, 1960s.

Age	Height		Children in large families shorter by
	Only children	3 or more siblings.	
5½	43·9″	42·9″	1·0″
14½	64·8″	62·7″	2·1″

OHE (1967) *Malnutrition in the 1960s.*

(10) *Decreasing quality of maternal care*

The Royal Commission on Population noted that 'the control which men and women exercise over the number of their children is one of the most important conditions of their own and of their country's welfare'.

Virtually all medical opinion seems to concur with this judgement, as expressed by one doctor:

> Twenty-five years of clinical experience have convinced me that many couples in the lower socio-economic groups could manage reasonably well with a family of two or three, but are swamped by the responsibility of looking after five, six or more children. Standards within the family unit deteriorate and parents, children and the community suffer.[13]

Table 7/8 shows the results of a survey of the decreasing quality of maternal care with increasing numbers of children among the families of 1,181 manual workers. The researchers found that the health visitors who made the assessments tended to 'make allowances' so that the larger families were often up-rated. The evidence presented later shows that this generalisation is not true of working-class families only, and that middle-class children suffer too.

Table 7/8

Decrease in the quality of maternal care with increase in the number of children. UK, 1950.

	Number of dependent children in family				
	1	2	3	4	5 or more
% of mothers rated 'among the best'	45%	33%	27%	16%	10%
Total numbers of children in each size-group	260	880	860	450	560 (est.)
Number of children not getting the best care	143	590	628	378	504

Mothers were rated by health visitors as 'among the best' 'average' or 'among the worst', with respect to these items:-

a. management of children.
b. adequacy of children's shoes.
c. adequacy of children's clothing.
d. cleanliness of the child.
e. cleanliness of the home.

Adapted from:- Douglas and Blomfield, (1958) 'Children under Five'.

(11) *Increasing ill health in mothers*
In 1967 an official publication, *Circumstances of Families,* demonstrated that the proportion of mothers reporting ill-health rose from 1·4 per cent for those with two children to 24 per cent for those with six children or more.

(12) *Delayed maturation: the outset of puberty in girls*
Table 7/9 shows the age of puberty by completed family size. If the onset of puberty is assumed to be a suitable indicator, maturation in girls appears to be progressively delayed, as family size increases.

Table 7/9

Delay in onset of puberty in girls with increase in family size. UK, 1960s.

| No. of siblings | Appearance of 1st menstrual flow | | | |
	Earlier than normal	Normal	Later than normal	Total %
0	53%*	28%	19%	100%
1	39%	36%	25%	100%
2	36%	34%	30%	100%
3+	33%	32%	35%	100%

Based on rounded data from:-
Douglas, J. W. B. (1964) 'The Home and the School'. (pp. 107 and 198).

* The apparently odd absolute distribution follows from the working definitions.

(13) *Increasing incidence of neurosis*
The authors of a survey conducted in the 1950s report that 'there was a higher than expected frequency of patients with neurosis in birth-orders five and over, and a lower than expected frequency in birth orders one, two, and three'.[14] The incidence of neurosis was 4 per cent lower in birth orders under four and 16 per cent higher in those of five and over. We might regard this as negative evidence in the field labelled 'intangibles'.

(14) *Reduced education and downward social mobility*
Even Colin Clark gives evidence, from a study by Bresard in France, to show that children in larger families are penalised:

In all . . . social groups, other than the 'larger business proprietors and professional men' . . . a larger family means . . . less education and a lesser chance of entering the higher social groups. The sons of farmers and small business men . . . have considerably less chance of entering their father's occupations when they are born into large families, and correspondingly more probability of becoming wage workers.[15]

89

He also refers to a supporting study by Berent: 'Here again we get the [same] result . . . and there are some *signs that this discrepancy is increasing*' (Italics added).

(15) *Decreasing intelligence test scores*
Table 7/10 shows the relationship between family size and intelligence as measured on a standard test—though *not* in this case expressed as a percentage. The table gives a breakdown by sex, by social class (determined by the father's occupation), and by family size. Families are divided into those with one or two children and those with four or more. It is important to note that the very marked decline in measured intelligence of the children of the larger families is to be observed for both middle-class and working-class families. There is one curious anomaly, however—the fact that the middle-class girls suffer a very much smaller penalty than any of the other groups; by contrast, the working-class girls are *worse* off than the boys.

Table 7/10

Falling intelligence test scores with increase in family size.
UK, 1960.

		Intelligence test scores (averages)	
Social Class	No. of children	Boys	Girls
Middle Class	1 or 2 children	57·27	56·28
	4 or more children	52·52	55·96
Manual Working Class	1 or 2 children	50·00	50·98
	4 or more children	45·53	46·07

Adapted from Douglas, (1964) 'The Home and the School.'

(16) *Decreasing reading ability*
The Inner London Education Authority's literacy survey bears out earlier findings that increasing family size is related to

poorer reading ability. Of the several reading categories used, only two are reported here, 'poor' readers at the bottom of the scale and 'good readers' at the top. Table 7/11 shows the proportion in each.

Birth position reflects a similar relationship, Only 13·5 per cent of first-born children showed up as poor readers against 32·2 per cent of those born seventh or later. 12·7 per cent of the first-born were good readers against only 3·3 per cent for the seventh plus. These figures are further reinforced by the fact that about twice as many single children lived in an 'atypical' situation—i.e. with only one parent—and that these had poorer reading standards. This indicates that if like is compared with like, i.e. only those in 'normal' families, the advantages of the small family would be even more emphasised.

Fig. 7/11

Fall in reading ability with increase in family size*. London, 1970s.

	Reading standard	
	Poor readers	Good readers
1 child	13·2%	14·3%
2–3 children	15·8%	11·3%
4 or more children	22·8%	5·6%

*Based on data from ILEA literacy survey. Private communication, January 1973. Some material is available in mimeo form.

(17) *Decreasing parental stimulation*
One of the factors related to academic performance may be the amount of stimulation given by the parents, and Table 7/12 shows that this, as assessed by teachers, is generally much lower for both manual and non-manual families, as family size increases. There is one exception to the rule: in the case of the non-manuals there is a small increase in stimulation from the one-child to the two-three child families. But in accordance with the general trend, there is a big drop to the 4+ families,

10 per cent less of the large families being judged 'stimulating' and 81 per cent more 'unstimulating'. In the case of the manuals the effect is greater still. Here 55 per cent less are judged 'stimulating' and 72 per cent more judged 'unstimulating', taking the one-child family as the basis of comparison through-out. Further research should reveal the answer to the interesting question of whether the families which become large are judged less stimulating over the years as they increase in size.

Table 7/12

Decrease in parental stimulation with increase in family size.
Breakdown by father's occupation. London, 1972*.

| No. of children | Occupation of father | | | | | |
| | Non manual | | | Manual | | |
	1	2–3	4+	1	2–3	4+
Stimulating	36·0%	38·9%	32·4%	10·4%	8·8%	4·7%
Average	54·6%	50·7%	50·5%	58·7%	58·5%	42·2%
Unstimula-ting	9·4%	10·4%	17·0%	30·9%	32·7%	53·1%

* Source. ILEA Research, 1972, private communication.

Note. Manual 5,645 cases, Non-manual 1,199 cases.

Economic factors

(18) *Improvement in the economic status of married women with decrease in family size*

Richard Titmus has written:

Above all, the decline in the size of the family has meant, in terms of family economics, *a rise in the standard of living of women which has probably been of more importance, by itself, than any change since 1900 in real earnings by manual workers.* Nor would it be hard to argue that *this factor was far more influential up to the Second World War than any additional benefits derived from the expansion of social services* and improvements in medical care.[16] (Italics partly original, partly added.)

Despite the general emancipation of women by the reduction in family size, many individual exceptions remain. As all parents know, the larger the family, the worse off it is until the children reach working age. This is so obvious that it would not be necessary to waste time on it were it not for the fact that at least one eminent scholar, Colin Clark, has argued the opposite case. The essential increase in the outlay on food leads to reduced spending on rent—one of the causes of the over-crowding to be found in large families—and of course on fuel, clothing and entertainment.

(19) *Decreasing proportion of owner-occupiers*
In the case of two-child families, 53 per cent of the parents own their homes, with four children the proportion is down to 38 per cent, and with six or more down to 23 per cent. The proportions[16]. (1957) *Essays on the Welfare State.*

In local authority houses rise from 26 per cent to 60 per cent, respectively, showing that, where housing is subsidised, the larger the family the heavier is the charge upon the ratepayers. Where fathers were sick or unemployed in the two or three child category, 24 per cent were owner-occupiers, whereas only 14 per cent of those with four or more children owned their homes. The percentages in local authority property were 50 per cent and 74 per cent respectively.

(20) *Decreasing amount of savings*
Circumstances of Families also demonstrated that the proportion of families with savings of £300 or more, excluding an owner-occupied house, decreased according to family size. Again we see a steady decline with each increase in the number of children, with a big drop from the five to the six or more children category: Of those families with up to two children 22 per cent had savings; but only 11 per cent of those with five children, dropping to 6 per cent of those with six children or more.

(21) *Increasing poverty*
Table 7/13 shows the proportion of families who not only had no savings but whose income was less than their requirements as measured by two standards, the National Assistance scale

and the Supplementary Benefits scale. On the National Assistance scale only 1 per cent of the two-child families were below minimum requirements, with three children it was 2 per cent, with four children 4 per cent, and with five children 7 per cent. With six or more children 14 per cent of the families were below requirements. According to the somewhat higher Supplementary Benefits scale, the percentages were, respectively 3, 3, 7, 9 for the five child families, and 21 for six or more children.

Although only 15 per cent of the *families* came into the four or more child category, 56 per cent of all *children* suffering deprivation through the family's lack of resources came in these large families. Well over a quarter of the mothers with four or more children had to go out to work to make ends meet, and the larger the family the more overtime the father works in order to cope. 64 per cent more of the fathers of five children work sixty hours a week or more, as compared with the fathers of two.

Table 7/13

Increase in poverty with increase in family size UK, 1960s.

No. of children	Percentage in poverty by family size					
	2 children	3 ch.	4 ch.	5 ch.	6 ch.	All fams.
National Assistance scale	1%	2%	4%	7%	14%	2%
Supplementary Benefits scale.	3%	3%	7%	9%	21%	4%
HMSO (1967) op. cit. p. 11.						

(22) *Increase in crime and delinquency*

Barbara Wootton examined twelve causal factors in crime, and top of her list came size of the delinquent's family. It seems that most criminals come from large families and many studies bear this out.[17]

A fairly typical one is that done by the Dumbartonshire Joint Probation Committee on the 518 juvenile cases coming before the court in 1966. This showed that the mean family size for male juvenile crime offenders was 5·06, while that for females was 5·04—roughly twice the mean family size for society as a whole. The second stage of the study concerned all male juveniles from the Borough of Dumbarton, 'charged with a criminal offence in the past five years' and once more, 'the mean family size was found to be 5·56'.[18]

(23) *Increasing aggression score among boys in an approved school*
The Home Office Research Unit carried out a series of studies in 1962 to measure the relationship between family size and delinquency, and to try to assess that between family size and aggression. Table 7/14 shows that the aggression score progressively increases with family size. Two thirds of the children from families of three or less show a 'low' score, against less than half of those from families of six or more, these values being reversed in the 'high' score column of the table.

Table 7/14

Increasing 'aggression' score with increasing family size.
13 year old boys in approved school UK 1961.

| Family size | Aggression score* | |
	Low score (1 or 0)	High score (2 or more)
3 or less	67%	33%
4 or 5	60%	40%
6 or more	49%	52%

NB (i) N = 257 (ii) % rounded
Adapted from: Field, E. et al. HMSO (1971) *13 yr.-old Approved School Boys* (p. 26).

The basic flaw
The flaw here, once again, is parochialism. The fundamental refutation is that even if it were true in all cases that large families produce adults who are vastly superior in every con-

ceivable respect, and that society directly benefits from being peopled by these mature and rounded individuals, it would still be impossible to adopt a policy encouraging or even permitting large families for the general run of parents, because of the finiteness of the earth and its resources. The only possibility would be to ally it to a drastic rationing system which prevented enough would-be parents from reproducing at all in order to compensate for the extra children produced in the large families allegedly needed in the national interest.

Part III

THE 'SCIENTIFIC' FALLACIES

Part II

CHAPTER 8

The biological argument: the fallacy of the growth curve

As a biologist, . . . I find the idea of a 'Population Explosion' nonsense. . . . The world population will double by the year 2000 but . . . the population of any biological species . . . rabbits, yeast, cells or men . . . tends to respond to a favourable change in its environment by increasing. And the increase follows an S-shaped curve, first slow, then fast and then slowing down again to a new equilibrium. Magnus Pyke.[1]

Dr Pyke directs a scientific research station for the Distillers Company, he is author of a number of books, and a well-known populariser of science—especially in the field of synthetic foods. He is now the Secretary of the British Association for the Advancement of Science. In what sense can we argue that a biological argument put forward by a distinguished biologist is fallacious? To answer this several strands must be disentangled.

In the first place Dr Pyke has a curious sense of the value of words. A doubling of the world's population from 3·5 to 7·0 thousand millions in less than half a lifespan, which Dr Pyke admits, because of the 'biologically favourable influence . . . [of] . . . applied science' is explosion enough for most people; and yet he says he finds the idea 'nonsense'. If we recollect that nearly three full doublings (from half a thousand million) have already occurred since the explosion began in the seventeenth century, and that another is thought likely half a lifespan beyond 2000, we can dismiss Dr Pyke altogether and go on to examine the substantive issue: whether or not S-curves exist, and how they relate to population.

Let us first state the fallacy of the growth curve in the usual logical form, as follows:

99

First premise: All population explosions follow the S-shaped growth curve and automatically become stationary.

Second premise: Populations which automatically control their own explosions present no problems and need cause no concern.

Conclusion: The human population explosion will control itself automatically, present no problems, and need cause no concern.

Now for the evidence.

Do growth curves exist?

The concept of the S-curve and its relationship to populations was first put forward by Verhulst in 1838, later rediscovered and explored at some length by Pearl and Reed in 1920,[2] and described as one of the greatest discoveries since Malthus by the sociologist Sorokin in 1928.[3] It is also called the logistic curve, the sigmoid growth-curve, the logarithmic curve, and, in chemistry, the curve of autocatalytic growth.

Let us look at a few examples and the mechanisms underlying them.

The two basic shapes of growth curves

Figure 8/1 shows the two basic shapes of growth curves—although there are complications, as we shall see. All living things tend to increase in numbers to infinity; there are no inherent constraints on the growth process and curve A shows what would happen to any population in an infinite environment. However, there are no infinite environments, and all populations must in fact follow some approximation to curve B as environmental constraints mount in effectiveness.

There are two further possibilities, not shown in Fig. 8/1, but these are variants on curve B rather than basically different types. For instance, if a population follows curve B somewhat unsteadily, the oscillations would tend to be little S curves superimposed on the major S curve, and the essential underlying process would not have changed. The other possibility rests on the fact that growth curves can be negative as well as positive (a fact already implied in the oscillations just men-

Figure 8/1.   The two basic growth-curve shapes

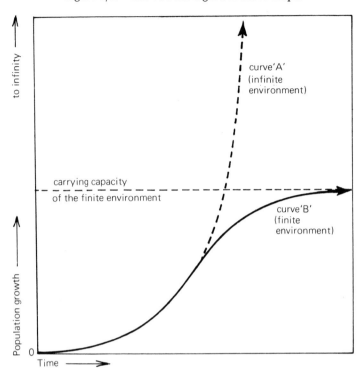

tioned), so that a population can expand to some apparently stationary level and then decline, possibly to extinction. Most populations which have existed in the evolutionary process have done just this.

Rate of growth and competition
Fig. 8/2 shows not one variable but three. In the centre is a classical S curve (No. 1)—in this case relating to the growth of a population of *Paramecium Caudatum*—while rising on the left and declining towards the right is the curve (No. 2) showing the *velocity* of growth, and sweeping up to the right is the curve (No. 3) showing the continually steepening rise in the intensity of the struggle for existence until the limit is reached when the population has stopped growing, the carrying capacity of the environment having been reached.

Figure 8/2.   Competition in a homogeneous population
of *Paramecium Caudatum* (After Gause.)

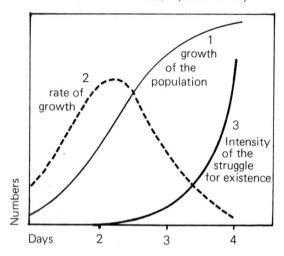

Table 8/1

Growth in a small population of rapidly breeding animals.

Years	(1) Aggregate Growth	(2) Velocity of Growth, i.e. numbers added per annum	(3) Rate-of-Growth i.e. increase per cent per annum
I	2	—	—
2	8	6	300%
3	24	16	200%
4	48	24	100%
5	72	24	50%
6	90	18	25%
7	100	10	$12\frac{1}{2}$%

After Glenday, R. (1944). The Future of Economic Society
(p. 52).

Table 8/1 reports in numerical terms the same type of information as that portrayed visually in Figure 8/2, in this case for

a population starting with a single pair of rapidly breeding animals. As the total increases, the 'velocity of growth' (measured by the number of animals added per year) also increases, but only to a maximum in the fourth year, after which it holds steady for two years, and then declines. The 'rate of growth' (the increase per cent per annum), however, declines rapidly from the very beginning—a rather puzzling fact until one thinks carefully through the whole process.

The growth-curve is S-shaped because of the relationship between the biological and physical factors in the system making up the population and its environment. In the case of a colony of cells comprising a human foetus, there appear to be built-in instructions telling them to interact with each other in such a way as to reach a genetically programmed maximum size or *as near to it as the environment permits*. We don't go on growing beyond this point, no matter how favourable the environment may be, and this 'stop-growing when you get to point *x*' rule is built into many living things.

Populations of separate individuals have a different rule: 'keep on growing until your environment stops you', as we see in curve A (Fig. 8/1). Of course the rule cannot float around in the population at large; it has to be inside the individuals, and therefore must take some form such as 'reproduce as much as you can'. However, the 'as much as you can' rule often requires some sort of definition, and many populations have supplementary rules built in to provide this. In the case of many species of birds, for example, extra rules are, for males: 'try to acquire a suitable nesting site', 'don't let other birds drive you out once you've got one', 'try to attract a mate', and so on; for females: it is 'try to find a male with a nesting site', 'don't have anything to do with a male without one', etc.

The environment automatically rations the number of nesting sites, then health, strength, aggressiveness and the social code apportion them, so that when the S-curve reaches its upper plateau, as we see in curve B (Fig. 8/1), the system remains stable until new forces enter it. Numbers are regulated by instinctive social arrangements, as Professor Wynne-Edwards has demonstrated,[4] rather than by Malthusian-type checks of hunger and disease, and some of them take strange forms. Among the flour beetle's rules is the injunction 'eat any flour beetle larvae you come across'; and a number of other creatures, such as the sea-horse, are enjoined to eat as many of their own young as they can, even while they are being born, if they are in a confined space such as an aquarium tank.

Populations affect their environment differently at different sizes and rates of change, and some authorities have argued that environmental resistance to further growth increases with the square of the size the population has already reached, so that the forces restricting further growth increase disproportionately until no more can take place.

Man may be the only living creature without inbuilt second-order rules modifying the basic rule, 'reproduce as much as you can'—unless there is a supplementary rule: 'when in difficulties use your brains'.

The growth curve applied to a human population
One of the few attempts to fit the growth curve to a human population was made in the United States by Pearl and Reed.[5] These authors worked out an equation giving an S-curve from 1790 to the year 2100, making the pivotal date 1 April 1914. Thus, according to A. J. Lotka was a period of

> peculiar interest . . . representing the point when the population passed from a progressively increasing to a progressively diminishing rate of growth . . . If the . . . United States continues to follow this growth curve . . . it will reach a maximum of some 197 million souls, about double its present population, by . . . 2060 or so. Such a forecast as this, based on a rather heroic extrapolation, and made in ignorance of the physical factors that impose the limit must, of course, be accepted with reserve.

Lotka did well to hedge his scientific bet so thoroughly because, although the calculated curve fitted the actual population curve with 'remarkable faithfulness' up to 1910, as he claimed and as we see in Table 8/2, the predicted settling-down at 197 millions by the year 2060, according to the graph in Figure 8/3 was catastrophically wrong.

Figure 8/3 shows Pearl and Reed's positive growth curve (they also computed a negative growth curve showing a much

Table 8/2

Data for an S-curve fitted to a human population.
USA, 1790–1910.

Year	Observed Population	Calculated Population by Equation (14)	Error
1790	3,929,000	3,929,000	0
1800	5,308,000	5,336,000	+28,000
1810	7,240,000	7,228,000	−12,000
1820	9,638,000	9,757,000	+119,000
1830	12,866,000	13,109,000	+243,000
1840	17,069,000	17,506,000	+437,000
1850	23,192,000	23,192,000	0
1860	31,443,000	30,412,000	−1,031,000
1870	38,558,000	39,372,000	+814,000
1880	50,156,000	50,177,000	+21,000
1890	62,948,000	62,769,000	−179,000
1900	75,995,000	76,870,000	+875,000
1910	91,972,000	91,972,000	0

After Lotka, A. J. (1956). Elements of Mathematical Biology (p. 73).

larger and entirely hypothetical population approaching the same equilibrium point by contraction instead of growth). If we were to superimpose upon this a third growth curve— that representing the facts as we now know them—we would see that the American population had reached 200 millions by 1967, and is heading for an estimated 300 millions by the year 2000. By 2020 the curve would reach 400 millions, and by the year 2060—when the levelling out at 197 millions was supposed to take place—it would be somewhere in the region of 900 millions and still growing at a greater rate than before; always provided that nothing happened to change the trend meanwhile. Of course, the curve will have to flatten out in due course, however wrong these calculations were and no matter how steeply it rises.

Figure 8/3. Growth curve for a human population.
USA, 1790–2100.

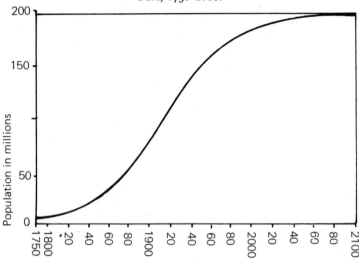

The four main possible growth curves for man
Figure 8/4 shows the four main possibilities—'main' because
other things *could* happen, as we saw in the 'surprise' futures in
Chapter 4. If there is a God he could transmit a rider to the
old injunction to 'increase and multiply'. He could add 'only
up to the optimum level, not until you wreck your environment!' If those flying saucers *do* land, their occupants could
establish themselves at the top of the food-chain and crop us
at some appropriate level as a protein source.

However, ignoring these and many other possibilities, let us
return to Figure 8/4 and examine the four main curves and
the two subsidiary ones, leaving the B curves until last.

A: The spontaneous 'control' curve
This expresses the situation which is possibly on the point of
arising in some countries like Sweden and a few of the People's
Democracies, countries which have no policy of population
optimisation or control in the strong sense of that term (although
they all have population policies of some sort, often to increase
the birth rate) but in which births have dropped—temporarily

Figure 8/4.   Human populations. The four main
types of growth curve

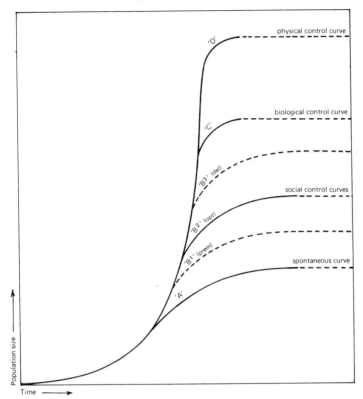

at least—to around the long term replacement rate. At the
present time we cannot say whether or not these countries have
really reached a long-term population stabilisation.

C: The biological control curve
This describes a state in which numbers are limited or reduced
—as they all too often have been in history—by biological
controls, notably starvation, disease, and violence, factors
which are still operating. Some 10,000 people are said to die
of starvation every day and many millions more die of disease
exacerbated by hunger, and by violence.

A point which must be made here, however, goes beyond the sad historical record. Even if man begins to behave himself and orders world society rationally in all spheres save that of population control, so that we are peaceful and tolerably nourished, we must eventually press heavily on the carrying capacity of the environment in other respects, through shortage of space, materials, amenities, and so on. It could be that at this point biological factors other than starvation and violence would come into play: stress, anomy, apathy, homosexuality, and so on; there are many and various possibilities which we can do little more than guess at.

D: The physical control curve
If C turned out to be misconceived, and no biological controls supervened, then obviously the final crunch would come on elementary physical grounds: factors of space, matter or energy would eventually prevent further growth, as we saw in Chapter 6.

B: The social control curves
This curve—shown with three variants, 1, 2, and 3—represents a situation which has occurred so often and so widely that it might be reasonable to describe it as the norm. It is one in which a society has experienced or foreseen what overpopulation means and taken the necessary steps to avoid it by means of social control, with law, custom, and morality ensuring an effective use of such measures as sexual abstinence, birth control, abortion, infanticide and cannibalism.

The three variants are shown because it is obviously possible to control population socially without producing an optimum. The curve B 1 (prem.) represents a population brought *prematurely* to the stationary state, giving insufficient people to realise the values built into the definition of the optimum; B 3 (del.) is the curve in which control is *delayed*, producing a state which, though overpopulated, is nonetheless viable; B 2 (opt.) represents the curve for a controlled entry into a stationary state at the *optimum* level. The last state could, of course, subsequently be redefined and adjusted, in the light of changing circumstances, as often as its citizens wished.

Figure 8/5.   Four 'quality of life' S-curves

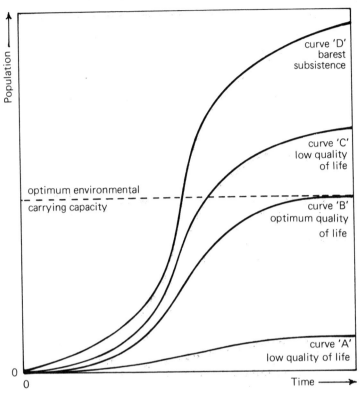

Carrying capacities with differing qualities of life

In the case of lower animals the level of subsistence is fixed by instinctive mechanisms—birds seem happy enough with a nesting site and enough food and water—but with man the 'quality of life' is a very flexible concept. There appear to be no inherent limits to our desires. Many individuals do opt out of the acquisitive race, but a large number do not so that the species as a whole is pushed ever upward (if that is the right word) in terms of consumption of material things. From this it follows that where the supply of goods and amenities is limited—as it mostly is—the more we want to have for each person the smaller the final number of persons must be. Taking the example of land, for instance: other things being equal, if we are content to live in a small space in a tower block there can be more of us than if we want a detached house and garden for each family, and many more than if we want to keep enough agricultural land to grow our own food or to preserve some areas of wilderness. If we all felt, as some people do, that a satisfactory quality of life requires the ownership of a few hundred acres of grouse moor, the total population would have to be very small indeed.

Figure 8/5 illustrates this point with four S-curves coming up to differing environmental carrying capacities, each determined by a differing level of attainment and aspiration. The scale is of course arbitrary and the graph merely illustrates the general principles. Curve A shows a 'low' quality of life (though it would be 'high' in some respects—with low levels of noise, pollution, and crowding and a large amount of raw materials per capita), because there are not enough people to produce all the basic goods and services—especially communications—we have come to expect. Curve B shows an optimum carrying capacity for a high (possibly the highest) number of people at the highest standard of living thought desirable and possible. Curve C shows another 'low' quality of possible life—low in this case because there are now too many people for the available resources. Curve D shows the maximum carrying capacity of the environment, at bare subsistence level.

Carrying capacity and self-sufficiency

It will be obvious by now that there are problems in defining the limits to the carrying capacity of an environment. Britain has been incapable of feeding herself for over a century, yet the greatly increased population lives at a higher dietary level than when we could produce all our own food. The reason for this is that we have traded other goods and services to make up the food deficit—a process that has involved exploitation of other peoples, as well as the digging up of a sizeable chunk of the island for sale and consumption as coal. We now do this with building aggregates and plan to do the same with our oil.

An even simpler way of living above your carrying capacity is to persuade other populations to help keep you by sending you their surpluses more or less free, which is the ostensible object of foreign-aid programmes; and though there is a good deal to be said for this in the short run—especially as a recompense for past exploitation—it can hardly be a viable way of life for more than a few small populations or for more than short periods.

In the case of Britain we cannot by any means be certain that half our food will continue to be available on the world market, even if we continue to be able to obtain enough raw materials—which in itself is in some doubt—to produce a surplus of goods and services to dispose of in exchange. As Fred Hoyle put it in his inimitable way some years ago: 'Soon everyone will be trying to exchange goods nobody wants for food nobody has got'.

While we don't need actually to *be* feeding ourselves at any given moment—there is nothing wrong with a just exchange of goods and services—we ought always to be *able* to feed ourselves at very short notice and at the cost of a not too drastic change in our way of life. Being in the Common Market may make it less likely that we shall find ourselves in the situation of having to provide all our own food.

Carrying capacity long-term and short-term

So far I have argued as though the carrying capacity of an environment were a fixed and unchangeable quantity, but of course it is not. Man has clearly increased the carrying capacity of the earth for human populations in three major steps as there have been no fewer than three population explosions.[6] The question is not *whether* it can be increased, but by how much and for how long? This raises the question of whether the carrying capacity of an environment should be boosted by short-term measures, if in the long run these will not only prove ineffective in maintaining the larger population but will also damage the environment so that even the original carrying capacity cannot be sustained. In the case of local populations, man has come up against this problem on many occasions, creating dust-bowls and deserts by over-intensive agriculture or grazing. Even where the environment is not being damaged, it is obvious that an over-large population can be partially supported for a time—the time, that is, that it takes its members

Figure 8/6.   Carrying capacity before
and after overpopulation

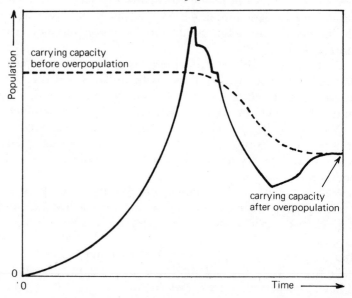

to starve to death. Figure 8/6 shows diagrammatically how carrying capacity can be exceeded and then reduced. The question we now have to ask is whether it is possible that man has already overshot the long-term carrying capacity of the earth; and, whether he has or not, what that long-term capacity is.

Some growth-curves for Britain

It is almost impossible to show a complete growth curve for a human population because the baseline would have to be so long to take in the full history. However, if we ignore the greater part of that history and simply take a few thousand or a few hundred years, the task becomes feasible. Figure 8/7 shows the UK growth over the past 500 years, with the 1972 projection for 2000, and some possible alternative stabilisation levels up to 2500. It is important to note that in Britain we are already a long way above the carrying capacity of our island if we insist on a fairly high quality of life in conventional materialistic terms.

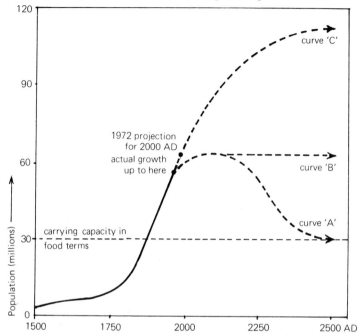

Figure 8/7. UK Population—three possible growth curves

A: the food self-sufficiency curve
This shows, very approximately, how our growth-curve might tail off if we decide to become self-sufficient in food with a fairly high-quality diet with a population of 30 millions, roughly half the 1973 level, as suggested by Sir Joseph Hutchinson.[7]

B: The curve for stabilisation by 2075
We see here how it would look if we managed to bring population growth to a halt at the level projected in 1972 for 2000, but by slowing it down gradually so that is it not reached until a lifespan afterwards.

C: the 'final' doubling curve
This illustrates the situation if population is allowed to double once more (the *last* doubling being within living memory) by the year 2400 or so, before being held stationary by one of the mechanisms described earlier.

The fallacy of the unattainable optimum

I have argued that we should decide upon the social control curve for our population, which—if it is neither too early nor too late—must by definition lead to an optimum population. The concept of the optimum population has traditionally been annexed by economists, who defined it as the size at which per capita income is highest and then rejected it (along with most academics) as useless for all practical purposes. Dr Eversley, the demographer, made a typical statement on the BBC Third Programme: 'I deny . . . that there is some magic 'optimum' population. . . .'[8] The prefix 'magic' has the effect of ridiculing the allegedly utopian aims of those who support a population control policy.

The Parliamentary Select Committee's report on Population found itself in difficulty in this issue because expert witnesses hedged and twisted so.[9] The Ross Committee falls into the same trap: 'we do not know the optimum size of Britain's population nor do we see how . . . any such optimum might be calculated.' However, their commonsense triumphs in the end when they add: 'Our analysis nevertheless leads us to the conclusion that Britain would do better in future with a stationary rather than an increasing population.'[10]

Another common ploy for rejecting the optimum was adopted by Geoffrey Hawthorne in a Fabian pamphlet: 'We cannot usefully employ the notion of an optimum population because it assumes constant technology and capital.'[11] Yet I have never seen any argument for a fixed optimum, valid for all times and conditions. *Every* writer in favour of population policy stresses the tentative, interim, and shifting nature of the optimum definition, with the consequent need for reappraisal and redefinition as things change—not just capital and technology, but values and customs, too. We organise all our social action in the knowledge that things will be different in *n* years, but do the best we can meanwhile. Most 'primitive' societies have without the slightest difficulty defined and realised their optimum population over several millennia, and if they can do it, why can't we?

Finally, I have put forward as an interim measure the concept of the 'quasi-optimum': 'A population size which is reasonably acceptable to a democratic society and which the environment can sustain as far into the future as can be foreseen.'[12]

Is there any reason why we shouldn't ask the voters and be guided by the majority on this issue as on most others?

Misuse of the growth curve

The problem here is not that Dr Pyke, say, has got his facts wrong, but that he completely fails to mention some of them— the factors equal and opposite to the 'biologically favourable influences' now causing fast growth. These opposing factors are the biologically *unfavourable* influences which soon make the new growth slow down and then stop. On the important question of *why* the curve flattens out at the top the apologists remain silent. 'Scientific' statements about how populations in general tend to behave do nothing whatever to counter reasonable fears about what might happen to particular groups, indeed whole nations, if world or local populations are allowed to increase to the point at which they *have* to flatten out. The very factors which make Dr Pyke's statement true—that growth curves do flatten out in the long run—are the ones which would cause damage to the individuals comprising those populations and their environments, and which provide rational grounds for concern.

Correctly used, the growth curve argument can help us to understand and solve our population problems. Where the 'spontaneous' curve fails to manifest itself (as it may have done in Sweden, say), we ought to take hold of population growth and control it in accordance with the 'social' control curve. However, Britain is already a long way past the 'spontaneous' and 'optimum' social control curves, and the longer we leave it the lower will be the resulting quality of life.

Can any moral or rational creature—let alone one claiming a touch of divinity—deliberately opt out and allow the world population's growth-curve, or any other, to be flattened out by brutish natural processes rather than by sympathetic involvement, foresight, and applied intelligence.

CHAPTER 9

The demographic argument: the fallacy of
the population cycle

'Thus, in industrialised countries, birth rates have been brought into the closest match with death-rates . . . population growth in the developing nations—ought to be brought into balance by the same means that have already succeeded elsewhere—through the material progress of society. . . . It is this view with which I wish to associate myself'. Professor Barry Commoner.[1]

Professor Commoner vehemently rejects any suggestion of population control, even where it is mutually agreed in a democratic society; and, since he sees only too clearly the increasing conflict between population and resources, he is driven to seek another way out of his dilemma, seizing—as so many other apologists do—on the fallacy of the 'population cycle' or 'demographic transition', to give the concept its technical name. (It is sometimes also called the 'Thompson-Notestein' theory.)

This fallacy may be formulated as follows.

First premise: All nations which have become materially prosperous have automatically attained the goal of a stationary population.

Second premise: All nations with exploding populations should be helped to attain the stationary state.

Conclusion: All poor nations should be helped to become materially prosperous.

Let us now examine the evidence.

Does the demographic transition exist?
The demographic transition *is* a fact of life; what is in dispute is not whether it exists, but whether it cures the population

problem. The reasons why this theory falls down are three-fold. In the first place the facts are carelessly collected. In the second place the argument is weakly constructed: the logical structure is feeble and no causal relation is stated; and in the third place the language in which the argument is expressed is too loose and imprecise to be practically useful.

A further problem is that this theory finds its way only too often into the mouths of apologists innocent of any real knowledge of population fact or theory. I do not suggest that only experts are entitled to opinions on these questions. I argued in *Population Versus Liberty* that it is not only the right but the duty of all citizens—especially those in authority—to read the writing on the demographic wall and to take action accordingly. However, a certain amount of homework is required before going into print[2] and Professor Commoner, for example, whose book is quite well documented on pollution and ecological issues, contains virtually no references to population titles. He evidently believes that population questions are amenable to a commonsense approach and do not require serious study. (In carelessness typical of the apologists, his chapters and notes to chapters do not coincide, the numbers are all wrong, the book starts at page 11 and there are two pages of notes for a chapter which does not exist.)

What is the demographic transition?
Kingsley Davis, one of the earlier writers on this topic, described how, in the days of high infant mortality, women 'experienced the drain and danger of childbearing often to no purpose'. 'Too much effort', he went on, 'was spent in trying to bring each new generation to adulthood; too much energy . . . lost in sickness, malnutrition, and mourning. . . . The new . . . demographic balance released a large part of this energy . . . for other things . . . an astounding gain in human efficiency'.[3]

The transition to which he referred has been stated in a number of ways, differing mainly in the number of stages which go to complete it; but all writers agree that it is a process of change from a situation of high birth and death rates to one of low birth and death rates *and zero or very slight population growth*. It is always implied, though rarely stated and never documented, that population growth was very high before the transition started, and that it has prevented any problem of overpopulation both currently and for the future. The main reason for the transition is often said to be economic change, which sets in train a whole series of social, psychological, and moral developments.

The social scientist Maurice Duverger, falling into the same trap as most of his fellows, wrote:

> Rising standards of comfort and the development of education and individualism increase voluntary birth control so that *in the end a demographic equilibrium is established*, based on a low birth rate coinciding with low death rate. The population increases, but slowly.[4] (Italics added).

The implications of this viewpoint are:

(1) If only the poorer countries of the world can be raised by their bootstraps into and through the economic 'take-off', they will automatically choose low fertility for themselves so that the population problem will be solved;

(2) It is therefore unnecessary and immoral to talk about population problems—much less population control—and all efforts should be bent towards increasing economic growth and aid to the poor countries.

One difficulty with this argument is that there is some evidence of a possibility that beyond a certain point in the growth of affluence, fertility may tend to rise again, as the American studies of Lee Rainwater[5] show. He found that the norm on family size can be expressed as 'one should not have more children than one can support, but one should have as many as one can afford'. In his research the desired family size for those with no financial worries averaged $3 \cdot 2$, a long way above replacement level; Myra Woolf's recent studies in Britain show an even more marked trend, her figure being $3 \cdot 4$, as we saw in Chapter 2.

A theoretical representation of the demographic transition
Figure 9/1 shows a representation of the demographic transition from Ralph Thomlinson,[6] a reputable commentator on population questions. Its smooth and symmetrical geometry is

Figure 9/1.   The demographic transition in theory

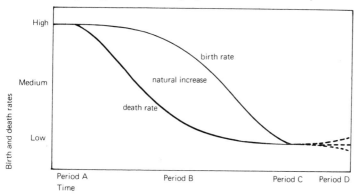

no preparation for the ragged reality that follows. After Kingsley Davis, Thomlinson calls the conditions at the beginning and end of the transition—top left and bottom right, respectively—the 'old balance' and the 'new balance'. The difficulty is that this 'balance', like beauty, lies in the eye of the beholder.

Different formulations of the transition theory

All formulations contain the same basic elements, but it is instructive to review them briefly in order to demonstrate the lack of precision and concensus among social scientists. Let us look at three-stage and five-stage formulations, bracketing the target of the four-stage theory which is perhaps the most precise and informative of them all and so will be considered last.

Figure 9/2 illustrates the three-stage form of the transition. This shows a smoothing and streamlining comparable to that in Figure 9/1, although it is much more realistic than Thomlinson's curve. Petersen describes the three-stage transition model as follows:

> The population growth of an area undergoing modernisation is divided into three stages:
> (1) A more or less static population at a high level of fertility and mortality;
> (2) A period of constant fertility and falling mortality, with a consequent rapid increase in population;

(3) *A more or less static population* at more efficient levels of birth and death control.[7]

Figure 9/2.   Three-stage model of the demographic transition

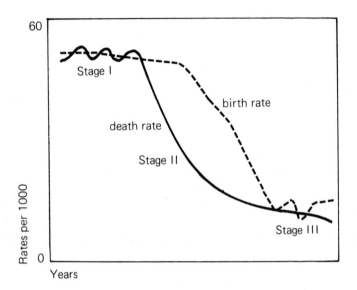

He winds up with a criticism of sociologists who 'have usually been content with this roughest and most simplistic of models'.

Anthony Barnett has used a five-stage formulation.

The demographic cycle . . . has five phases. The *first* is one in which both birth and death rates are very high: in times of peace and abundance the population rises; famine, pestilence, and war at other times cause decreases. There is no steady trend up or down.

In the *second phase* better social organisation leads to a fall in the death rate, while the birth rate remains high; the population increases, though not rapidly.

In the *third phase* the death rate declines still further and although the birth rate also tends to fall the rate of population increase is high.

With the *fourth* phase *approximate stability is reached* with both birth and death rates low. The net reproduction rate is about unity; *not only does the population show no marked trend up or down but, unlike a population in the first phase, it also escapes violent fluctuation.* . . . Finally we come to the *fifth phase* in which the fall in the birth rate is so great that the population, despite a low death-rate, declines steadily: this is largely hypothetical, since only one country, France, has ever reached it, and today the French population has returned to the fourth phase.[8] (Italics added.)

In a radio discussion with Lewis Frank, an American publicist of population problems, Norman St John Stevas, MP, discounted any possible need for population control by reiterating the fallacy of the population cycle. He explained away the obvious fact that population goes on rising by saying that in wealthy societies the birth-rate 'tends to rise again *for a time*'.[9] However, he gave no justification for this assertion or any hint about the likely duration of this fifth phase, how and why it would end, or by how much population would increase in the interim.

In the admirable though now somewhat dated PEP book, *World Population and Resources* four 'revolutions'—in agriculture, science and industry, medicine, and birth-control—were described as leading to 'a fairly regular pattern known as the 'population cycle' . . . which has four stages . . . well illustrated by the example of England and Wales'. Figure 9/3, reproduced from the PEP book, shows the four stages, and it is instructive to compare the shape of the diagram with the geometric precision of Figure 9/1. They were described as follows:

(a) *High Fluctuating stage* . . . the normal state of mankind before the scientific and industrial revolutions of the last 200 years; a period of high birth and death rates (about 35 a 1,000) . . . very slow and irregular increase of population.

(b) *Early expanding stage.* About 1750 the death rate in England and Wales began to fall rapidly, the birth rate remaining constant for another 130 years; in the latter part of that period births were about 34 a 1,000 and deaths about 21. . . . Over the period the population trebled. . . .

(c) *Late expanding stage.* Suddenly, about 1880, the birth rate . . . began to fall. Fifty years later it was about 16 while the death rate, continuing to decline, was about 12 a 1,000: . . . population increased by more than half.

Figure 9/3.   Four-stage model of the demographic transition,
England and Wales, 1750–1950

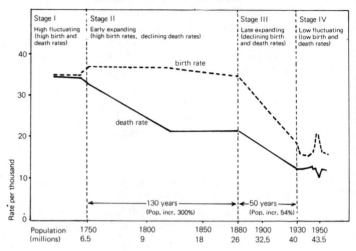

After PEP (1955) *World Population and Resources* (p. 10).

Figure 9/4.   The demographic transition in Sweden, 1750–1950

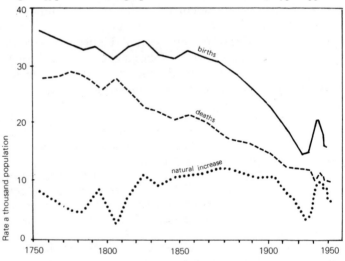

Note. Figures are 10 year averages from 1751 to 1930. 5 year averages from 1931 to 1940
and annual figures thereafter

After PEP (1955) *op. cit.* (p. 236).

(d) *Low fluctuating stage.* Although in England and Wales, like all other western countries, there was a sharp rise in the number of children born immediately after World War II, *birth and death rates soon became stable* at about 16 and 12 a 1,000 respectively, *resulting in a small and steady growth of population.*[11] (Italics added.)

Figure 9/4 shows the transition in Sweden. The diagram does not bring us quite up to date, but it has the advantage of showing the natural increase, as well as births and deaths. This fluctuated widely during the transition (the bulge in the 1940s is very near to the highest ever recorded) and settled down for a time at about three-quarters of the rate at the beginning, 0·6 per cent as against 0·9 per cent per annum. The Swedish birth-rate may not be quite high enough for replacement in the long term, although the population is nonetheless growing fairly rapidly under the influence of an 'artificially' low death rate and substantial immigration. (Death rates in many countries are lower than they must be in the long run, about 13·5 per 1,000 with a life expectancy of 74 years, because the medical revolution is not yet complete and age structures are distorted.)

William Petersen has used the case of Holland to provide a striking refutation of the transition fallacy.[12] Table 9/1 shows that the average annual increase in population rose from 0·72 per cent in the early nineteenth century to 1·35 per cent in the 1940s and 1950s, having been even higher in the 1920s and 1930s. This approximate doubling of the rate of increase is even more striking if we look at the absolute numbers. The 0·72 per cent yearly increase in 1800 was on a population of just over 2 millions, while the 1·35 per cent of 1960 was on one of over 11½ millions, the increases in numbers per decade being 152,000 and 1,377,000 respectively. The *rate* of increase was 88 per cent higher and the *numerical* increase 800 per cent higher. By 1971 the Dutch population had reached 13·1 millions, giving the highest density in Europe, and was increasing at 1·1 per cent a year, equivalent to an annual increment of 144,000 and a doubling-time of sixty-three years.

England and Wales may be considered in detail, rather than Great Britain or the United Kingdom as a whole, because

Table 9/1

Population growth during the transition. Netherlands, 1795–1960.

Year	Population (—ooo)	Percent *Average Annual Increase* During Preceding Period
1795	2,097	—
1829	2,613	0·72
1839	2,861	0·91+
1849	3,057	0·67—
1859	3,309	0·80
1869	3,580	0·79
1879	4,013	1·14
1889	4,511	1·18
1899	5,104	1·24
1909	5,858	1·39
1920	6,865	1·45
1930	7,935	1·46
1940	8,923	1·18
1950	10,200	1·35
1960	11,577	1·35

[1] As of December 31 of the designated year, except for 1849 (November 19) and 1869 (December 1). Figures from 1795 to 1930 are from the census; thereafter from the population registers.

After Peterson, W. (1964) op. cit. (p. 174).

these regions are more homogeneous and better documented over the two centuries, approximately, that the transition took.

The PEP diagram (Figure 9/3) shows a fact not allowed for at all in transition theory—a *rise* in the birth-rate at the beginning of state 2. This increased the explosion of numbers (from 6·5 to 26 millions) during the 'early expanding' stage, by about ¾ per cent per annum, a substantial factor over the 130-year period. The fall in both death and birth rates in stage 3 is clearly marked, as is the striking instability of stage 4.

Now although this diagram demonstrates the elements of the demographic transition and the point I am most concerned to stress—its failure to produce a stationary population—some important ambiguities show themselves. The names of stages 1 and 4—the 'high-fluctuating' and 'low-fluctuating', respectively—are normally taken to mean high and low rates of population growth. The outcome of this interpretation—quite unjustified by the facts—is that once the 'low' stage is reached population problems are virtually over: as the PEP study puts it, there is 'a small and steady growth of population'. What the terms really mean is high and low birth and death rates *regardless of population change*. Even if one looks only moderately carefully at Figure 9/3 one can see that the natural increase in stage 4 is about seven times that in stage 1, and simple calculations based on ten-year periods before and after the transition bear this out to a most striking degree.

Pre-transition

1740 population	5,990,000*
1730 population	5,940,000*
Increase in numbers, 1730 to 1740:	50,000

Increase as a proportion: $\dfrac{50,000}{5,940,000} \times 100\% = 0\cdot84\%$

Post-transition

1961 population	46,105,000
1951 population	43,758,000
Increase in numbers, 1951 to 1961:	2,347,000

Increase as a proportion: $\dfrac{2,347,000}{43,758,000} \times 100\% = 5\cdot37\%$

* Averaged from Rickman and four other authorities. Taking the worst possible case, the *lowest* for 1730 and the *highest* for 1740, the post-transition numerical increase is still over 300% greater. The *median* figures would slightly reduce the ratios in the main text.

Growth before and after the transition compared

i.   Change in % rate of increase per decade.

$$\frac{5 \cdot 37\%}{0 \cdot 84\%} = 6 \cdot 39$$

This is about $6\frac{1}{3}$ times greater, equivalent to an increase of 539% $((6 \cdot 39 - 1 \cdot 00) \times 100\%)$

ii.   Change in numerical rate of increase per decade.

$$\frac{2,347,000}{50,000} = 46 \cdot 9$$

This is about 47 times greater, equivalent to an increase of 4,590% $((46 \cdot 9 - 1 \cdot 00) \times 100\%)$

Commentators often choose a datum-point rather arbitrarily set some time after the transition has started, which distorts the overall picture still further. Even J. M. Thoday, an admirable commentator on population problems, does this.[13] He starts at 1851, when the birth and death rates were about 34 and 23, respectively, and going up to 1931 when they were about 16 and 12. This shows the natural increase falling by about two-thirds—from 11 to 4 per 1,000. But if we look at the numbers again we get a very different picture. In 1851 the population was 17·9 millions, so that a natural increase of 11 gave 197,000 more each year, whereas in 1931—the population now being 39·9 millions—a natural increase of 4 increased numbers by nearly 169,000 each year. The huge drop of 64 per cent measured as a *rate* of natural increase, turns out to be a drop of only 14 per cent when measured *numerically*. If this exercise were to be done again, starting on the natural increase somewhere near the beginning of the transition—say around 1800—and carried up to 1960, an apparently large drop in growth would turn out to be a very large increase in growth, more than a doubling of the numerical rate.

Wealth and the birth-rate

Although it is true that, in general, fertility falls as death rates fall, and that these both fall as wealth increases, there certainly is no level of wealth which automatically produces a replacement birth-rate. It is true that some wealthy societies such as Denmark, West Germany, and Sweden, may be approaching the stationary state, but some of the wealthiest societies the world has ever seen have birth rates for above the replacement-rate as Table 9/2 shows.

Table 9/2

High wealth coupled with high fertility. Selected countries in 1971.

Country	GNP per capita US$	Crude births (per 1000 per annum)	Doubling time* (yrs)
USA	3,980	18·2	63
Kuwait	3,540	43·0	9
Switzerland	2,490	16·5	63
Canada	2,460	17·6	41
France	2,130	16·7	100
Norway	2,000	17·6	78
UK	1,790	16·6	140
Iceland	1,680	20·7	58
Netherlands	1,620	19·2	63

Source: Population Reference Bureau (1971) World Population Data Sheet.

* The apparently arbitrary relationship between births and doubling-times is due to the fact that the death rates, not shown, vary considerably. The long-term doubling-times would all be greater because death-rates must rise.

In 1971 the population of the United States was increasing at 1·1 per cent per annum giving over 2 millions more each year and a doubling time of sixty-three years. Only two of the nine countries listed have doubling-times appreciably longer than one lifespan, and most have considerably shorter ones. Since 1971 the fertility-rate in the United States has dropped suddenly and inexplicably—unless concern about overpopulation is the cause—so the country may be heading for the stationary state in a generation or so. On the other hand, the fall may be a temporary phenomenon caused by anomie due to the Vietnam war, racial stress, crime and violence, political corruption, the energy-crisis, the economic crisis, environmental destruction—what you will.

One thing we can be quite certain about, however, is that the fall to long-term replacement level was *not* due to an increase in wealth, as this has been marginal in the brief period concerned.

Most people seem to expect to keep on getting better and better off and many feel that the more prosperous you are the more children you ought to have, as we saw in Chapter 4 on population projection. If these expectations can be realised, improbable though it seems at the moment, the whole process might go into reverse and produce a true fifth stage of the demographic transition along the lines suggested by St John Stevas, but more or less permanent—or as permanent as biological and physical constraints permit.

Population cycle of the world

The population of the world is not homogeneous. By and large the wealthy Northern and Western nations are in State 4, while the Southern and Eastern populations are now getting well into Stage 2—some being in Stage 3 already. If the world as a whole follows the pattern of the wealthier countries—and we might reasonably expect that the transition will be a good deal quicker than in Europe—then birth and death rates will in the future be appreciably lower, but population may well be growing a great deal faster than before the cycle started, albeit slower than during Stages 2 and 3, the time of the greatest explosive force.

Splitting the world population into the categories—'developed' and 'underdeveloped'—provides a further test of the efficacy of the demographic transition in producing stationary populations. If we compare the 'developed' countries which are supposed to have completed it with the 'underdeveloped' countries, which have not, we see that the latter are expected to increase at 2·7 per cent a year during the 1970s and 1980s, whilst the developed countries are expected by the UN to continue expanding at 0·9 per cent a year, giving a doubling-time of seventy-seven years.[14]

Conclusion

We have seen that all industrialised societies have gone through the first three stages of the demographic transition, and are now in Stage 4, although a few seem to have gone through into Barnett's Stage 5 for a time, later returning to Stage 4. The populations of the poorer countries appear to be launched into the same cycle, and we can confidently expect a similar end-product—greatly reduced birth and death rates.

In this sense then, the phenomenon we can reasonably call a 'demographic transition' is empirically verifiable. What does not exist is a whole class of stationary populations—i.e. one in every developed society which has completed the transition. The end-product is mostly far from 'birth-rates having been brought into the closest match with death-rates' as Commoner asserts, or Barnett's 'approximate stability'.

Although it is true that in a few countries birth rates are down to the long-term replacement level—or even slightly below if present trends continue—the more typical transition is from Stage 1 (Very low population growth at high birth and death rates) to Stage 4 (High population growth at low birth and death rates). We saw that in the case of England and Wales the increase in numerical growth was 4,590 per cent and this is the typical nature of the demographic transition.

Transition theory rests on poor observation, lax conceptualisation, and loose terminology, even when used by experts, and all those who have really thought about the matter now reject it except as a useful rule-of-thumb generalisation. Finally we must recognise that, even if populations did arrive at a stationary state all by themselves, in accordance with the popular interpretation of transition theory, there is no evidence that they will remain in this state or that it would be the most desirable one—that the process must inevitably have led to an optimum population. The belief that this would be so—even *must* be so—is too much like the 'invisible hand' theory of classical economics, now completely discredited, to be accepted.

Part IV

THE ECONOMIC FALLACIES

CHAPTER 10

The general case: the fallacy of more people, more wealth, better lives

'I assert that in any given state of civilisation a greater number of people can collectively be better provided for than a smaller. I assert that the injustice of society, not the niggardliness of nature, is the cause of the want and misery . . . I assert that the new mouths which an increasing population calls into existence require no more food than the old ones, while the hands they bring with them can in the natural order of things produce more. I assert that, other things being equal, the greater the population, the greater the comfort which an equitable distribution of wealth would give to each individual. I assert that in a state of equality the natural increase of population would constantly tend to make every individual richer instead of poorer.' Henry George.[1]

'This [population] increase constitutes the most dangerous obstacle that faces the Egyptian people in their drive towards raising the standard of production.' *National Charter of the United Arab Republic*. 21 May, 1962.

There are a number of specific and more or less technical arguments used to justify population-growth on economic grounds. Some of these are dealt with later, but since they are generally imbedded in a whole matrix of factually and logically fallacious reasoning about the foundations of economics and its relevance to the wider society, let us first examine the general case.

In his chapter, 'Disproof of the Malthusian Theory', Henry George provided the most forthright statement I have yet discovered of what I am calling the 'economic argument', but nearly all modern economists appear to think along these lines, and they have instilled their belief in the minds of politicians and laymen of both left and right. Even people who feel we are already overpopulated, harbour the idea that population

133

control is to be conceded only reluctantly because of the economic benefits which will have to be foregone. Let us now examine some of the misconceptions underlying these attitudes.

It would be very hard to find a more enthusiastic contemporary devotee of increasing numbers than Colin Clark. He is a demographic determinist who ascribes almost magical properties to growth. In the preface to *Population Growth and Land Use* he says; 'Population growth has taken place, and will continue. . . . It is the only force powerful enough to make . . . communities change their methods, and in the long run transform them into . . . more advanced and productive societies'. In the chapter, 'The Economics and Politics of Population Growth', he comes very near to ascribing everything desirable in human life to this one cause. He starts by quoting the fourteenth-century Arab philosopher-historian, Ibn Khaldun:

> The individual cannot satisfy his wants independently but must co-operate with his fellow men. . . . Food-stuff is not produced by one person's efforts. . . . In its production co-operate six or ten, blacksmith, carpenter, labourer, etc. Now when all these co-operate, they produce together a quantity of food-stuff by far exceeding their wants. (p. 254)

Ignoring the obvious fact that Khaldun is advocating not population increase but *co-operation* (the word appears three times in this short passage), Clark takes a quite unjustifiable leap in reasoning by implying that if ten workmen can produce better than five workmen than 10 billion can produce better than 5 billion.

Clark says:

> We . . . have historical evidence of a number of cases of the beneficial effect of substantial population growth in communities with a limited area of agricultural land, namely Ancient Greece about the 6th century BC and others . . . The world still marvels at the achievements of the Greeks from the 6th to the 4th centuries BC . . . in architecture, literature and philosophy . . . Their achievements in painting and music may have been very great too, but have been lost. (p. 273.)

134

The attribution of the lost achievements of the Greeks in painting and music to population growth is an especially nice touch.

Clark says that the success of the Dutch nation in the seventeenth century was due to its 'exceptionally high population density on only 8 million acres of land, much of which was heath land or swamp. . . . This small nation was then the world's greatest commercial, naval and colonizing power, founding New York, Cape Town and Jakarta within a few years of each other, able not only to defeat the English fleet but even to stand up against an Anglo-French alliance. . . . They . . . also produced some of the world's greatest painting . . . and substantial scientific achievements' (p. 254).

Holland has since undergone nearly three doublings, but Dr Clark does not explain why with its present density—one of the highest in the world—it is not performing with comparable brilliance. Instead he tells us that 'Dutch predominance . . . came to an end when population growth slowed down' (p. 276).

Clark uses France mainly as a negative case to prove the dire consequences of *not* having a large and rapidly expanding population. However, he does start by saying that before she 'began to restrict the growth of her population well before the end of the eighteenth century . . . the greatness of France was due to her exceptionally large numbers'—over 30 millions when the Black Death came. He almost seems to gloat over the fact that 'in . . . 1798, when Malthus was writing his book . . . Napoleon was successfully invading Egypt, and France, came near to dominating the world'. He continues:

If population limitation were the key to economic progress . . . then France would be the richest country in the world by now, for she has certainly practised it the longest. . . . French historians are now blaming the lack of population pressure for the . . . slow progress of French agriculture and industry in the nineteenth century. . . . Every Frenchman is now bitterly conscious that the decline in his country's influence in the world has been mainly due to its lower rate of population growth. The English . . . have been slow in reaching a similar conclusion. (p. 276.)

In addition, Clark cites 'Japan at the end of the nineteenth and the beginning of the present century—[which] has made substantial contributions to science' (p. 273) and 'Britain in the latter part of the eighteenth century'.

> Turning to Victorian England, regarding its performance in the visual arts, perhaps the less said the better; but this should not divert our attention from the very great achievements of the Victorians both as poets and as scientists.

He winds up his eulogy for population growth with the words: 'We may now be witnessing a similar sequence of events in India beginning at the middle of the twentieth century' (pp. 272–3).

Clark shamelessly selects and slants his evidence. He ignores the other 140 or so countries which have also had population explosions, and the periods in his small handful of selected countries when population continued to expand rapidly without any display of brilliance in politics, economics, or the arts. The evidence which *is* presented is scrappy in the extreme; and even where he does quote some of the substantial evidence against his case, it is ignored in the summing up.

For example, in the case of Holland most of his material is taken from the seventeenth-century commentator Sir William Petty,[2] and he is objective enough to quote his mentor on some of the many non-demographic factors which tended to make Holland prosperous. These included good natural communications; good natural defenses against land attack, which permitted relatively low investment in defence and proportionately more in commerce; good natural harbours; cunning design of artificial harbours, concentration on commerce and industry combined with a somewhat risky reliance on migrant labour, mercenaries, and imported food, etc.

Perhaps the most damning indictment of Clark's special pleading is that his justly celebrated work, *The Conditions of Economic Progress* (published in 1951, long before there was any general awareness of the population explosion), contains few words on the subject of population and none at all on population pressure as a prerequisite of economic development. It does, however, contain detailed evidence that in ancient Greece population fell throughout the third and second centuries BC, a phenomenon accompanied by a substantial drop in rent and interest rates' probably an indication that money and capital were becoming abundant in relation to population (pp. 564–5).

Let us now look at some ideas on population and economic change in the work of other possibly less biased commentators.

Conditions for economic growth: Two classical theorists

(1) *Adam Smith*

According to Adam Smith, the author of *The Wealth of Nations* and the father of modern economics, there is (in the absence of corrupt, dissolute, and authoritarian regimes) a 'Natural Progress of Opulence', stemming largely from the division of labour. He stresses the vital importance of individual freedom, the pursuit of economic self interest (though not to the point of total egocentricity), of good government in general, and of law and order in particular. However, he thinks the division of labour is the most important single factor, the extent of which is limited by the size of the market and not by the size of the population:

> This great increase of the quantity of work which, in consequence of the division of labour, *the same number of people are capable of performing*, is owing to three different circumstances . . . the increase of dexterity . . . the saving of time . . . passing from one species of work to another; and . . . the invention of a great number of machines which facilitate and abridge labour. (Bk. I, Ch. I) (Italics added)

(2) *Karl Marx*

Marx the authors of *Capital* and founder of Communism, believed that in the development of the power of production lay the key to the proper understanding of the whole historical process. Increasing production through technological innovation not only was not *caused* by population increase, but did not *require* it; rather, it created its own law of population, as does every mode of economic organisation. 'Capitalist accumulation . . . constantly produces . . . a population larger than

137

suffices for the average needs of the self-expansion of capital . . . in short, a surplus population'.

Marx had no general theory of economic growth, restricting himself in the main to the progressive accumulation of wealth by capitalists, as long as both state and industry are organised on a class basis through the progressive transformation of 'surplus value' (obtained by exploitation of the workers) into capital for further investment. 'Accumulation resolves itself into the reproduction of capital on a progressively increasing scale. Simple reproduction moved in a circle; but now . . . this circle has been changed into a spiral.'

The aggrandisement of the capitalists was accompanied by the production of a vast body of unemployed, the 'industrial reserve army', as we have seen, and the progressive impoverishment of the workers, so that summing up the resultant change in the economy—to see whether or not there had been net growth—would be a difficult task. Eventually the 'contradictions' of capitalism would ensure its demise, a major step on the way to the end of the process of social evolution leading inevitably, via the dictatorship of the proletariat, to the classless society, a truly communist state of which the guiding principle would be: 'From each according to his abilities, to each according to his needs.'

Economic growth would be a meaningless concept in such a society and Marx's theory has the merit of a steady-state ending, be it ever so remote.

Conditions for economic growth: Some modern theorists

(1) *W. A. Lewis*

Perhaps the most widely respected commentator on the topic of economic growth today is Professor W. Arthur Lewis. In the preface to his work, *Theory of Economic Growth*[3] he says: 'My title is misleading if it suggests that there can be a single theory of economic growth. The factors which determine growth are very numerous, and each has its own set of theories'. He argues later in the book that population growth makes economic growth 'desirable' without guaranteeing that it will come about, and he dispassionately points to some cases in which rapid population growth has not prevented even more rapid economic growth, notably the United States.

Nowhere in this scholarly volume is there any suggestion that economic growth is caused by population growth, and his judgement on the fact that 'population and food supply may be racing neck and neck' goes as follows: 'It requires no elaborate argument to establish the proposition that if death rates fall from forty to ten, the world will soon be in a mess unless birth rates fall to much the same extent.'

(2) *W. W. Rostow*

No other theorist of major status—or, for that matter, of minor status either—attributes economic growth solely to population pressure. In his important work, The Stages of Economic Growth,[4] W. W. Rostow classifies societies into five stages of economic development. The first and second are 'traditional society', in its early quiescent state and in its later phase as it develops the 'preconditions' for economic 'take-off'; third comes the 'take-off' itself; fourth, the 'drive for maturity'; and fifth, 'the age of high mass-consumption'.

In none of these stages is any potency attributed to population pressure as a factor inducing economic development or growth. At the critical stage of developing the preconditions for take-off, Rostow gives most weight to a powerful disturbing factor from the outside on a 'well-established traditional society'; 'The . . . general case in modern history . . . saw the stage of preconditions for take-off arise . . . from some external intrusion by more advanced societies . . . which shocked the traditional society and began or hastened its undoing'.

Rostow believes that in some circumstances population growth can aid economic growth, once it has started, provided that the population growth is modest and balanced. He points out, however, that rates of population increase in the poorer countries are vastly greater than those obtaining when the developed countries experienced their economic take-off and that this fact must impose severe strains in many spheres. (Rostow takes his analysis further in *Politics and the Stages of Growth*, published in 1971.)

(3) *S. Kuznets*

Simon Kuznets sets forth in his work, *Modern Economic Growth*,[5] the argument that societies surge forwards from time to time under the influence of an 'epochal innovation' which may be social, technological, political, or other. With respect to economic growth over the past two centuries, he says the epochal innovation is 'the extended application of science to problems of economic production' (p. 9) which led to 'feedback effects upon the growth of science itself—a kind of self-stimulation of further economic growth' (p. 11). He goes on to spell out the *Weltanschauung* or world view 'which permits and fosters the application of science to economic technology', typified in this case by 'three terms, secularism, egalitarianism, and nationalism' (p. 12).

With respect to population Kuznets argues that given certain crucial assumptions, which may or may not be justifiable, moderate population increase can help economic growth in some ways, but he also balances his case by pointing to the negative aspects of population growth.

(4) *B. F. Hoselitz*

The only other theorist there is space to consider here is B. F. Hoselitz, who has produced what is possibly the most complex theoretical model of societies displaying differing economic growth patterns.[6] He first of all makes the useful distinction between 'economic' and 'non-economic' theories—that is to say between those explaining economic growth solely in terms of other economic variables, and those including non-economic variables. He points to the great gulf in our knowledge by arguing that 'what is needed . . . is a theory relating economic development to cultural change' (p. 24). He also draws attention to the very important part played by cities in economic growth, some being 'generative' and positively aiding the development of the region in which they are situated, while others are 'parasitic', leaching away and dissipating the vital forces of the surrounding area. In this latter category he places Rome from the third to the fifth century AD, Constantinople from the mid-twelfth to the mid-fifteenth century, and the cities of the Iberian peninsula in the seventeenth and eighteenth centuries.

His main theme, however, is the classification of societies along three dimensions; firstly, according to whether they are territorially 'expansionist' or 'intrinsic', as he labels it; secondly whether they are 'dominant' or 'satellitic'; and, thirdly, whether the economy is 'autonomous' or whether the government intervenes to bring about 'induced' development. Putting these together produces eight basic types of economy, ranging from the expansionist, dominant, autonomous—as in the United States from 1830 to 1890—down to the intrinsic, satellitic, induced, such as those of most of the present People's Democracies. With regard to the relationship between demographic factors and economic growth, his reference to the 'population obstacle' shows clearly how little positive weight he attaches to population pressure.

A more detailed analysis of some of the factors

(1) *Technology and economic growth*

Most commentators seem to agree that technology is one of the most important factors, and a number of researchers have made detailed studies of the relationships between technology and various potential factors affecting the standard of living. One of these is the American sociologist, W. F. Ogburn, who looked at the effect of population, economic organisation, technology, and natural resources, in China, India, the United Kingdom, the Soviet Union, and the United States. He concluded that 'technology is much the most important of the four factors in explaining the variation in the standard of living'.[7] He also quoted another study, of eighteen countries this time, showing a large positive correlation between standard of living and technology ($+0\cdot7$), and a negative correlation with population density ($-0\cdot3$).[8]

A number of authors have examined the social forces related to the production and exploitation of inventions, the basis of technological development, and all of them agree that this is one of the basic forces producing economic growth. One of them, Jacob Schmookler, believes that 'long term economic growth is primarily the result of the growth of technological knowledge' both in quantity and kind.[9] Existing knowledge is more widely diffused and new knowledge is produced by the innovators, provided that the socio-economic climate is conducive to these processes.

Lewis Mumford has argued that these social forces have such a profound effect that, once the process had acquired a certain dynamism, 'invention had become a duty . . . people agreed that inventions were good, whether or not they actually provided benefits'.[10]

This is the foundation of the belief that 'technological determinism' now afflicts our society, a state of affairs in which the technologically possible becomes the economic and political necessity. If a Concorde *can* be built it *must* be built. However, as Leslie Sklair points out in *The Sociology of Progress*,[11] inventions by no means always lead to economic and social innovation in any significant sense. Hero's steam turbine of the first century AD provides a notable example of this possible gap between the inventor and the economy. We have to explain not only the psychological, social, economic, and environmental factors conducive to inventions, but also how these same variables combine so as to foster or impede their subsequent adoption and use. Underlying the processes of both invention and innovation is the long social, psychological and moral build-up to the point at which they can take root and flourish. As Mumford points out:

> While people often call our period the 'Machine Age', very few have any perspective on modern technics or any clear notion as to its origins. Popular historians usually date the great transformation in modern industry from Watt's supposed invention of the steam engine, and in conventional economics textbooks the application of automatic machinery to spinning and weaving is often treated as an equally critical turning point. But the fact is that in Western Europe the machine had been developed steadily for at least seven centuries before the dramatic changes that accompany the 'Industrial Revolution' took place. . . .
>
> Behind all the great material inventions of the last century and a half was not merely a long internal development of technics there was also a change of mind. Before the new industrial processes could take hold on a great scale, a reorientation of wishes, habits, ideas and goals was necessary.[12]

But technology, to which this and other writers attribute such weight as a determinant of growth, can backfiire, not only in the form of pollution of the environment but in the alienation of man. As Toynbee put it: 'The sheer technical expertise which has enabled Man to conquer and control his outer environment may frequently be the seal of his doom if he proves incapable of surmounting the challenges that impinge on his soul from within'.[13]

(2) *Natural resources and economic growth*

Ogburn's study, referred to earlier, did not rate natural resources highly but it is obvious that without access to some natural resources a society cannot exist at all. Without a fairly adequate supply it cannot achieve wealth, merely subsistence, and without a plentiful supply it cannot pursue a policy of increasing prosperity. Picture the nineteenth-century Eskimo or Bedouin attempting to launch an industrial revolution.

It is equally obvious that even in an environment providing an ample supply of natural resources, the more people there are the less per head there must be, provided that there are *enough* people to develop them for use at all. If the population of Britain were only half its present size, our coal, oil, natural gas, and other resources, would, other things being equal, provide equal prosperity for twice as long. On the basis of finds up to April 1974, our North Sea oil supplies are expected to rise to a peak production of 115 million tons a year in 1981, and then to fall rapidly from that figure to 40 million tons a year by 1990.[14] Estimates of potential up-grading of existing discoveries and yields of others yet to be made show that production could be sustained at around 150 million tons a year throughout the 1980s before the decline sets in.

Other things being equal, with half the population our North Sea bonanza would take us well into the next millennium before our oil-based economy must change drastically.

(3) *Education and Economic Growth*

Another factor often left out of account is education, and attention has already been drawn to its importance with respect to the rapid growth of Japan in economic power and world influence. For instance, Yoichi Okazaki said:

> Among the factors which promoted the amazingly rapid modernisation process of Japan, the importance of an invisible factor, education, has particularly drawn attention recently. Already at the Meiji Restoration in 1868, the starting point of modernisation, the level of education in the public was considerably high, because the continuance of peace over 200 years under the Tokugawa regime contributed to improve the level of culture in general and spread education on the populace. Moreover the new Meiji Government decided to place special emphasis on the education as a part of modernisation policies [*sic*]'.[15].

In a table Okazaki shows that while material capital has increased by a factor of approximately 6·9, since 1905, educational capital has increased 23 times.

(4) *Religion and economic growth*
R. H. Tawney said

> For the middle classes of the early seventeenth century, rising but not yet triumphant, the enchanted mirror was puritanism. What it showed was a picture grave to sternness, an earnest, zealous, godly generation, scorning delights, punctual in labour, constant in prayer, thrifty and thriving, filled with a decent pride in themselves and their calling, assured that strenuous toil is acceptable to heaven, a people like those Dutch Calvinists whose economic triumphs were as famous as their iron Protestantism— 'thinking, sober and patient men, and such as believed that labour and industry is their duty towards God.'[16]

Max Weber also showed the importance of religion in the development of capitalist society in America and elsewhere.

The importance of the religious factor stressed by Weber and Tawney can be reinforced by evidence pointing in the opposite direction—that is, evidence that a religiophilosophic system with different values may *prevent* economic growth in spite of population pressure. Lewis Haney wrote:

> One of the most striking characteristics of both Hebrew and Hindu . . . thought . . . was the conflict between economic stimuli

and ethico-religious ideas . . . characterised by such a lack of individualism and materialism, such a disapprobation of industry other than agriculture and relative indifference to wealth, such a degree of passivity and fatalism, that its dominance made any great industrial civilisation impossible.[17]

(5) *A psychological need for achievement and economic growth.*
David McClelland, in a very penetrating study of the interaction of different religious beliefs and other social factors, coupled with an analysis of environmental resources and economic change, has postulated a 'need for achievement', culturally induced in individuals and objectively measurable, which 'is an important factor affecting the rate of economic development'.[18] One of his main points, however, is how complicated socio-economic systems are and how difficult it is to pin down the effects of particular causal factors. There are many other factors which would have to be considered for a thorough-going analysis.

The opposite case: Population growth as a negative factor in economic growth
Many commentators have argued the exact opposite to the case of George and Clark. One of these is Ellsworth Huntingdon, who wrote in 1945: 'Throughout . . . history all countries have normally contained about as many people as they could support at the stage of culture . . . then . . . reached. . . . At all times and places there is a powerful tendency toward population pressure'.[19] He gives numerous examples of countries enjoying greater prosperity when population pressure was lower, and one of these was India.

> In the days of the Mogul emperors . . . there were . . . probably 30 or 40 million people in an area [Northern India] which now contains about 180 millions [vastly more now, of course]. This relatively small population utilised only the most fertile land and therefore presumably got a greater return per acre than now. . . . The size of family holdings was also greater. . . .
> In AD 1600 a labourer's daily wage bought twice as much food as in 1900 and a still larger amount compared with today. . . . The peasants were oppressed by heavy taxes and rich landlords

but they must have been better fed than now. . . . They had such a surplus that rice, wheat, millet and grain cost only half as much in proportion to a day's wages. . . . It is especially significant that mutton and especially ghee or butter were even cheaper than cereals. . . . The peasants not only had more but better food than now.[20]

Beneficial effects of a drop in population

Huntingdon also demonstrates that there was frequently a blossoming of culture and prosperity when population pressure was *reduced*, usually after one of the all too frequent catastrophes:

A famine which began in 1595 continued four years and was so terrible that children were sold for a song and cannibalism became frequent. It was accompanied by a pestilence so violent that the roads were actually blocked with corpses. Again in 1630, three years of poor rainfall were followed by a complete failure of the rains. Famine, cannibalism and pestilence again ensued. Such conditions usually lead to extreme poverty and misery for a while, but after a few years the people are actually better off than before. Their numbers are temporarily less than formerly, but the same amount of land is available. . . . Thus the food supply is enlarged in comparison with the population. . . . After the famine of 1630 wages went up because the workers were scarce, but the price of food . . . went back to the old level . . . and people lived more comfortably than before.[21]

Huntingdon continues:

The 1630 famine . . . was followed by the reign of Shah Jahan . . . a time 'of increasing order and tranquillity' . . . The Mogul empire attained its greatest magnificence and the lovely pearl mosque at Agra and the . . . stately Taj Mahal were erected. There can be little doubt that one of the conditions which made . . . possible . . . such buildings was . . . an increasing food supply because of the decimation of numbers through famine. This made people more healthy than usual . . . more vigorous, more contented, and better able to pay taxes and work on public projects.[22]

Reduction in population and the liberation of the English serfs

We saw earlier that Clark claims that the English serfs were liberated by population growth; historians appear to be unanimous that the opposite is true. M. W. Flinn, for instance says:

The immediate effect of the Black Death . . . was to convert the shortage of *land* into a shortage of *labour*. Wages rose steeply. . . . Lords faced the prospect of drastic loss of income unless they could succeed in attracting new tenants. Economic forces swung in favour of tenants *whose power of bargaining* to secure manumission and commutation of labour services *was doubled overnight*.[23] (Italics added.)

The first English wage-freeze was triggered off by this true manpower gap so that, Flinn continues,

In an effort to stabilise wages the government, acting needless to say in the interests of the lords rather than of the common people, issued first an Ordinance of Labourers in 1349, and later a Statute of Labourers in 1351 . . . [forbidding] the payment of wages in excess of those . . . between 1325 and 1331, and required compulsory service in employment of all able-bodied men and women under sixty . . . *though vigorous attempts were made to enforce these laws, they fought a losing battle against the superior forces of economic pressure*. Lords competed against each other for labour . . . *higher wages were the inevitable response to the drastic shortage*. (Italics added.)

Ireland: falling population and increasing quality of life
The PEP study referred to earlier argued that population pressure in Ireland led not to power, wealth and brilliance, but to disaster.

Overpopulation led to a disastrous famine, the shock of which caused the people at large to . . . stop fragmentation of farms and . . . population growth. This was achieved in spite of the success of a powerful church in opposing birth control. . . . The people embarked on a new way of life which is continuing even today. . . . late and limited marriages and very high emigration . . . which has reduced the population by half during the last century . . . are both mainly due to the spontaneous reaction to the overwhelming catastrophe of the 1845 famine. . . .

At the beginning Ireland was exceedingly poor, at the end it was not rich but it had a much higher standard of living. It seems highly probable that this is mainly due to the reduction of population.[24]

Here the study quotes an Irish scholar, R. C. Geary: 'with a low population, life in Ireland is relatively easy and pleasant, and we have been spared most of the stresses and strains which have afflicted other people in this terrible century'.[25]

The Industrial Revolution

Rather surprisingly, Clark does not attempt to explain the industrial revolution in population terms, but some authors do—L. C. A. Knowles, for example:

> It is at first sight remarkable that the industrial revolution should have started here in a country only containing about 9 million people between 1780 and 1709, when France had 26 million in 1789 and ought to have afforded a better market for manufactures produced on a large scale. . . .
>
> *Possibly the explanation lies in the fact that the English population was so small that, to deal with the growing export trade, machinery was essential, as there were not people enough to satisfy by handwork the increased demand. . . .*
>
> *England had to supplement her small population with machines.*[26] (Italics added.)

Later on the impetus for innovation was partly lost, and Knowles comments: 'The coming of machinery was probably delayed owing to the rapid increase of population in the nineteenth century, which made it less urgent to introduce machinery in the older trades as more hands became available'.

The costs of population growth

Population growth costs money; it consumes wealth which could have gone into raising standards for the existing populations. However, apart from 'opportunity costs' and other economic drawbacks, rapid population growth creates obvious and immediate problems in other spheres which are hard to evaluate on a purely economic basis. E. P. Thompson, speaking of Britain during the Industrial Revolution, puts this very well:

> The unprecedented rate of population growth, and of concentration in industrial areas, would have created major problems in any known society, and most of all one . . . whose rationale was

148

to be found in profit-seeking. . . . The slums, the stinking rivers, the spoilation of nature, and the architectural horrors . . . occurred because all happened so fast, so haphazardly, under intense population pressure.[27]

Even relatively slow population growth in wealthy industrialised societies creates problems which no country has yet solved. There are *never* enough teachers, schools, roads, hospitals, telephones, houses, prisons, and so on. The investment required is never forthcoming on a large enough scale, and many have to go short. Over vast areas in the world, population pressure is forcing hundreds of millions of people off the land and out of a traditional occupation and way of life into a wretched existence of unemployment, poverty and desolation in urban shanty towns—the necessities of life simply do not exist, and probably never will while the flood of numbers continues unabated.

After two centuries of industrial revolution and increasing production we in Britain are only just beginning to look at the size of the bill for all this growth, in both numbers and 'wealth', and to toy with the idea of repairing the havoc wrought upon the environment; and still the rate of population growth—reduced as it is—is making it much harder, if not impossible, to catch up.

Rich and poor
It follows from Clark's analysis that if it is population pressure alone which causes economic development, then the greater the pressure the faster the development. The world's past and present trends show the exact opposite. Figure 10/1 illustrates the distribution of population and wealth in the world in 1968. In the case of population, the rate of growth of the poorer peoples is vastly greater than that of the richer ones—Southwest-Asia's 2·9 per cent per annum, typically, against the 0·6 per cent of Western Europe—but in the case of wealth the situation is reversed, the richer ones rapidly growing richer still, so that the 'gap' grows wider every year. The average annual growth per capita for the poor countries, according to the World Bank figures for 1960–1966, was 2·3 per cent and that for the rich ones 3·9 per cent—70 per cent greater. For

Figure 10/1.   Population and wealth in the overdeveloped
and underdeveloped worlds 1969

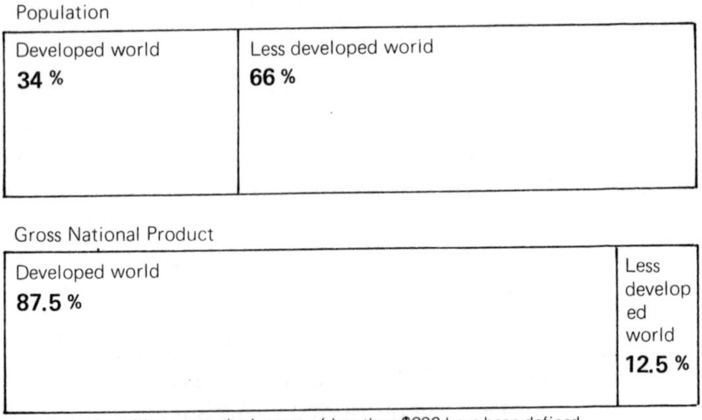

Population

Developed world 34 %	Less developed world 66 %

Gross National Product

Developed world 87.5 %	Less developed world 12.5 %

All countries with a per capita income of less than $300 have been defined
as 'less developed' for the purposes of this diagram

most of the poorer countries there is no question of catching up
on the rich countries, on present trends; but even for the few
growing more rapidly the prospects are daunting. It would take
Malawi 730 years and Pakistan 1,760 years to catch up with
the United States today.[28]

I have never heard of a single economist or any other observer who thinks that this situation can be altered without changes
in world politics and economic systems so drastic and far-
reaching as to beggar the word 'revolution'.

Human capital and the demographic investment
Even in the simplest societies the birth of a human being consumes wealth, the savings of the community, though if both
child and society are lucky it will grow up and repay the
investment, perhaps several times over. Some authors have
tried to work out what, in strictly economic terms, human
beings are worth. Claude Dupin estimated in 1748 that a
Frenchman was worth $353\frac{1}{2}$ hundredweight of corn, Barriol
thought that by 1910 he was worth 1,171 hundredweight and
Alfred Sauvy raised his price in 1958 to 2,750 hundredweight.[29]
Since then the figure has risen still further. The point is that
all this investment has to come out of the existing fund of

wealth, because it is a long time before the new citizen becomes productive. Where a population is growing, all these socialisation costs add up to the 'demographic investment'—the investment required in order to prevent capital per head from falling. The demographic investment in India in 1966 was $5,070 million.

It follows that, if population growth can be reduced, then there is a saving on the demographic investment, which can then be used for other purposes. If population control also costs money, as it does, then the question arises of profit and loss on the investment in birth control. The technical term for this is 'returns to fertility control', and many economists think that in a country with high population growth the greatest social return on investment capital is to be obtained in the field of birth control.[30]

Demographic 'Neighbourhood Effects'
'Neighbourhood effects' is an American term which I prefer to the British one, 'externalities'. Both refer to the 'external' consequences of economic transactions. If A and B get together to manufacture, sell, or buy an economic good, it may be a purely private transaction affecting no one else in any significant way so that the economist says it has no external consequences. If it *does* affect a third person the transaction could do him either good or harm. If it does him good is has 'positive' external effects, if harm, 'negative' external (or 'neighbourhood') effects. For example, if several owner-occupiers on an unmade road get together and have it surfaced, despite the fact that one or more refused to pay their share, all gain equally. Conversely, if two or three of them get together to buy a powerful record-player and amplifier which they then use at full blast to assuage their thirst for pop music, all the others suffer more or less equally.

Many, perhaps most, economic transactions have neighbourhood effects and, as more and more people consume more and more goods and services, their consequences tend to be increasingly negative; danger, congestion, pollution, and noise and nuisance are neighbourhood effects we suffer from every day. Only slowly and reluctantly are we realising that society must intervene and moderate the sovereignty of the individual supplier and consumer when the consequences of their actions are too damaging to others.

Population growth, poverty and violence
Francis Bacon said:

> The matter of seditions is of two kinds—much poverty, and much discontentment. . . . Rebellions of the belly are the worst . . . and . . . generally, it is to be foreseen that the population of a kingdom . . . do not exceed the stock . . . which should maintain them.[31]

Some commentators would want to modify this and argue that below a certain level of subsistence people have neither the will nor the energy to rebel; but the historical evidence shows that overpopulation and want have frequently caused expansion and war. The piracy of the Scandinavians, the Barbarian invasions of Europe, and the Crusades were all caused at least in part by overpopulation. So too was the militarism of the Japanese in the 1930s, according to Petersen and other writers, and the territorial ambitions of the Germans. With respect to contemporary society, studies done by the US Defense Department show that the poorer a country is the more it is involved in major outbreaks of violence (not crime). Only 4 per cent of the countries with a per capita income of $750 a year were involved in national violence, against 84 per cent of those in the 'very poor' category, less than $100 per head per year.

If we accept that population pressure causes poverty and that poverty (above starvation level) causes violence, then population pressure causes violence in man as in many other creatures.

The World today
The Director of the World Bank, J. H. Adler, recently commented:

> The most disconcerting aspect of the world economy since 1950 has been the high, and rising, rate of population growth. This is not . . . a new discovery. . . . What is new . . . is the heavy concen-

tration of high rates of population growth in the poorest countries. . . . These are . . . alarming because of the limitations . . . they impose on economic advancement. . . . There is an inverse relationship between population growth and growth . . . [in] income. . . . High rates of population growth . . . [are] a major factor which bears directly on their growth prospects.[32]

U. Thant, a moderate man, went even further, saying just before his retirement as Secretary General of the UN:

> I do not wish to seem over dramatic, but I can only conclude from the information available to me as Secretary General that the members of the UN have perhaps 10 years left in which to subordinate their ancient quarrels and launch a global partnership to curb the arms race . . . improve the human environment . . . defuse the population explosion, and supply the required momentum to development efforts.
>
> *If such a global partnership is not forged within the next decade, then I very much fear that these problems will have reached such staggering proportions that they will be beyond our capacity to control.*[33] (Italics added.)

The problem of social change

What Clark and other apologists are really talking about is not economic growth as such but social change accompanied by economic growth. All commentators seem to agree that economic growth by itself is impossible; there must be new values, new behaviour patterns, and new social institutions to compel—or at least to permit—the newer forms and/or greater intensity of economic life. More, and—hopefully—better production and consumption. Clark ascribes virtually all change in society to population pressure, but there is no support for anything remotely approaching this in the literature of the social sciences. The consensus is that social systems are so complex that no valid universal theory of social change is possible—certainly not at the present state of knowledge—except in the most general terms.

Sorokin, one of the greatest sociological scholars of our age, has argued that there are three basic kinds of explanation, the the *externalistic*, the *immanent*, and the *intermediary*. The first implies that change in a society must come from a source outside itself, the second that such systems not only *can* change without external influences but are hardly in a position to *prevent* change occurring: '*The problem of why a sociocultural system changes is falsely set forth.* Its change is neither a mystery nor difficult to explain. Much more difficult would it be to understand a case of unchangeableness . . . if one had ever occurred.'[34] The third type of explanation, the *intermediary*, is the one Sorokin accepts for himself. Societies can change because of both internal and external forces, and we find out why change occurred in particular cases by studying the evidence.

W. F. Ogburn, one of the founding fathers of American sociology, published in 1922 *Social Change*, which became a classic. In this he argued that cultural evolution can be explained by four factors—invention, accumulation, diffusion, and adjustment—which he linked to his twin theory of 'cultural lag', the biological and the social. The biological theory of cultural lag is that, in spite of his high cultural attainments, man is basically still the same creature that he was in the Stone Age. Our culture changes quickly while our biological nature changes slowly, so that the second tends to lag behind the first. Ogburn's other, and perhaps better known, theory of cultural lag relates to the alleged gap between our 'material' and 'adaptive' cultures, where again the second tends to lag behind the first. The basic sources of progressive change are found in material inventions, materials, tools and processes which enhance the material culture. This in turn interacts with the rest of our institutions and values which, given time, tend to adapt more or less successfully to the demand of, and opportunities created by, new elements in the material culture. The key phrase here is 'given time', because for a good many reasons spelt out by Ogburn—vested interests, habits, social-pressures, and others—the adaptive culture tends to lag behind the material culture, which is the dynamo generating change.

Revolutionary versus evolutionary change
In the case of revolutionary as distinct from evolutionary change, we saw in Chapter 4 that Eric Wolf believes that population pressure has frequently been an important factor

in toppling a long-established regime and bringing about drastic change. It is doubtful, however, whether he allows enough weight to the fact that there must have been quite a lot of change to permit the population pressure to build up in the first place. It may be that in these circumstances an explosion of numbers may be an intervening variable rather than a cause. Whatever the merits and demerits of the argument, however, not many people will welcome the population explosion on the ground that it is likely to produce a series of revolutions. Most of us seem to prefer evolutionary change without a demographic pistol held at our heads.

Grand theory: the rise and fall of whole civilisations
Beyond the problem of understanding moderately short-term change lies the more fundamental problem of explaining long-term change in social systems, and it is impossible to go very far into this field without coming up against theories which are not merely philosophical but religious. In brief, the theories of change over the long run can be classified under three headings. Firstly, those postulating cyclical change—as in some Eastern philosophies; secondly, those on progressive change, societies evolving towards some golden age; and, thirdly, theories of progressive-regressive evolution, such as Oswald Spengler's, in which, after their brief heyday, societies slide back into oblivion.

The real problem underlying the phenomenon of economic growth, as Clark approaches it, is why some populations develop civilisations which burst forth and flourish while many—perhaps most—others merely tick over, making the faintest of impressions on the pages of history; others again, whether they have shone or barely existed for a period, quietly go under.

Arnold Toynbee is perhaps the best known modern theorist on this great question of the genesis, efflorescence, and demise of whole civilisations, and for him all static societies may be likened to a climber resting on a ledge with a precipice below him and another above. However lowly the society may now appear, it must nevertheless have ascended a good way out of the abyss of man's primeval state:

Their companions . . . have only just left this same ledge and
started to climb the face of the precipice above; and, since the
next ledge is out of sight, we do not know how high or how
arduous this 'pitch' will be. We only know that it is impossible
to halt and rest before the next ledge, wherever that may be, is
reached![35]

To answer the question why some societies are recumbent
on a ledge whilst others are tenaciously scrambling higher and
still others—those who tried and failed—are crashing to their
deaths in the abyss below. Toynbee puts forward the theory of
'challenge and response'. If societies continue to exist, they are
forced from time to time to meet challenges to their capacity
to adapt and survive. These challenges can come from many
different quarters, from a harsh environment such as that faced
by the Eurasian nomads, or the prehistoric jungle-swamp of
the Lower Nile valley, now the fertile Nile delta, or the ab-
normally light and stony soil of Attica, the basis of the great
civilisation of the ancient Greeks; from social, religious, or
political persecution, such as that undergone by the British
Dissenters of 1660, the American Mormons two centuries later,
and the Jews throughout the ages; or, in some cases, from pressure of population.

Toynbee thinks that pressure of numbers forced ancient
Sparta into an ultimately stultifying militarism, while Athens,
leaving it almost too late 'until the pressure threatened to find
vent in a social revolution', was pushed into 'agricultural
specialisation . . . and manufactures . . . for export, and then
developing her political institutions so as to give a fair share of
political power to the new classes which had been called into
being by these economic innovations' (p. 41)—in other words,
to invent democracy.

Whether a society will be able to respond to a major new
stimulus is unpredictable: 'The initiative that is taken by one
or other of the live parties to an encounter is not a cause; it is
a challenge. Its consequence is not an effect; it is a response'
(p. 97). 'The factor that tips the balance either towards success
or towards failure . . . is the spirit in which Man responds to
the challenge of the sum total of Nature' (p. 96).

However—and this is especially relevant to the challenge of population pressure—Toynbee argues that a challenge can be so great that a society, instead of being stimulated to unprecedented effort, is simply broken on the wheel of fortune. To produce the appropriate level of stimulation, a 'challenge' must be optimal—not too large and not too small, and of just the right kind so that it 'not only stimulates the challenged party to achieve a single successful response, but also . . . to acquire a momentum that carries him a step further: from achievement to fresh struggles' (p. 136).

For Herbert Spencer, perhaps the greatest social theorist of all time, all systems—social, biological, and physical—must continue to evolve, the direction being that 'in which the aggregate of opposing forces is least', but there is no guarantee that evolution is in a desirable direction.

> The cosmic process brings about retrogression as well as progression, where the conditions favour it. Only amid an infinity of modifications, adjusted to an infinity of changes of circumstances, do there now and then occur some which constitute an advance.[36]

Conclusion

Demographic, economic, and social change are related on a many-cause many-effect basis, not a single-cause single-effect basis, and in many cases we don't even know the direction of causality. In his zeal to establish the case for unlimited population growth, Clark doesn't even stop to consider whether—far from a 'large' population 'causing' greatness, in the case of ancient Greece or seventeenth-century Holland—greatness causes a large population, or whether some third factor or combination of factors produces both a large population and greatness together.

The American sociologist, Sorokin, has summed up the question very cogently:

> In brief, if there is a correlation between demographic factors and the forms of social and political organisation (which is probable), it is so remote, so complex, and so strongly masked by the interference of other factors, that we must regard it as potential or intangible, rather than as a factual correlation. . . .

157

I would mention only one type of correlation which appears to me more or less valid . . . that, with an increase in size and density of the population, its social differentiation, whatever may be its form, and its technical division of labour, are likely to increase also. . . . But . . . even this broad correlation is far from being close, and the lines of both processes do not always go parallel.[37]

Where amidst this welter of facts and theories is the 'correct' or 'best' answer to the problem of human economic social, psychological, esthetic and moral development? Surely at the present stage of knowledge, the answer is open-mindedness and eclecticism. We must recognise that ecosystems containing human societies are of such complexity that they may never be fully understood, much less become predictable, so that we have to learn to live in humility with our ignorance and uncertainty. Nonetheless, we do know not only that nations can disappear and whole civilisations perish but also that living species mostly become extinct through failing to adapt to new environmental 'challenges', to use Toynbee's term.

The odds are heavily against the survival of our species, judging by the evolutionary record, but man is unique—in our corner of the universe, at least—in that he can to some extent foresee and be concerned about alternative prospects in train for the future. Because of this unique property he can —given the will—shoot the evolutionary rapids in his frail canoe indefinitely. To use Gabor's terminology he can 'invent' his own future, a prospect open to no other creature before.

Further reading on economic growth
Baran, P. A. (1973) The Political Economy of Growth.
Barkley and Seckler (1973) Economic Growth and Environmental Decay.
Denison, E. E. (1970) Why Growth Rates Differ.
Gould, J. D. (1973) Economic Growth in History.
Harcourt and Laing (1971) Capital and Growth.
Heller, W. (1968) Perspectives on Economic Growth.
Hicks, Sir J. (1965) Capital and Growth.
Hicks, Sir J. (1969) A Theory of Economic Growth.

Hodson, H. V. (1972) The Diseconomies of Growth.
Hoselitz, B. F. (1960) Theories of Economic Growth.
Inagaki, M. (1970) Optimal Economic Growth.
Johnson, H. G. (1970) International Trade and Economic Growth.
Kalecki, M. (1972) Selected essays on the economic growth of socialist and mixed economies.
Kindleberger, C. P. (1967) Europe's Postwar Growth.
Kregel, J. A. (1972) The Theory of Economic Growth.
Markov, M. (1968) Technology, Dependence, Monopoly and Growth.
Meade, J. E. (1962) A Neo-Classical Theory of Economic Growth.
Mills, J. (1972) Growth and Welfare.
Mirrlees and Stern (1973) Models of Economic Growth.
Mishan, E. J. (1969) Growth, the Price we Pay.
Morishima, M. (1969) Theory of Economic Growth.
Mun, T. (1664) England's Treasure by Forraign Trade, etc.
OECD (1967) Social Change and Economic Growth.
Powelson, J. P. (1972) Institutions of Economic Growth. A Theory of Conflict Management in Developing Countries.
Richardson, H. W. (1973) Regional Growth Theory.
Rosenberg, N. (1972) Technology and American Growth.
Shone, Sir Robert (1966) Investment and Economic Growth (Pamph.)
Turgot, A. R. J. (1766) Reflexions sur la formation et la distribution des richesses.
Vanek, J. (1968) Maximal Economic Growth etc.
Wiener, A. J. (1971) Faust's Progress. The Changing Economic and Social Climate for Technological and Economic Growth.
Williams, P. R. (1973) Science and Technology in Economic Growth.

There is also a vast literature on economic development which is rarely distinguished from economic growth.

CHAPTER 11

The manpower argument: the fallacy of the labour shortage

'By this time any child ought to have known that our man-power situation was extremely menacing.' Quintin Hogg.[1]

'This need to increase the working population is not a temporary; it is a permanent feature of our national life.' Economic Survey.[2]

'Nothing would make us so uncompetitive in the world's markets as long-term acute labour shortages.' D. E. C. Eversley.[3]

'A key point . . . is that . . . an expanding population . . . should help to solve our longer term manpower shortages.' Harold Wilson.[4]

'Would we be right in deducing from your figures that there is more likely to be a shortage of labour than the reverse. . . .?' Chairman of the Parliamentary Select Committee on Science and Technology. 'I agree with you entirely.' Expert witness: (Mr Whybrew, Economics Adviser, Research and Planning Division, Department of Employment and Productivity).[5]

It will be seen from the quotations at the head of this chapter that there has been a fervent and widespread belief in a shortage of manpower in post-war Britain, and in its over-riding importance for the economy and the general welfare of the nation. It is a theory with a long history.

If we go right back to the ancients we see that most of their sages were only too acutely aware of the problems of overpopulation, poverty, disease, and violence, and of the need for a balance between numbers and environmental carrying capacity. Many of them were also convinced of the desirability of *optimising* the sizes of societies rather than *maximising* them. However, in the Middle Ages other economic and political philosophies evolved in the West—perhaps partly under the influence of the 'increase and multiply' aspect of Christianity

—which began to stress growth and size in both population and wealth.

One of these was mercantilism, a philosophy of growth lasting for about 250 years from early in the sixteenth century. This was militaristic and expansionist in the political as well as the economic sense. The chief goal was power; power came from wealth; true wealth lay in stores of precious metals; these came from foreign trade; and for a thriving foreign trade as many hands as possible were required.

The German form of Mercantilism, called Kameralism, lasted well into the nineteenth century, and this placed an even greater stress on population size and growth as a source of wealth.

One of its representatives, Von Loen, concluded: 'All legitimate means must be used to maintain a constant increase of the population'.[6]

Let us now examine some of the evidence about population, manpower and wealth.

Structure of the manpower argument

First we must make a distinction between a general and diffuse shortage of manpower of the sort described by the mercantilists (i.e. between the present work force and a potential future work force) and a specific gap in a contemporary industry or even an individual plant. Most recent commentators, though not all, have concentrated on the last problem—the alleged shortage of labour in a particular sector of the economy. Again the essence of this fallacy can be expressed as a syllogism.

First premise: Manpower shortages are caused by population shortages.

Second premise: Some British industries have manpower shortages.

Conclusion: Britain has a population shortage.

Let us look at some of the evidence.

Some historical examples

One way of identifying a manpower shortage or gap is to look for instances where an existing population has been suddenly depleted by natural or man-made catastrophe or by social mechanisms such as emigration. According to Gordon Childe, one of the main reasons for the fall of the Western part of the Roman Empire was lack of manpower. Continuous wars had meant a ready supply of slaves to till the land and work at manufacture, but these prevented settlement by native families whilst generally leaving no offspring behind themselves. 'With the beginning of the Augustan reign of peace, wars ceased, and the source of the slave supply was cut off . . .; the question became more insistent with each generation—who was to get the food out of the ground?'[7] Land fell into disuse, wealth and population declined and soon the barbarians—themselves thrust inexorably onwards by population pressure from behind —were at the gates of Rome. 'People ask why the Roman Empire fell! Childe concluded. 'Why did it last?'

After the Black Death struck in 1348, the population of England was rapidly reduced by about a third. Many historians believe that a reduction was helpful in the long run, because the country was overpopulated at the time and the arable land 'plough sick', according to Olaf Stapledon. Chambers and Mingay claim that: 'Only catastrophe could rescue the medieval peasantry and it came in the form of a drastic pruning of peasant households by the Black Death'.[8]

A statute of Edward III, promulgated in 1350, said:

A great part of the People, and especially of Workmen and Servants lately died of the Pestilence, and many . . . will not serve unless they receive excessive Wages . . . Considering the *grievous Discommodity*, which may . . . hereafter come . . . of the *lack of Ploughmen* and such Labourers, We have . . . ordained:
1. Every Person able in Body under the Age of Sixty Years, not having the wherewith to live . . . shall be bound to serve him that doth require him, or else be committed to the Gaol. . . .[9]

However fortunate for the survivors this may have been, plagues are not very precise instruments of population control, and many regions found they had switched almost overnight from overpopulation to underpopulation, farms and other existing enterprises were unmanned, and in many cases whole villages became deserted and slowly went back into the soil; we are still finding their remains to this day. In this sense, then, there was a real shortage of manpower for a time; but it is an ill wind which blows no one any good, and this situation led to the first wage freeze, as we have seen (somewhat ineffective then, as now), the emancipation of the serfs, and the socio-economic revolution which made possible the subsequent growth in the carrying-capacity of the environment.

Ireland is an interesting case in this context. The population of what is now the Republic was reduced by a half as a result of the great famine and heavy subsequent migration of the nineteenth century but because the country was grossly over-populated before the famine and a high rate of natural increase has continued there has never been a manpower shortage. Indeed Ireland, both north and south, has had a labour-surplus economy ever since, and substantial emigration continues to this day.

Facts and figures about the labour 'shortage'

Before launching a drastic manpower policy, it seems a reasonable precaution to ensure that the figures it is based on are more or less right. If they cannot be guaranteed, then the likely margin of error should be estimated as accurately as possible and the policy made flexible enough to suit the range of conditions implied by the upper and lower limits. All too frequently this is not done, and crucial policies are based on a foundation of fantasy and hope.

Governments are among the worst offenders. Britain's National Plan, launched in September 1965, contained what George Polanyi has called 'the notorious assertion . . . that a 'manpower gap' of some 400,000 persons was likely . . . by 1970 . . . the difference between the labour force . . . then available and the total required for the planned 25 per cent increase in national wealth'.[10] The National Plan admitted that

> this was a small difference relative to the *total* labour force, about 25 million in 1964, but . . . nevertheless attached great importance to the projected 'gap' in relation to the total expected *increase* in the labour force up to the year 1970. . . . Regional policies . . . should be used to reduce the gap from 400,000 to 200,000. (Italics added.)

Polanyi, however, challenged the whole argument by showing that Government policy was based on an elementary statistical error.

A more explicit statement . . . would have pointed out that though the current estimate of the labour force at mid-1964 was 25·43 million, the margin of error of around 5% would mean that about 1¼ million persons might need to be added or subtracted. . . . Consequently, apart from the problems of forecasting employment and output per head over 5 years, any statement about a difference of the order of 400,000 (and more so of 200,000) . . . was liable to be devoid of meaning. As it happens the . . . working population in 1964 has since been revised to 25·89 million so that the manpower 'gap' has been closed . . . without the need for intervention by the planners.

Apart from the inherent lunacy of thinking of a figure for output and then working out the manpower required, instead of gearing the production goal to our known resources, anyone with any experience of large organisations knows how chaotic are procedures for making 'estimates' of future markets, output, and requirements. All too often, the task is shuffled about in the hierarchy until it falls on the desk of some unfortunate junior whose brief is, more or less, to make a few inspired guesses and then 'prove' them.

Alleged *present* manpower 'gaps' are so questionable that prognostications about gaps in the *future* must be virtually worthless.

Filling the 'gap' through immigration
The Royal Commission noted as early as 1949 how totally unreasoning was the hullaballoo about the alleged manpower shortage, and drew attention to the shortsightedness of 'filling' it by importing workers: 'Large-scale immigration was widely advocated as a means of bridging the 'gap' between manpower resources and requirements, with a complete disregard of the fact that the immigrants would have to be fed . . . clothed and housed' (paragraph 280). Seventeen years later, undaunted by such reflections, the *New Statesman* was still writing editorials like this: 'If we opened our ports to a million fresh immigrants,

most of our labour problems—which are driving the Chancellor to another 'tough' budget—would be eased' (29 April 1966).

The National Coal Board's former policy of recruiting Hungarian refugees for the mining industry should be remembered whenever we talk about recruiting manpower overseas. At the time of the Hungarian revolution in 1956 the NCB thought it was so desperately short of manpower that it sent officials post-haste to recruit refugees as they picked their way through the minefields into Austria. The aim was to get skilled miners if possible, but anyone prepared to be trained was acceptable, and about 4,200 were brought to Britain, where special hostels and schools were set up to teach them Basic English and British mining practice. Eventually attempts were made to introduce them to the pits, but unfortunately, although the National Union of Mineworkers had agreed this policy at national level no one had remembered to consult the miner's lodges about the proposed influx, and most of them refused. The miners were reading the signs like Indian trackers, they have a deep intuitive feeling about the state of the industry, and by the time the Hungarian crisis broke they knew that hard times were just around the corner. They were absolutely right, and a few months later, in February 1958, the NCB enforced a total ban on all recruitment. Although about 700 Hungarians did work in the pits or ancillary enterprises for a time, most soon left, many going on to the United States, apart from a possible humanitarian spin-off—the whole enterprise was a complete fiasco costing several millions which the industry could ill afford. Since then, manpower has been run down to a fraction of what it was.

The general picture of British migration since the Second World War is that gains and losses have been roughly equal. We might make the assumption that the balance roughly holds with respect to manpower, too. By 1966 we had 2·6 million resident immigrants (those born overseas, excluding their children born here), including 853,000 from the New (i.e. Coloured) Commonwealth[11] and 739,000 from Ireland, and the contribution these made to the labour force was about 1·75 millions. This was higher, proportionately, than that of the native labour force, but it is very small indeed compared with the manpower which could have been siphoned out of our national spare tank, as we shall see, and so far as the immigrants were recruited to fill manpower gaps the exercise appears to have been totally redundant.

We might think more realistically about the economics of migration if we had a policy of paying and being paid for immigrants and emigrants respectively, along the lines of what the Russians are doing with Jewish emigrants to Israel, but worked out equitably and without prejudice.

Manpower and mechanisation
We would expect on commonsense grounds that there would be some sort of relationship between the availability of manpower and the rate and kind of mechanisation and, more recently, automation. Joan Robinson bears this out: 'When a capitalist economy comes up against a scarcity of labour while the urge to accumulate is strong, it sets about finding labour-saving improvements in . . . production.'[12]

We have seen that at least one commentator thinks the Industrial Revolution occurred here partly because our population was so small and labour so scarce that mechanical invention was stimulated. However, the Industrial Revolution created a great surge in population growth and this—coupled with the earlier impetus given to investment and invention—soon created a surplus population ('the industrial reserve army', as Marx called it) which then hampered development. One Marxist historian, Christopher Hill, says there was a 'surplus of child labour for the factories'[13] and E. P. Thompson documents the wider ramifications: 'The very cheapness and superfluity of handloom labour *retarded* mechanical invention and the application of capital in weaving'.[14] Thompson goes on to argue that this manpower surplus did not hamper innovation but caused 'degradation' for instance of the weavers who 'had to work longer into the night to earn less' thereby lessening the chances of employment for others. Those

> displaced swelled the limitless supply of cheap labour for the arduous work of sheer human muscle in which the times were so spendthrift. There was little or no mechanisation in the mines;

in the docks, in brick works, in gas works; building; in canal and railway buildings; in caterage and porterage. Coal was still carried on men's backs up the long ladders from ship's holds; in Birmingham men could still, in the 1830's be hired at 1s a day to wheel sand in barrows nine miles by road, and nine miles empty back.[15]

Knowles also makes the point that in relatively new trades such as cotton spinning and engineering there could not be enough labour 'so that there would be an inducement from the outset to employ mechanical appliances'[16], and that newly developing districts with poor transport systems would stimulate development in the same direction.

Innovation was stimulated by labour shortage from quite another cause, strikes. Samuel Smiles reported of Nasmyth, the great engineering innovator, that

notwithstanding the losses and suffering occasioned by strikes, Mr Nasmyth holds the opinion that they have on the whole produced much more good than evil. . . . They have served to stimulate invention in an extraordinary degree. Some of the most important labour-saving processes now in common use are directly traceable to them. . . . Manufacturers could not be induced to adopt potent self-acting tools . . . the self-acting mule, the wool-combing machine, the planing machine, the slotting machine, Nasmyth's steam arm and many others . . . until compelled . . . by strikes.[17]

Modern Technological unemployment

Unemployment has recently been an increasing rather than a decreasing problem, and one of the reasons for this is increasing investment in labour-saving technology, creating the problem of 'technological unemployment'. It has been calculated that the passenger-controlled elevator put 40,000 operators out of work in New York alone. It has recently been agreed that £3,000 millions of taxpayers' money should be invested in the British steel industry with the object of so improving 'efficiency' that 50,000 jobs will be lost. Even in traditional industries like agriculture, the rate of displacement of manpower is very high and one group of writers has recently argued that 'the major ground for disquiet about future employment prospects in Britain is what is loosely described as the 'outset of automation' —the very real employment problem—in the USA—might come to Britain in the—next few years'.[18] This report further argues that 'fears of redundancy . . . have been shown to be one of the major barriers to industrial change', so that surplus manpower is locked up unnecessarily by the absence of an adequate policy on redundancy and redeployment; and that there is now a powerful tendency towards raising the technical quality of employable labour, leading to the likelihood of a 'perpetual underclass' of the unemployable, as Gunnar Myrdal has labelled it.[19]

We can sum up this section in the words of S. Silver:

> Technology has brought us to the threshold of a new industrial revolution. It has enlarged the possible sphere of automation to encompass almost every industrial process . . . the awesome aspect is a society which will have attained the ultimate state of freedom from labour and have nothing to do.[20]

There need be nothing terrible about all this. Man needs more leisure. An essential precondition for his using it well, however, is to stop treating human beings as commodities and breeding or importing them, or both, to cram into the insatiable maw of an economic machine.

Potential sources of extra manpower

We could use our existing labour force very much more effectively, and one of the obvious ways of doing this would be to cut out some of the frills and concentrate more on essentials. In recent years, for instance, the average household has spent far more on clothing and footwear than on either fuel, light and power combined, or on durable household goods. In 1970 the figures were £2,634, £1,489, and £1,846 millions, respectively. Except among the very poor, it is almost unheard of in our society for a garment to be used until it is even moderately shabby, let alone worn-out; high powered manipulation of tastes through fashion is the chief factor determining behaviour in this field, and our expenditure could easily be cut by half or more with no real loss in our quality of life. Such a reduction would save approximately £1,300 millions, and release over a million workers for more essential activities. (Those directly released would number about 700,000 but the operation of the 'multiplier', approximately 1·5, would tend to raise this to 1,050,000.*

There are many other spheres in which manpower is used wastefully, but let us work on the conservative assumption that everything we now consume is essential and must be provided. If on this basis there is now or were in future to be a genuine shortage of manpower—though it is hard to see how this could ever come about if we organised ourselves sanely—sources already exist which are so far largely untapped.

(1) Womanpower

We ought to supplant the term 'manpower' by one which is sexually neutral, but meanwhile we should at least be aware of the fact that our womanpower is grossly underused as compared with the Soviet Union, say, and we should recognise how grotesque a distortion it is to talk of a labour shortage when women suffer from the range of economic and social discrimination found in our society. I believe there is now only one profession from which women are totally excluded, but the priesthood of most churches and all professions except two— teaching and social work—operate such powerful taboos that women are in a tiny minority. Banking and medicine have especially strong prejudices against women. Although in the Soviet Union women form 75 per cent of the medical profession, in Britain—during a shortage of doctors so great that we import them from countries which need them even more than we do—we restrict women's entry into the medical schools to 15 per cent of the total, and further restrictions ensure that only 5 per cent of practising doctors are women.

In 1969 only 35·7 per cent (just over 9 million) of our labour force was comprised of women—more than in the Netherlands,

---

* The 'multiplier', a term introduced by J. M. Keynes, refers to the ultimate increase in national income which results from a given investment. Thus, if an investment of £1,000 leads to an increase in national income of £2,000 the multiplier is two.

Norway, Spain, Italy, or France (all under 32 per cent), but a good deal less than in Finland (40 per cent), Poland (44·6 per cent), and the Soviet Union (at 51·9 per cent) the highest in the world—apart, possibly, from China). If we could raise our proportion, say, by 9 per cent to that of Poland, this would give us an extra 2·3 million workers, and we could improve upon this increment still further by getting rid of sexual prejudices and using existing womanpower more effectively.

(2) *Technological power*
Shortage of manpower stimulates technological innovation, as we have seen, and this in turn can go on to afford more leisure and/or liberate scarce manpower for other purposes. Much scientific and technological knowledge simply lies around because of what Fred Hoyle calls social 'fossilisation'. Sometimes—though it is difficult to get hard evidence on this—the reasons are sinister, inventions being bought up for the purpose of suppressing them. We have all heard of everlasting matches and electric light bulbs and a few years ago Professor Scott of Aston University reported numerous attempts to buy up (some, he suspected, to squash) his soon to be perfected photodegradable plastic containers.[21]

Automatic tube trains have been possible since 1927 because the GPO has been running them from that year in London—admittedly with freight only. The London Victoria Line has done the same with passengers since 1969, and the Northern and Bakerloo lines are due to change over soon. However, this leaves a lot of trains with a lot of drivers—not to mention a lot of firemen on locomotives without fires—and a railway system which would collapse without massive input of immigrant manpower and hard cash.

According to the Department of Trade and Industry we could save £500 millions a year by applying the lessons of the new discipline of tribology (the study of friction), £550 millions through terotechnology (plant design, installation, and maintenance), and another £300 millions from the application of existing knowledge about corrosion and its prevention. Gilbert Hunt, Chairman of the DTI Committee for Industrial Technologies, has calculated that potential savings to industry alone from the application of existing knowledge—much of it provided by research funded by the taxpayer—could be £1,500 million a year. Again there is the problem of translating this into manpower, but if it all can be taken to represent labour, and given a 'multiplier' of 1·5 it is equivalent to some 1¼ million average wage-earners saved for other purposes.

(3) Patriarchal power

The place of the elderly in the economic balance is discussed in the next chapter, but here we may question the arbitrariness of our present arrangements. These more or less compel women and men to retire at 60 and 65 years respectively, and penalise those who want to keep on working by cutting down their pensions. In 1970 there were 8·8 million men and women over the retirement age, and if only an extra 10 per cent wanted to keep on working, this would add another 880,000 to the nation's work-force. Surely we can think of a thousand ways of using their services on a full-time or part-time basis, preferably in their own neighbourhood so they are out and about meeting people who will miss them if they fall ill. How about inviting some of them to deliver the mail or the milk, and read the meters, for example, in a few nearby streets?

(4) Persuasion power

We expend a great deal of wealth every year on advertising, for the purposes of informing people what is available on the market, a necessary and laudable function, and of persuading people to buy things they would otherwise not buy, a highly questionable activity which should surely be particularly closely scrutinised when we are concerned about overpopulation, resource-depletion and pollution.

Manpower here is wasted in two ways. The advertising industry itself consumes substantial resources in both men and materials to create artificial demand, the satisfaction of which then requires still greater resources. In 1972, advertising cost in money terms £680 millions, and over 17,000 people were promoting it, making and transporting the materials, doing art work, printing, publishing, and so on, and many hundreds of thousands—possibly millions—more in supplying the extra

demand created by the advertisers. It is difficult to translate
all this into manpower figures, but if we allow that one-third
of the advertising effort goes into the useful 'informative'
function and two-thirds into the useless 'badgering' function,
then about £450 millions a year was then wasted in this way
and at least as much again in the economic activity thereby
stimulated: £900 millions all told. With a multiplier of 1·5 at
the then current average wage it represented around three-
quarters of a million workers, and at 3 per cent of the work
force this sounds a conservative estimate.

(5) *Pupil power*
Children contribute a good deal to the economy of some
societies, minding animals, gathering food and fuel, helping
with simple manufacturing processes, and of course they
contribute something to our own. In bygone days children
played a very important part in our economy, working twelve
hours a day or more from the age of six or seven and although
gross exploitation of this kind is a thing of the past, children
still perform many economic functions, doing errands and
odd jobs, attending pumps at petrol filling stations and dis-
charging a wide range of other tasks. (The Newsom Report
showed in 1963 that 42 per cent of the boys over fourteen had
paid employment.)

In higher education, vacation jobs are much like those of
full-time workers and students make a sizeable contribution to
the economy *outside their educational activities*. However, inside
centres of learning, educational tasks are usually so defined as
to exclude anything of direct and immediate benefit to the
economy. The one exception is to be found in the sandwich
courses put on by some colleges and universities. Why is it that
'education' in general may not be contaminated by usefulness
or direct value to the community?

In 1970 8·6 million children aged from five to fourteen were
at school, plus another million or so aged fifteen and over, and
another half a million in full time higher education—say
10 million in round figures. If 10 per cent of their effort went
into useful work (leaving 90 per cent of the curriculum for
education as pure and traditional as you like) and this was half

as effective as adult labour, then another 500,000, effectively, would have been added to the work force.

(6) *Fossil power*

This doesn't relate to the fossil fuels but to the manpower locked up in an outdated and inefficient—i.e. fossilized, division of labour leading to 'restrictive practices'. This has been especially bad in some of the traditional craft industries, like shipbuilding, where 'rivetters' and 'boilermakers' have to be found work on welded ships propelled by diesels, but it goes right across the board, and some of the older professions—such as law—are notoriously restrictive and protectionist. Economic efficiency and the public interest figure nowhere in these role definitions and everyday we see people idling their time away when there is work to be done: the lorry driver who stands and watches all day while the tools and materials he brought are used by his mates, the Post Office clerk twiddling his thumbs on 'pensions' while his neighbour is run off his feet on 'stamps', and so on, all the way up the hierarchy—there was even a case recently in which a fire was allowed to burn for nearly two months in a corporation building yard because it was nobody's job to report fires.

How much this adds up to in manpower equivalent is anybody's guess—at least a million, surely—but I propose to allow only 470,000 to make the total a nice round figure.

(8) *Unemployed manpower*

During the whole period of hue and cry about the shortage of manpower there has been a substantial reserve army of registered unemployed, a number of divisions of unregistered unemployed, and a further phalanx of underemployed (not to mention a good few battalions of leisured folk, mentioned again later, who live by the sweat of other people's brows). The number of registered unemployed has fluctuated between 300,000 and 500,000 for most of the period since the Second World War. The lowest point was reached in 1951 at about 220,000, and there was a marked rise from 1967 up to a peak of around 900,000 in 1972. All of these figures need to be reduced by the number of unfilled vacancies e.g., on February

173

11th 1974, the registered unemployed totalled 600,000 in round figures and the unfilled adult vacancies 352,000. See Department of Employment Gazette. It seems reasonable to argue that, given job mobility and industrial change, a small amount of unemployment is inevitable, but surely the reserve does not need to be so high. Greater forethought should have kept jobs and workers more in balance and obviated the need for massive recruitment overseas. With a saner manpower policy and better organisation, it might be reasonable to assume that, on the average, another 250,000 persons could be helped to join the active labour force from the ranks of the unemployed.

(8) *Military manpower*
All modern states have substantial numbers of men and women tied up in their armed forces whose contribution to the economy is virtually zero; they exist mainly as an insurance policy for the preservation of the integrity of the state. Although the armed forces are only rarely called on to discharge their military function, and we all hope that they will never be called upon again, we define and control military training and duties as we do education, to exclude as thoroughly as possible anything of possible use to the community. General Eisenhower said 'war is synonymous with waste', and we can extend this truism: peace is synonymous with waste, too, so far as the armed forces are concerned.

The armed forces and their huge and expensive back-up force in the armaments industry are by and large a total drain on the economy. Although the regulars may be called in to do civilian work in national emergencies, such as general strikes and flood disasters, we do not even make them clear away their own military litter—old pill boxes, barbed wire entanglements, rifle ranges, and the often lethal detritus of explosives scattered around the countryside. Surely every unit should have a conservation function in peacetime and at least clear up its own mess as it goes.

The Chinese have a different view of the role of the military. They call theirs a 'people's' army—something which could never be said about ours—whose function is to 'serve the people'. They interpret this to mean service in war *and in peace*, soldiers salute civilians instead of each other, and as far as possible the units are self-sufficient. John Gittings recently described[22] a visit to the 196th Division of the People's Liberation Army, which spends 50 per cent of its time on military affairs, 30 per cent on political, and 20 per cent on agricultural work. It runs a pig farm, a vegetable patch for each company, a small factory producing bean curd, soya paste and other items, and another—run by the officer's wives—turning out medical supplies. They had just finished making their own firing range and had so designed the earthworks that a swimming pool could be thrown in as a bonus. The 196th division was claimed to be completely self-sufficient in vegetables and meat, and only 20 per cent short on rice. It is interesting to compare this with the peacetime activities of the British Army (counting periods of service in Northern Ireland as wartime), which appear to include substantial stints on blancoing, boot and button polishing, and living it up in the Naafi. Apart from the obvious economic advantages, which of these alternative peacetime strategies is the best for morale, the more democratic, dignified and humane?

Our own armed forces in 1970 contained 372,000 (only 14,000 of them women), and if we allowed them a 50/50 military/economic allocation of man-hours we would effectively add another 176,000 to the workforce, in this case nearly all men in their prime who should be above the average in productivity.

(9) *Manpower lost through industrial accidents*
Lord Robens's committee on industrial accidents reported that every year about 1,000 people are killed at work, half a million injured, and about 23 million work-days are lost.[23] The economic cost—quite apart from the enormous amount of suffering involved—may be as much as £900 million a year. A 10 per cent reduction of casualties on the industrial battlefield would liberate 92,000 workers from the bondage of injury, suffering, and deprivation, and enrich the economy in that proportion. There would need to be added the further 75,000 or so liberated by the £90 million reduction in the economic costs of industrial accidents, making a round total of 170,000.

(10) *Invalid power*

There are over 3 million and possibly as many as 4 million adult 'impaired persons', defined as those 'lacking part or all of a limb, or having a defective limb, organ, or mechanism of the body', and although some of these will never be able to contribute to the productive process, and many others contribute a good deal already, could we not train, encourage, and equip the rest to be more active members of our economic system and of the wider society? Even as low a proportion as 5 per cent of 3 million could give the equivalent of 150,000 more workers.

(11) *Patient power*

In 1970 there were on average nearly half a million people in hospital. Many of these were very sick, many both sick and very old or very young, but equally, a sizeable minority in the normally healthy working age-group must have been there because of faulty preventive medicine—an area in which we invest very few resources. Could we not keep people healthier and therefore more productive, and use in-patients with spare capacity to help each other and the professional staffs to run the hospitals on a more economical as well as a more neighbourly basis, thereby liberating some of the nearly three quarters of a million workers who look after them? If 10 per cent fewer persons were allowed to fall ill that would give 40,000 extra workers; and if 10 per cent of the staff could be liberated by the cooperation of the patients, that would add another 70,000. This leaves out of account the further possibilities of reducing the number of out-patient attendances (58 million) or the huge number of man-years lost by sickness not leading to hospital treatment.

(12) *Drop-out manpower*

This is perhaps the most difficult category of all to quantify without a good deal of research, some of it of the face-to-face kind. No one drops out of the economic process in his role as consumer, but a substantial number abdicate from that of producer. The first category is that of those who are genuinely 'drop-outs', as the term is normally understood, who would probably be counted in the statistics of the unemployed. The second category is that of the full-time criminal, some of whom again may show up in unemployment statistics. The third is that of the idle rich, a group not normally thought of as drop-outs although they obviously are in the sense defined above.

It is clear that not all the rich are idle. A number of the noble, rich, and merely comfortably off—both inherited and nouveaux—work very hard, either in the economic field (making their own pile even bigger or doing more or less routine professional jobs for society), or in the social field (doing voluntary work to plug some of the gaps left by the State, local government, and private enterprise), or both. It is equally clear, however, that there are a number who are plain parasites on the body economic, taking a lot out and putting nothing back. What they add up to in manpower is hard to measure— I asked the Communist Party for their estimate but they haven't done their homework, either, so it is anybody's guess. My own would be at least a quarter of a million, but that is intuitive and so chancy that I will leave it as a possible bonus, together with the other two categories of dropouts, and refrain from adding it to the total.

The manpower reckoning

The possible savings suggested can now be totted up to see how much of our presently under-used manpower we might harness to the economy. Table 11/1 shows the result, about 7 million more workers—something over a quarter of the existing labour force—simply by quite marginal adjustments to our existing social and economic policies and the use of a modest part of the existing knowledge at present being allowed to lie fallow.

This pool of reserve labour is four times as large as the total immigrant labour force in 1966, and over seventeen times as great as the alleged manpower gap forecast by the National Plan.

World manpower

Far from there being a shortage of manpower in the world as a whole, there is a problem of unemployment which is already so huge as to defy the imagination and is rapidly getting worse.

177

Table 11/1

Summary of potential extra manpower

Potential workforce	Manpower equivalent (thousands)
i. Womanpower	2,300
ii. Technological power	1,250
iii. Patriarchal power	880
iv. Persuasion power	750
v. Pupil power	500
vi. Fossil power	470
vii. Unemployed manpower	250
viii. Military manpower	170
ix. Industrial victims	170
x. Invalid power	150
xi. Patient power	110
xii. Drop-out manpower	?
Total manpower reserve	7,000

As overpopulation and rising aspirations drive people away from traditional pursuits and off the land into towns, already grossly oversaturated in many regions, so modern technology tends to bring about a relative reduction in new job opportunities. 'Relative' is used here in the sense that though a new steel works in India, say, will make some new jobs, the higher the technology involved, the greater the cost per job and the smaller the number that will be created.

An international conference on overseas development at Cambridge in 1968 concluded: 'No rate of industrial expansion ever achieved can conceivably absorb the expected increase in the labour force. . . . The spectre of the 1970s will be . . . large scale unemployment and attendant threats to the political order'.[24]

Conclusion

If we continue the present free-for-all it is difficult to the point of impossibility to assess the manpower needs of the future and the National Plan was a fiasco in this respect. The only footnote required to George Polanyi's calm exposition of the drolleries of the government's manpower forecasting is to mention that no immigration was required—nor any extra effort on the part of parents—to fill the manpower 'gap'.

We saw from historical examples that there can be a true manpower gap when a previously existing population is removed by some means or another. But in the absence of drastic events like the Black Death, we must ask when there is alleged to be a shortage of labour: is the existing work force optimally deployed, is an industry overdeveloped, and why was allegedly scarce labour wasted in building a factory which cannot be manned? We must also ask if it is reasonable to worry about temporary labour shortages when the main problem of the future is likely to be technological unemployment on a massive scale?

I would like to see all the proposed measures in this chapter tried out: more of our people brough more·effectively into the process of producing the wealth we consume, with staggering of working hours and weeks to ease congestion, improved use of our existing capital, especially knowledge and skills, all coupled with a general increase of leisure for those doing most of the donkey work now. Work and the things work produces are not the be-all and end-all of human existence but the work which *does* have to be carried out should be honourable, done well, and equitably shared and rewarded.

CHAPTER 12

The burden of dependency argument: the fallacy of the ageing population

'If we do not have at least one young worker to replace every one that retires, the old become an impossible burden on the community.' D. E. C. Eversley.[1]

'A reduction in the number of children . . . would mean that by the year 2001 we would have an aged dependant population of . . . over 7 million that we are unable to support.' Dr P. H. Millard.[2]

'If the population stabilised . . . we would find ourselves with a rising proportion of elderly people supported by a work force of stable size.' Frances Cairncross.[3]

'We have what is quite likely the heaviest burden of old-age dependency in the world. If we are to carry it without imposing an impossible task on those who do the work we shall need all the children parents are prepared to have.' Sir John Walley.[4]

Population, manpower and dependency
The most basic economic division of society is perhaps that between producers and consumers, or, rather—since all producers also consume—between producer-consumers and consumers only. The demographer, Cox, talks of 'producer-units' and 'consumer-units'.[5] Clearly consumers-only depend on the producer-consumers and for this reason they are often called 'dependants', from which follows the rather gloomy technical expression, the 'burden of dependency', used by the Royal Commission among other authorities, to describe the fact that most societies discharge the twin tasks of rearing their young until they can start producing, and maintaining their old after their long productive period is over. The Annual Abstract of Statistics talks of the 'economically active' and 'inactive'—a queer definition implying that consumption is not an economic process—and L. H. Jones argues[6] that none of us are consumers, we are, because of the laws of conservation, simply *users* of matter and energy.

Figure 12/1 shows the producing-dependence structure of a population in terms of four basic categories: the *working force*, those actually employed in some economic producing activity; the *labour force*, the workers plus the unemployed, those who want work and can't get it; the *manpower force*, the first two plus those who are able to work but are neither working nor seeking to; and the *dependants*, the young and the old, who are not expected to seek work. Of course this tidy little scheme is inadequate to represent reality, though it is a reasonable

Figure 12/1. Population, producers and consumers

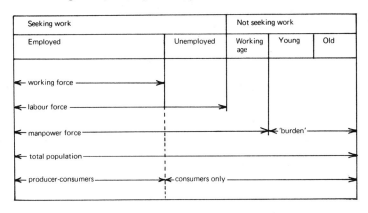

approximation. Housewives and daughters housekeeping for elderly parents wouldn't normally be counted as part of the labour force, however long and hard they labour, and many children and old people contribute to our economy although they are officially dependents. By the same token some of those nominally in the labour force take such good care not to work themselves out of a job that one might be forgiven for considering their reclassification, and some of those just outside it are not striving too bumptiously to get in.

The 'burden of dependency' is obviously a variable quantity which needs to be measured. This is done very simply by working out *dependency ratios*, as follows:

$$\text{Youth dependency ratio} = \frac{\text{population under working age}}{\text{population of working age}} \times 100\% = `x'\%$$

$$\text{Aged dependency ratio} = \frac{\text{population over working age}}{\text{population of working age}} \times 100\% = `y'\%$$

$$\text{Combined or total dependency ratio} = \frac{\text{young + old}}{\text{workers}} \times 100\%$$
$$= `x' + `y'\%$$

It might be better to use the still simpler formula:

$$\text{Combined DR} = \frac{\text{non-workers}}{\text{workers}} \times 100\% = ?\%$$

This would, however, present difficult problems of definition and data-gathering and the 'official' formula is at least as simple to apply.

Structure of the argument

The quotations at the head of the chapter show that a lot of people—including many in influential positions who really ought to know better—believe in this hoary fallacy, which can again be expressed in logical form:

First premise: An increase in the number of aged dependants can be met only by an increase in the number of workers.

Second premise: The number of workers can be increased only through an increase in births.

Third premise: The number of aged dependants is increasing.

Conclusion: The number of births must increase.

Another formulation would state that births must remain above the replacement level. Whatever the form of expression, however, and regardless of the fact that the argument is logically valid, the conclusion is false because the first two premises are completely false and even the third is shaky.

Factual refutation

First premise. It is not true that an increase in aged dependants can be maintained only by an increase in the number of workers. If there were to be an extra burden it could be met by having the fit members of the old carry on working, by having the workers work harder or longer, or both, by increasing productivity through investment and/or research and development. In fact it is the Government's aim to increase productivity by 5 per cent a year, with only a modest increase in the labour force, which means that wealth doubles every fourteen years—roughly twice per generation or five times per lifespan. If no old people ever died again, the burden of the aged would increase at a maximum figure of only 5 per cent in the first year, the increment gradually declining as the population of the old increased. From this we see that the increase in productivity is many times greater than any possible increase in the 'burden' of the old.

Second premise. Most of the last chapter was spent on a demonstration of the manifold ways in which the working force can be increased without an increase in population.

Third premise. This, though not false, is shaky, because what is really happening is that the number of the aged, expressed proportionately and taking the long view, is fluctuating. It is increasing at the moment it is true, but not by much and not for long, and here we need some figures to show the pattern.

Historical changes in the dependency-ratio

Table 12/1 shows the manpower force and differing burdens of dependency, both separately and combined, from 1821 to 2011. Let us look at past changes first:

(1) *Manpower.* The manpower force has fluctuated between 56·2 per cent in 1821 and 70·3 per cent in 1931, in later decades hovering just below the two-thirds mark.

(2) *Aged burden.* Between 1821 and 1921 the aged burden of dependency increased steadily and then more sharply from 1921 to 1971. Over the whole period the aged burden increased more than four-fold, from 3·0 per cent to 13·1 per cent.

(3) *Youth burden.* Although the youth burden declined by more than a half between 1821 and 1941, (41·2 per cent down to 20·5 per cent) rising slightly by 1971, the peak year in this century, it is at all times much greater than the aged burden. In 1821 it was nearly fourteen times as great, in 1901 six and a half times, in 1931 three times, and from 1941 to 1971 around twice as great.

(4) *Combined burden.* Despite the great increase in the proportion of the old the combined burden fell dramatically between 1821 and 1931, from which year it has started on a steady rise which will continue until the peak in 1981. *Over the whole period* the combined burden fell by more than one-eighth (from 44·2 per cent to 38·4 per cent).

Table 12/1

Approximate burdens of dependency. England and Wales 1821–2011.

Year	Pop. millions	Burden of dependency Young	Old	Combined	Manpower force	Dependency ratio	Productivity index
1821[a]	10·0	41·2%	3·0%	44·2%	56·2%	0·787	100
1861[b]	20·1	35·7%	4·6%	40·3%	59·7%	0·675	159
1901[c]	32·5	30·4%	4·7%	35·1%	64·9%	0·541	339
1911	36·1	28·7%	5·2%	33·9%	66·1%	0·513	355
21	37·9	25·8%	6·0%	31·8%	68·2%	0·466	316
31	40·0	22·3%	7·4%	29·7%	70·3%	0·423	351
41[d]	37·9	20·5%	10·0%	30·5%	69·5%	0·439	479
51	40·0	20·9%	11·0%	31·9%	68·1%	0·468	451
61	46·1	22·9%	11·7%	34·6%	65·4%	0·529	640
71[e]	48·9	25·3%	13·1%	38·4%	61·6%	0·623	1077
81	50·1	24·5%	14·3%	38·8%	61·2%	0·634	1190?[f]
91	53·0	24·6%	14·1%	38·7%	61·3%	0·631	1314?
2001	55·5	24·7%	12·9%	37·6%	62·4%	0·603	1451?
2011	58·3	24·0%	12·6%	36·6%	63·4%	0·571	1603?

NB (1) These figures are not strictly comparable, partly because of the vagaries of earlier statistics, and partly because I have taken the same retiring age for men and women. But the discrepancies are small.

NB (2) Productivity index based on data from Deane and Cole (1964) *British Economic Growth, 1688–1959.*

[a] Age groups 0–14; 15–60, and 60+
[b] Age groups 0–14; 15–64, and 65+
[c] Age groups 0–13; 14–64, and 65+
[d] The 1941 figures exclude the armed forces.
[e] Age groups 0–15; 16–64, and 65+
[f] From 1971 onwards increase in productivity per head is reckoned at the fairly conservative figure of 1 per cent per year.

(5) *Increase in wealth.* During the period 1821 to 1971 there has been a very large rise in per-capita wealth which should have enabled us to bear these 'burdens' with ever-greater ease.

Future changes in the dependency ratio

(1) *Manpower.* Between 1971 and 2011 the manpower force will increase from 61·6 per cent to 63·4 per cent.

(2) *Aged burden*. This will continue rising gently to its peak in 1981, and then—in the absence of a medical breakthrough in the 'cure' of aging—decline moderately for the rest of the period, being lower in 2001 then in 1971 and lower still in 2011.

(3) *Youth burden*. The youth burden will decline steadily (making the doubtful assumption that there will be no more baby booms) from 1971 to the end of the period, apart from a barely perceptible upturn in 2001.

(4) *Combined burden*. This is the important variable and it will increase marginally to its peak in 1981, remain almost constant for a decade, and then decline fairly substantially throughout the rest of the period. reaching the 1966 level again by 2011, a level which was first passed (also on the way down) some time late in the Victorian era, and again in the 1960s (on the way up, this time). The final figure is about 5 per cent less than that for 1971.

(5) *Wealth*. This is very problematical for the future, but the uncertainty need not trouble us unduly for reasons dealt with in the next passage.

Outcome of the comparison
Figure 12/2 shows the various figures graphically, making the changes immediately apparent. Even on the assumption that there will be no economic growth or even moderate negative growth for some time into the future, because of the crisis of resources—particularly energy—there should still be no burden of dependency problem. The combined burden was nearly 8 per cent lower in 1971 then it had been about a century before, in 1861. The worst figure in modern times, expected in 1981, will still be 6 per cent lower than the 1861 figure and no less than 20 per cent lower than in 1821, the first year for which we have detailed figures.

Burden of dependency with zero population growth from 1971
Table 12/2 compares the burdens associated with a growing population, as projected, and with one which is stationary from 1971 to 2011. The numbers of old people will be the same in both populations over a period as short as this, but of course their percentages get larger for a time on the stationary one.

Figure 12/2. Burden of dependency, England and Wales 1821–2011

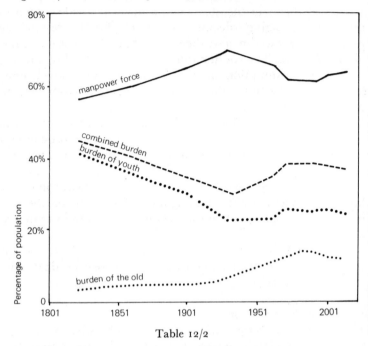

Table 12/2

Reduction in burden of dependency with stationary population.
England and Wales, 1971–2011.

Year	Population As projected	If stationary	Dependency As projected	ratios with stationary population	Improvement (reduction) in dependency ratio
1971	48·8	48·9	0·623	0·623	
1981	50·1	48·9	0·634	0·527	10%
1991	53·0	48·9	0·632	0·507	20%
2001	55·5	48·9	0·602	0·144	31%
2011	58·3	48·9	0·578	0·325	44%
Steady state		48·9		0·608	

Births are reduced to compensate exactly for deaths and the youth burden is smaller by the same number so that their proportion of the total population goes down with a bump. The

186

table shows that the combined burden is 10 per cent less by 1981, when the aged burden reaches its peak, 20 per cent less in 1991 when the aged burden starts to decline rapidly, and down by getting on for a half a generation later.

Burden of dependency in a steady state
The burden of dependency is not the same in the long term steady state as in the short-term ZPG situation. The reason is that zero population growth can be obtained at the present moment only by depressing birth-rates to an 'artificially' low level to match the temporarily reduced crude death-rate. In the future steady state—given life-expectancies comparable to those of the present day—the figures would be as shown at the foot of Table 12/3. Manpower is just under two-thirds, the combined burden just over one-third, and the youth 'burden' is one-third greater than that of the old.

Table 12/3

Dependency ratios based on the three Ross Paul population projections. UK AD 2051*

Population projection	Burden of dependency			Man-power force	Depend-ency ratio	Producti-vity index[a] 1967 = 100
	Young	Old	Com-bined			
'Low'	22·8%	16·5%	39·3%	60·7%	0·647	7,000[c] say
'Medium'	26·3%	13·5%	39·8%	60·2%	0·661	6,400
'High'	30·9%	10·5%	41·4%	58·6%	0·705	5,800[c] say
Eventual steady state[b]	21·8%	16·0%	37·8%	62·2%	0·608	?

*Adapted from: HMSO (1973) Report of the Population Panel (p. 96).
[a] Productivity increasing at the Government's 1973 target figure of 5% a year.
[b] Figures for this kindly supplied by the OPCS by private communication.
[c] Given a weighting of + and − 10%, respectively, to allow for the change in the demographic investment.

Dependency ratios in 2051

Table 12/3, based on the speculations of the Ross Committee, shows what the dependency ratios will be in the middle of the twenty-first century on three separate population projections, 'low', 'medium', and 'high'. These show that the 'high' projection compared with the 'low' gives a 'burden of the young' greater by 8·1 per cent (30·9–22·8 per cent) and a 'burden of the old' lower by 6·0 per cent (16·5–10·5 per cent), the overall burden increasing with fertility and population all the way.

When we settle down to the inevitable steady state the overall dependency-ratio will have fallen appreciably from the lowest of these figures down to the level of the late 1880s and 1960s and the early 2000s. The right-hand column shows by how much productivity would have increased over the eighty-four years between 1967 and 2051 at the Government's target figure of 5 per cent growth each year. At this rate productivity doubles every fourteen years, in round figures, so that in eighty-four years—one long lifespan—it would have doubled six times and be sixty-four times greater. Of course there is in fact no chance of this growth rate being realised.

World dependency-ratios

In general the poor countries have dependency-ratios very similar to those in Britain in the 1820s. South-East Asia in 1960 had 41 per cent under fifteen and 3 per cent over sixty-five. By 1980 their over sixty-fives will have increased to 4 per cent, while their under fifteens will still be at 41 per cent, giving a slight increase in the total dependency-ratio. In 1960 the Middle East, Africa, and Latin America had 43 per cent in the youth category—more than we ever had (as far as the figures go)—with the same percentage of old people as our 1820s figure.

By 1980 the poorer countries will average 39 per cent in the under fifteen group and only 4 per cent over sixty-five, so clearly their main economic burden is going to be coping with excessive fertility rather than with the old age. In fact the number of births will seriously hinder their capacity for giving the old a square deal.

Our own aged DR is higher throughout the period, though

more and more marginally towards the end—Europe as a whole will be 13 per cent by 1980 (against our peak of 14·3 per cent)—and Japan and the Soviet Union will be climbing rapidly as ours starts to fall.

A logical analysis of the 'remedy' for the increased burden of the old
We have seen that Eversley and many others are worried about the fact that we are going to have a few more old people to support for a decade or two and that their remedy is to increase the number of children to counterbalance the extra load. We can demonstrate and analyse this argument by means of the simple equation put forward earlier.

Stage 1: 'Normal' population.

$$\text{Aged burden} = \frac{\text{old}}{\text{workers}} \times 100\% = \text{`x'}\%$$

Stage 2: Increase in old people.

$$\text{New aged burden} = \frac{\text{Old} + \text{extra old}}{\text{workers}} \times 100\% = (x + ?)\%$$

Stage 3: To compensate for extra old people, add extra children:

$$\text{New youth burden} = \frac{\text{children} + \text{extra children}}{\text{workers}} \times 100\% = (y + ?)\%$$

Stage 4: To work out new combined burden, combine stages 2 and 3:

New combined burden =

$$\frac{(\text{old} + \text{extra old}) + (\text{children} + \text{extra children})}{\text{workers}} \times 100\%$$

or:

$$\text{New combined burden} = \frac{(x + ?) + (y + ?)}{\text{workers}} \times 100\%$$

The combined dependency ratio after the recommended prophylactic measures have been taken is obviously greater by both the extra old people and the extra children. The object of the exercise was to make the 'burden' as bearable—i.e. small —as possible, but it has produced the opposite result.

The logic sounds less hare-brained if the case is argued that the aged DR is going to increase some years in the future and the children should be born *now* to grow up and join the manpower force. Even this is unrealistic, however, for it takes no account of the 'opportunity-cost' of a greater than replacement birth-rate and the raised demographic investment over the intervening years which could have gone into higher productivity and therefore coped with the extra old people without a delayed increase in the work-force.

In any case, it is a bit late in Britain now as our school-leaving age—the time at which a part of youth joins the manpower force—is sixteen, whereas the peak of the aged DR is in 1981, only five years away. The bulge in manpower would miss the bulge in old age by eight years, only to become an old age bulge itself forty-nine years later.

A potential reinforcing argument stems from the fact that the case has been argued as though consumption by both young and old were the same. In fact the old probably consume less per head than the young (apart from very small children), and if this is true then the burden-of-dependency argument is further weakened.

Conclusion

The 'burden of dependency' argument is even more nonsensical than most. The 'burden' is made up of the old plus the young, so that if the number of the old increases the last thing we want to do is to increase the burden of youthful dependence as well. This would compound the disaster, if disaster it were, but of course it is no such thing.

It is true that the proportion of the old has increased, but over the same period the burden of the young has gone down, compensating for the extra old people nearly twice over, while productivity and income per head have increased by an enormous factor. The aged dependency ratio will increase a little further in the future, but the youthful ratio is still going down, and will go down still further if we manage to attain a replace-

THE BURDEN OF DEPENDENCY ARGUMENT

ment birth rate, so that in future the total dependency ratio is never going to increase above the figure for 1890 or so. Throughout the twentieth century, the combined burden has been appreciably lower than in the first half of the nineteenth century, which will continue unless there is an extraordinary rise in fertility, or a 'cure' for aging. Shall we be less able to support our proportionately smaller number of dependants after the industrial revolution than we were before it?

However, once again the fundamental refutation rests on an exposure of the parochialism underlying the argument. Even if it were true that the aged dependency ratio were going to continue increasing from now until the crack of doom and that a higher birth rate would help to support it, there would come a time when we would simply have to put up with it because there was no room in our country (or on the earth) for more people.

CHAPTER 13

The economies of scale argument: the fallacy of ever-increasing efficiency

'It is an obvious conclusion that there are many cases in which production is made much more effective by being conducted on a larger scale.' John Stuart Mill.[1]

'It seems very probable that considerable economies of scale . . . would be realised if our population were to increase to 100 millions.' *The Economist.*[2]

'A large and growing population will facilitate the establishment of large scale production industries.' Open University textbook.[3]

'When I am able to make more, it will cost less, and I am—er— hoping that in time I may be able to make so much that it will cost nothing. After that, of course, the more I can make the more—ah —profitable it will be.' Professor Branestawm.[4]

Historical antecedents

Compared with some economic theory, this belief is a newcomer and I have not been able to trace any references to it before Adam Smith published *The Wealth of Nations* in 1776. Engels was well aware of the positive scale effect (there is a negative, too, as we shall see), so was Marx in *Capital*, and John Stuart Mill said it was 'obvious', as we saw in the quotation at the head of the chapter.

The pioneers in the field ignored all of the problems and concentrated on the benefits of production on a large scale, leading to the formulation by Marshall of the 'Law of Increasing Returns' as a counterweight to the 'Law of Diminishing Returns' which had caused so much gloom from Malthus's day onwards. This seems to have been what economists were looking for and the philosophy of increasing returns seems to have provided the psychological underpinning for most economic thought since.

Structure of the argument

This is one of those population fallacies with a good grounding in fact. The only trouble is that, in the first place, people don't get it quite right, and, in the second place, they then work it to death.

Once again we can state it in logical form, as follows:

First premise: Unit production costs must always be reduced where possible.

Second premise: The larger the scale of production the less is the cost of each unit produced.

Third premise: The larger the market the larger the scale of production.

Fourth premise: The larger the population the larger the market.

Conclusion: Population must be increased where possible.

Meaning of the term 'economies of scale'

There is a concept in economics called 'returns to scale', and this has been defined as follows:

> Returns to Scale (Increasing and Decreasing), an economic law used to describe the relationship . . . in the long run . . .

between the scale of input of all the factors of production, used in unchanged proportions . . . and the output of commodities . . . at small scales of production . . ., efficiency . . . can often be increased by increasing size.[5]

Three essential points must be noticed here: it is stressed that its primary relevance is 'at small scales of production' not at *all* scales of production; this 'law' is *conditional*, saying that efficiency can 'often' be increased by increasing size, not 'always'; it cuts both ways, since returns to scale can be both positive or negative, 'increasing' or 'decreasing', and there is an optimum point beyond which increases in scale may *decrease* productive efficiency. All of these qualifications are ignored by the growthmen.

The Law of Diminishing Returns—a possible source of confusion
The 'returns to scale' concept, positive and negative, applies when *all* the factors of production are changed together and in the same proportion (and the results assessed in the long run) so that decreasing returns to scale are eventually produced when a whole enterprise gets too big—too much land, capital, labour, raw materials and the rest.

The Law of Diminishing Returns, on the other hand, describes the effect on output in the *short* run when the proportion of one factor is increased relative to the other factors. It states: 'As equal increases of a variable factor are added to a constant quantity of other . . . factors, the successive increases in output will after a point decrease.[6] This is sometimes called the 'Law of Variable Proportions', clearly distinguishing it from decreasing returns to scale which, in a sense, is a law of *constant* proportions of all the factors of production. The first relates to the optimum input of a single factor and the second to the optimum size of the system.

A further point worth making is that in the 'Diminishing Returns' argument the factors which remain constant often are not changed because they cannot be: they are 'fixed'. The classic example of this is land. We can allocate it in different ways and apply more and more fertilisers, labour, irrigation, and other inputs, but eventually, if we go too far, not only shall we stop getting more and more out of it, we shall progressively destroy its productive capacity.

Truth in the scale argument

The economies of scale argument is at least logical—the conclusion follows from the premises; but what about the truth of the premises? Here commonsense reinforces what *Everyman's Dictionary of Economics* sets out academically: 'Increased efficiency, measured as increasing returns, may follow increases in scale because of the wider scope for specialisation of labour and equipment.'

At the commonsense level in everyday experience, this generalisation is obviously valid. If we want a bag of 1-inch oval nails we go to the ironmonger, who in 1975 will sell us a pound for 15p or so, and not to the blacksmith who—if he could be found and prevailed upon to make them—probably couldn't do it for less than £5, even though his nails wouldn't be as good as the mass-produced variety. The reason why the ironmonger can supply us so much more cheaply, despite transport and storage costs and three profit margins—his, the wholesaler's, and the manufacturer's—is that somewhere there is a firm manufacturing nails on a large scale, whereas the blacksmith would have to use his forge, hammer and chisel, anvil, vice and grinding wheel to make and sharpen each nail separately.

Reasons for positive returns to scale

There are many reasons why, up to a point, economies of scale occur, and among these are the facts that more capital can be invested in equipment and that both equipment and skills can be increasingly specialised.

Dividing up work so that people can specialise and become experts is a very old idea. There may have been a time when everybody did everything, but from very early times—long before the Industrial Revolution—there was specialisation within the family, especially between the sexes, which developed into the definitions of crafts, trades and professions. Plato talks of job specialisation and according to Gordon Childe there was a shield factory employing 120 artisans in ancient Greece.[7] Cicero also commentated on this arrangement in *De*

194

Offiiciis, as did David Hume much later, so there was a solid historical foundation for Adam Smith's classic analysis of the division of labour in pin making. For this he detailed no fewer than eighteen operations, and went on to argue that further divisions were limited only by 'the extent of the market'.[8]

A modern industrial state has many thousands of job roles, and a single large enterprise may embrace several hundreds of them. The British Army has sixty classifications for junior trainees, another 220 for adult 'other ranks', and the full range of professions, with many sub-divisions, among the officers. It is easy to see that, as skills become more and more minutely specialised, the problems of understanding and integrating them into a coherent pattern increase rapidly.

Indivisibles

Major items of capital equipment have been recognised as important for a long time. They are now called 'indivisibilities' or 'indivisibles', which have been defined as follows:

> The technical or physical characteristics of a factor of production . . . which prevent its being used except in minimum quantities. Most machinery and capital equipment must be used in 'lumps'. . . . A workman is also an 'indivisible' unit in this respect; the hands used for an assembly line cannot be separated for the legs that could be simultaneously used for messenger work.[9]

Any tool is an indivisible, however small; you can not get half a hammer. Where the investment is small it doesn't matter too much if an indivisible is acquired for only occasional use; but in the case of large and expensive indivisibles, such as combine harvesters, to be used only one week out of the fifty-two, individual purchase is an expensive and wasteful business. Three farmers sharing the combine, and using it one after the other, have unit costs reduced by two-thirds. The special nail making machines referred to earlier can only be supplied and used effectively by an economy large enough to provide the demand to keep them going. Really massive indivisibles such as canals, docks, and railways require very substantial utilisation to make them feasible. But we must on the other hand not allow ourselves to become too impressed by the difficulties: Iceland with less than a quarter of a million people has most of the amenities of civilised life, Luxembourg with less than half a million has more, and Eire and New Zealand with less than three millions each have them all.

What bearing do these elementary truths have on the scale of manufacture in large complex societies? Would we expect, because one manufacturer mass producing nails can do it better than 10,000 blacksmiths in their own forges, that a factory making 50 million cars a year would do it better and cheaper than one making only 1 million? Unlikely though this extrapolation is, many otherwise intelligent and informed people seem to make it, linking it with the population question. Because of fairly obvious barriers to international trade (tariffs and quotas, distance, poor communications, and political tensions), the assumption is normally made that increasing production to take advantage of 'economies of scale' means increasing the population of a particular nation, or producing/consuming unit. This is supposed to increase the size of the market and thereby permit the output of larger productive units to be absorbed economically.

Example of public transport
It is obvious that a very small society will not be able to afford much in the way of public transport, and that an increase in population would be an advantage from this point of view. It could also be true that after the population has become large enough to build and sustain a public transport system, still further increases would enable it to be utilised more efficiently, so reducing costs per passenger mile. Equally clearly, however, if the population goes on increasing there must come a time when the system is saturated and a bigger and better one is required.

It would obviously be short-sighted to rebuild or extend transport capacity only to the point at which it can cope with the existing overload—or even the load forecast for five or ten years ahead. The only sensible thing would be to design a system with the capacity to deal with the load as far into the future as can be reasonably foreseen, and that might well be half a lifespan. Of course, in some cases, it needn't all be *built* immediately, but a certain amount of spare capacity would have to be incorporated in the immediate programme in addition to the provision for still further expansion later on (for example, building railway tunnels to take two tracks even if only one is strictly necessary at the moment). This inevitably means higher capital costs for the community, and consequently larger payments per head in one form or another.

Region in which indivisibilities argument is valid
The only region in which the 'indivisibles' argument is valid— other things being equal—is between a population size too small and one just right for the economic use of a particular indivisible. Beyond this point the indivisibles argument goes into reverse and should be used—on precisely the same grounds —*against* further population increase, unless the increments of population can be sufficiently large and rapid to make full use of an extra indivisible (a new harbour or whatever) more or less immediately it was constructed. The only way to achieve this would be by means of massive and concentrated immigration.

We see, therefore, that once an indivisible is saturated, the last few people added to the population are the straw that breaks the camel's back. They could lead to a colossal increment in expenditure to make the transport system big enough to take them. In other words, as a population grows beyond the point of economic use of its indivisibles and into the region of saturation, increases in numbers become disfunctional rather than functional for the system.

A conference of the International Economic Association on economics and size concluded in 1957, in the words of Professor Robinson's Introduction to the 'Proceedings': 'It is easy to exaggerate the importance of scale among the many factors that influence productivity . . . *most of the major industrial economies of scale can be* achieved by a relatively high income nation of 50 million'. (Italics added.)[10]

The human cost
Even if larger-scale production never failed to produce economic benefits, the human costs can still be so high as to more

than outweight them. Marx's concept of the 'alienation' of large numbers of modern citizens from their work is now almost universally accepted. Millions work at jobs so dull, boring, and repetitive that their minds either atrophy or drive them into rebellion against the soullessness of large-scale production. Indeed, so far has the process gone that there are now counter-vailing tendencies towards 'job-enrichment' and a reversion to production in small groups as in the new Volvo factories at Kalmar and Söveda. If industrial units had not become so huge in pursuit of economies of scale, then no cure for aliena-tion need have been sought. I have never heard of a village blacksmith who needed job enrichment.

Conclusion

At the commonsense level there is a large nugget of value in this idea of economies of scale, but it is a far cry from this to the slogan, 'Bigger is always better'. Many other factors would come into a full discussion and refutation of the scale fallacy: efficiency, organisation, distance, communications, trade-barriers, politics, science and technology, opportunity cost, neighbourhood effects and many others. There isn't much point in concentrating the whole of Britain's nail production in one place in England, if the cost of transporting them to Wales and Scotland outweighs the possible extra cost of manu-facturing them on a smaller scale locally. There can also be very high human costs in over-large production units: patho-logical division of labour, bureaucracy, frustration and aliena-tion.

However, although we have seen that the way the scale argument is used is fallacious in itself, the really fundamental fallacy is to be found underlying it. This is, once more, that, even if it could be demonstrated conclusively that *every* increase in scale *always* gives huge increases in productivity, we must recognise the elementary fact that these are not possible for more than a very limited period because the earth and all it contains are finite.

CHAPTER 14

The market stimulus argument: the fallacy of increasing demand

'An expanding population . . . means an expanding market . . . and this should induce investment and technological development.' Harold Wilson as Prime Minister.[1]

'MORE PEOPLE mean MORE MARKETS
Sign beside the US Department of Commerce population clock.

'The slowest progress in wealth is often made where the stimulus from population alone is the greatest. . . . Population alone cannot create an effective demand for wealth.' Malthus.[2]

'The 'demand' that economists talk about is not real demand and the 'consumption' they talk about is artificial. . . . Economists limit demand to that made by consumers who have an equivalent to offer for what they receive.' Engels.[3]

'Want and effective demand are not the same thing. If they were, the poorest nations would be the ones to display the most vigorous demand.' Joseph Schumpeter.[4]

These quotations show that the relation between population and demand has been interpreted in many ways but the two main ones are that population growth automatically increases demand, and that, population growth need not increase demand. The first formulation probably reflects most popular opinion, and a good deal of professional opinion too, while the second is that held by the small minority who have stopped to study the facts and reflect on their implications.

Perhaps the most frenzied population zeal has been shown by the United States, whose great population clock has been ticking and flashing away since 1926. At first it was shown at various expositions around the country, but since 1952 it has had a place of honour in a public part of the US Department of Commerce. It is reset monthly to keep it running at the right speeds and in January 1973 its blue 'birth' light flashed every 9½ seconds and its purple 'death' light every 16 seconds, while the green 'immigrant' light came on every 87 seconds and the red 'emigrant' light every 15 minutes. The white 'population increase' light, summing all these, flashed every 18½ seconds and there is a digital counter which shows the latest score.

Basis in economic theory
Demand, along with supply and exchange, is one of the three most basic concepts in economics, and there is a theory, called Say's Law—after J. B. Say (1767–1832)—which states that supply creates the necessary demand so that economic systems tend towards equilibrium. This has been said to have had an important effect on the history of economic thought, but it was heavily criticised by Keynes, and supply and demand have proved to be almost permanently out of balance, so it is now out of favour. The relationship between earning power and spending power, on the face of it very straightforward, is complicated by psychological variables, since most of us don't automatically exercise our full spending power, and Keynes invented a further concept to help explain this complexity. This was the 'propensity to consume', explained by Seldon and Pennance as follows: 'Whenever income increases (or decreases), consumption spending will also increase (or decrease) *but not by as much as the change in income.*'

Statement of the demand fallacy
This fallacy involves the belief that numbers create demand in a simple and direct way.
First premise: Economic demand must continue to increase.
Second premise: Population growth is the means of increasing economic demand.
Conclusion: Population must increase.
   Stated thus baldly, it is fairly obvious that although the logic is correct this is a bad argument. It is by no means obviously true that demand must continue to increase, as the first premise states. The second premise is wrong in two ways;

in the first place it is false—or at least true only in the long term because an extra baby creates extra *need*, not demand— and in the second place it implies that there are no other ways of increasing demand, which is not merely false but absurd. What population increase creates (provided it is in the form of babies rather than migrants) is extra *need*, not extra demand. Demand is a technical term meaning 'spending-power', and no one with any acquaintance with economics should misuse it. *Everyman's Dictionary of Economics* defines it as follows:

> Demand, is the quantity of a commodity consumers wish and are able to buy at a given price in a given period. Demand in economics thus goes beyond the everyday notion of 'desire' or 'need'; unless the desire is made effective by ability and a willingness to pay it is not demand in the economic sense.[5]

A moment's reflection shows that although an increase in population has created new mouths to be fed, new bodies to be clothed, housed and kept warm, it has added nothing to the capacity of the population to buy these things. Until the increase in population has reached the productive stage it can be fed and cared for only diverting existing wealth from other purposes. In our culture the norm is for men and women to work until they get married, after which division of labour occurs. When they set up home together—or at least when the first baby arrives—society's definition of the man's role lays on him the onus of earning the living while the woman runs the home. Even if the mother returns to work after childbirth a third person is often called in to look after the infant. In other words if the mother becomes productive, economically speaking, it is at the expense of the productivity of some third party. The outcome then is typically that instead of two people feeding two mouths there is now one person feeding three mouths. In economic terms income has gone down from two units to one unit—'demand' necessarily having gone down with it—while need has increased from two units to three units.

How is the baby's need translated into economic demand? This is done by switching. Whereas previously a sizeable proportion of the parent's income may have gone on things like clothes, cars, football pools, records, books, travel and probably savings, some must now be switched towards such things as baby food, nappies, perambulators, toys and so forth, while the ties of parenthood usually reduce opportunities for leisure spending. Thus it becomes clear that the arrival of the new baby, i.e., an increment to the population, has done nothing whatever to increase demand. If the mother has stopped working, total demand has in fact decreased by the amount of her former income. The real difference in demand is that a small sector of the economy, the one dealing with the things babies require, will have gained a little at the expense of a much greater loss to other sectors of the economy.

This remains a fact even if society to some extent compensates the family for its new need through welfare payments and/or tax relief; and it is modified only if the birth of the new baby induces the wage-earner to work overtime, seek promotion or 'moonlight' (get a spare-time job). This basic economic point explains the paradox that the world contains hundreds of millions of hungry people, while there are at the same time local surpluses of food and other consumable goods elsewhere. The undoubted *need* of these starving millions is not *demand* in the economic sense.

Investment, confidence and demand
The argument that population growth is essential for sustained economic demand is sometimes formulated in a slightly different fashion from the one we have just discussed. This—though slightly more sophisticated-sounding—comes down to the same essentials and may also be formulated as a syllogism.
First premise: Economic growth must continue.
Second premise: Economic growth requires increasing investment.
Third premise: Increasing investment requires increasing confidence.
Fourth premise: Increasing confidence requires increasing demand.
Fifth premise. Increasing demand requires increasing population.
Conclusion: Population must continue to increase.

With the Fifth Premise we are back with the fallacious argument which has just been dealt with. But it is also untrue to say that economic growth can take place only through extra investment (productivity can increase through new ideas, better methods, harder work and so on). It is not true that increasing investment can come about only through increasing confidence on the part of private entrepreneurs—these are other sources of capital, notably public corporations and the State—and, it is not true (or at least not demonstrated) that the confidence of entrepreneurs can be had only on the basis of continuously increasing population size. Denmark, Sweden, and Luxembourg are all thriving with largely private-enterprise economies and populations approaching the stationary state; West Germany is said to be a veritable powerhouse of economic energy with a birth-rate possibly even below the long-term replacement level; and the economy of post-war Japan astonished the world as her birth-rate dropped towards the replacement level.

If we could instil into the minds of our credulous entrepreneurs the nature and dimensions of the demographic investment, so that they understood that fewer children can mean more wealth for investment in productivity, and therefore greater earnings and increased demand, the whole self-fulfilling prophecy could go into reverse and work quite happily in the opposite direction. It might be better still, however, to encourage them to think of the wider society and the longer term and become optimisers rather than maximisers.

Population, demand, and the self-fulfilling prophecy
There may be a paradoxical sense in which growth of need may stimulate growth of demand even though it 'shouldn't't'—i.e. it wouldn't if we were rational and fully informed. This is the phenomenon of the 'self-fulfilling prophecy', an idea first given wide currency by Thomas and Znaniecki, two of the founding fathers of American sociology, who wrote that 'if men define situations as real, they are real in their consequences', and called this concept the 'definition of the situation'.[6] Robert Merton coined the term 'self-fulfilling prophecy', which he defined as 'a *false* definition of the situation evoking

203

new behaviour which makes the originally false conception come *true*.[7]

If businessmen *believe* that a baby-boom is good for business, as they certainly did in the United States and to some extent still do, then they will act accordingly. They will tend to invest more than they would have done without this belief. Their feelings will then be reinforced by the actual growth in those sectors of industry which benefit from the switching of demand as needs change under the impact of population change. They will see demand increasing for building materials for schools and houses, for clothing, education all requisites, prams, toys, furniture, and many other items, and in their optimistic frame of mind may fail to notice the related diminution of demand in other sectors. This extra investment for the 'wrong' reasons may increase productivity because of more and better capital equipment and the accompanying optimism, so that people will tend to earn more, thus creating a situation in which demand really is greater than it would have been without this wrong belief and the population growth which triggered it off.

Conclusion
Of course population does play *some* part in determining the level of demand. It is difficult to imagine the income per head which would give Iceland, say, with 220,000 people, the level of demand typical of the United States, with 210 million. But the choice is not normally between a tiny population and a huge one—or over long historical periods—but between a largish population now and one which is only slightly larger next year, and the year after, and so on.

However, the basic refutation once again is parochialism. Even if it were true that more population always meant more demand there must come a time when we have to do without further increase in demand because of the lack of room for the extra people allegedly required to produce it.

CHAPTER 15

The technological argument: the fallacy of increasing production

'With every mouth God sends a pair of hands.' Popular saying.

'The road to world survival . . . does not lie in neo-Malthusian prescriptions to eliminate surplus people, nor in birth control, but in the effort to make everybody on the face of the earth productive.' Josue de Castro.[1]

'The real solution of the problems is . . . to be found . . . in a renewed scientific and technical effort on man's part to deepen and extend his dominion over Nature.' Pope John XXIII.[2]

'It is . . . a highly bizarre . . . fact that the strongest demand for birth control should have come precisely when the possibilities in the way of food production are seen to be virtually illimitable.' Malcolm Muggeridge.[3]

'Development of production, science, and technology always surpasses by far the rate of population growth.' Leader, Chinese Delegation, Stockholm Conference, 1972.

Slogans like 'With every mouth God sends a pair of hands' are mindless; they pay no heed to logic or the facts. The mouth is fully operational from birth, while the hands may not start providing until the age of twenty or more in an advanced society. In even the most primitive cultures the hand will not begin to be productive until five years or so when children can take on jobs like minding goats. Between the start of the consumption process and the start of the production process there is a large, critical and irremovable gap, which must be bridged by the production of the middling age groups. At the end of the lifespan, there is another gap to be bridged, arthritic old pairs of hands gradually lose their productive capacity while the mouth remains operational until death, which may come many years later. We all have to go through the first stage of

dependency, and in a developed society most of us can expect
to go through the second. We know that society must help us
through the first and we can reasonably expect it to see us
through the second if we have given our fellows what was in us
to give. We must always remember, however, that what is
consumed by the unproductive young or old, can only be at the
expense of reduced consumption on the part of the producers
on whom a rapidly growing population must impose a constantly
increasing pressure.

Malthus stated the general principle that the numbers of
living creatures tend to grow in 'geometrical progression', as a
mathematician would say, whereas production of food and
other necessities tends towards 'arithmetical progression'—
i.e., 'multiplicative' growth with compound interest and
'additive' growth with simple interest, respectively. The
reasons for this basic difference are easy to see. If at some given
time a population of animals containing equal numbers of
males and females pairs off, with each pair producing four
surviving offspring, it will double every generation; each pair
producing two pairs, who in turn produce four pairs, who go
on to produce eight pairs, and so on. In the case of food production, however, if human labour causes two ears of corn to grow
for this year's harvest where only one grew for last year's, no
inherent tendency will cause these two to become four and the
four become eight in the two succeeding years. What causes
productivity to rise is human effort, and generally speaking
the only way to get twice as much out is to put at least twice as
much in. Eventually, of course, the law of diminishing returns
operates and stops even this happening. Indeed, without
constant endeavour, productivity can and often does slip back.

A graphical demonstration of the two forms of growth would
show the geometric curve for population climbing ever more
and more steeply, illustrating Malthus's central point that
there is an inherent tendency for population growth to leave
growth of food production behind. Of course the geometrical
curve cannot ever leave the arithmetical curve behind—there
can never be an actual gap—because the larger population
represented by the higher curve would have nothing to live on.
The ever-present *tendency* for population to outgrow resources

is normally held in check by natural constraints, social controls, and 'the improper arts', (Malthus's term for birth control). Since Malthus's day it has become more clearly understood that productivity can also increase geometrically and often does, but his basic point still holds good: for the greater part of humanity throughout the known past, the population curve has been straining above the food production curve with the result that ever-increasing numbers of people are in need.

The technological fallacy in its strong form, as put forward by the Chinese delegation to the Stockholm Conference, and vehemently reiterated at the World Population Conference, and by Pope Paul, states that there is not and never can be a population/production problem. In its weaker form, it is based on a recognition that there is now or soon will be such a problem—either in the world as a whole or in some specific areas—but that it can be prevented or cured if only we really try to raise production. In both cases it is insisted that there is no need to restrict population growth.

Once again the argument can be expressed in logical form.
First premise: Population growth depends on increased production.
Second premise: Increased production depends on increases in science and technology.
Third premise: There are no foreseeable limits to progress in science and technology.
Conclusion: There are no foreseeable limits to population growth.

It is easy to run this question into that posed by the problem of the finiteness, or otherwise, of the resources on which scientific and technological processes depend, but they ought to be kept separate; so I am dealing with the production fallacy in two parts, first concentrating on science and technology as though the resources they need were infinite, then speculating on the finiteness of the real world, on 'limits to growth'.

Under pressure, the proponents of this argument will usually admit that in practice it seems to be rather difficult to raise production quickly or extensively; but they go on to claim that if only we really put our backs into it the task would be feasible. They usually make moral exhortations to the wealthier countries to share their surpluses and aid the poor, but fail to consider the colossal practical problems involved—psychological, social, religious, economic, military, political, geographical and scientific.

The second part of the fallacy is that not only can the production-curve be forced and kept above the population curve in the near future but that this can go on for ever. In a strictly literal sense it is impossible to envisage a point at which it could be conclusively demonstrated that we cannot grow 1,000 ears of corn where one grew before. However, a moment's reflection shows this does *not* mean that we can go on increasing productivity by ever-increasing amounts and compensate for any conceivable increase in population. One of the few things we can be certain about in a very uncertain world is that productivity is not 'illimitable'.

It is also true that no one can set bounds to scientific progress, so how can one say there are limits to growth for the sort of knowledge which can be used to increase human numbers? There are several senses in which such limits can be postulated, and the most fundamental concerns the apparent nature of the universe, on which all empirical science is based. This is expressed in basic scientific 'laws' such as the laws of motion, conservation of matter and energy, and so on.

Another potential limitation lies in possible limits to the growth of science itself. The number of scientific journals has been increasing exponentially since about 1730, and it is obvious that this must cease in the not too distant future. Growth in investment in science has been exponential for so long that this too must come to a halt soon. Lord Todd, then Chairman of the Advisory Council for Scientific Policy, wrote as early as 1965; 'We cannot continue indefinitely to double our expenditure every five years as has been done for the last fifteen years'.[4]

Manpower also poses a potential limit to the growth of science. About 95 per cent of all the scientists who have ever lived are alive now, and if the present rate of increase were to continue for a little longer, everyone—man, woman and child —would be a scientist. Derek de Solla Price, perhaps the world's leading authority on the growth of science, has written:

Science has been explosively filling the world at an exponential rate, faster than that of any population explosion . . . for . . . centuries, so that at all times past we could look around and see that almost everything known in science had been discovered only recently. . . . Now, something is suddenly new, we have witnessed for the last decade a steady and mounting decelera- tion. . . . The 'overdeveloped' countries, the US, the USSR, and perhaps the UK and a few other nations, are suffering from a sort of ecological disaster . . . information pressure . . . an over- population of scientists and scientific papers manifested in a flood of publications, of abstract and index journals, and of biblio- graphies of indexes ad infinitum. We witness also the cybernetic damping effects caused by lack of national funds, lack of motiva- tion toward the hard and basic sciences, and, to crown it all, an onset of machine murder, mysticism, drugs, and contemplation.[5]

There are also severe limitations on the use for productive purposes of *existing* science and technology. It is one thing to produce new knowledge and equipment, but quite another to educate people into an awareness of its existence and uses and a readiness to discard the old ways and get on with the new. If the flood of knowledge and present pace of change continue, there could be a reaction against it—as there has been in many areas against the green revolution—and an even bigger gap between what could be and what is.

However, a moderate proponent of the productivity argu- ment could still put forward the case that productivity, even if not 'illimitable', may be greatly improvable far into the future. This is a much more plausible argument at both the commonsense and scientific levels. It is common knowledge that vast amounts of food are wasted after they have been produced, through faulty storage and transit, unsuitable economic institutions, social taboos, incompetence, corrup- tion, theft and so on. A World Health Organisation paper on pollution states:

Human infestation with worms, transmitted mainly by polluted soil, is so massive that over half of the food produced and con- sumed is metabolised by the parasitic worm population infesting . . . man. . . . Half the work of the sick peasantry goes in the culti- vation of food for the worms that make them sick.[6]

Huge extra quantities could be produced simply by putting existing knowledge to practical use, further large increments could be gained by more intensive research and experimentation, and it is very tempting to accept this seemingly reasonable argument as sufficient ground for dismissing the population/food problem. Colin Clark does this, as we have seen, arguing that pressure of population is the only issue powerful enough to compel governments to change their ways, modernise, and raise productivity.

This view overlooks the central fact that productivity, like politics, is 'the art of the possible'. Human societies normally lag a great deal behind their theory, and it is improbable that they will change sufficiently in this respect; practical *reality* in the future is likely to remain as far out of touch with theoretical *possibilities* as it has been in the past. This prediction is not intended to deny the *possibility* of a genuine breakthrough, but the *probability* is that there will be no universal revolution embracing science, technology, economic institutions, politics and religion, enabling most of what is theoretically possible to be realised in fact.

Food production and hunger
Views on this vary so widely that it seems almost impossible to come to a sound conclusion, but it is of great moral and practical importance to try to reach some assessment of how many people in the world are hungry, who and where they are, how hungry they are, and what can be done about it.

None of the rich countries has overall food problems—excepting occasional crises of 'over-production'—although most have such internal inequalities that some people are grossly overfed and many go hungry. In the United States, for example, the wealthiest and most materially productive society the world has yet seen, some 35 millions were living in poverty as late as 1965. Clark is perhaps the most optimistic of all observers, but since he finally fails to offer any estimate of the amount of hunger and malnutrition in the world it is difficult to ascertain quite what his case is. In his most recent publications he argues that the 'real subsistence level' is seen in 'any community whose food supply is 250 kg of grain equivalent per person per year' but that 'we do not have evidence of any whole countries at or near true subsistence level. . . . The poorest country for which we have information . . . is Guinea with an output of 351. Not far above is India with 382'.[7] It seems to follow from this that not only is there no problem of hunger in the world but that even India—with her frequent food-riots, famines, and emergency food-aid imports—which most of us think of as a country pretty firmly on the bread line, is actually 53 per cent above minimum requirements, a very comfortable margin one would have thought.

In another publication Clark argues that far from there being a world food shortage, we are suffering from a minor crisis of over-production and the rate of increase should be cut down by about one thirteenth: 'Since the mid-1950s, the world rate of expansion of agricultural production has been $2 \cdot 7$ per cent per year—the desirable rate of growth would appear to be only about $2 \cdot 5$ per cent . . . per year.'[8] The FAO target figure is a minimum of $3 \cdot 9$ per cent increase each year to prevent food supply falling still further below what it regards as demand, but Clark does not think very highly of this organisation.

For a view quite pessimistic enough for most of us, we need only look at the official FAO statistics; we need not go to the Paddocks, Borgstrom, or even the Erhlichs, have been dismissed as doomwatchers, often by people who have done very little homework on the subject themselves.[9]

A. H. Boerma, Director General of FAO wrote in connection with the Indicative World Plan for Agricultural Development:

By the . . . second half of this century there were ominous signs of a steadily widening gap between supply and demand for food in the developing countries . . . which . . . was reflected in rapidly rising imports of staple cereals . . . and by mounting requests for food aid. . . . National and international action is needed to re-dress the alarming imbalance . . . in the race between food and population. . . . 85 out of every 100 additional persons . . . by 1985 will be in the poor countries . . . many of which are already overburdened by . . . their population. Growth of population alone would require an 80 per cent increase in food supplies by 1985 without any improvement in . . . individual diets. Continuation of the present trend in food production would result in only a quarter of the extra animal protein required . . . being produced domestically . . . and a need for cereal imports exceeding 90 million metric tons (nine times the 1962 level).[10]

He went on to show that 'good cultivable land is becoming steadily scarcer' and that intense population pressure has already led some countries to pursue short-term expedients in food production which have 'sometimes led to the permanent destruction of valuable resources for a relatively short-run gain in agricultural output'. In spite of the 'widespread alarm over DDT', he argues that the need for food is so great that putting 'a brake on technical progress at the risk of widespread famine cannot be contemplated. A calculated short-run risk must be taken'.

In his foreword to the FAO Annual Review *The State of Food and Agriculture, 1972,* he is no more optimistic:

> The Second Development Decade seems to have got off to a poor start. . . . In the developing countries the rise in production was between 1 and 2 per cent, which is much less than in recent years and well below the target of . . . 4 per cent. . . . They suffered not only a further decline in their share of world agricultural exports, but also a fall in absolute terms in agricultural earnings. . . . If urgent measures are not taken to redress the situation, the whole international strategy . . . could well be in jeopardy.

The body of this report is extremely unsatisfactory because the FAO's former policy of having clear graphs showing at a glance increases in population and food production and the resulting changes in per capita consumption has been superseded. Most of the information is now buried in tabular form in the Production Yearbook, a daunting volume of microscopically printed statistics. However, if one searches diligently enough one can find snippets about the sad facts; for example:

> According to clinical surveys . . . the prevalence of moderate protein/calorie malnutrition (PCM) varied between 4·4 and 57 per cent in children up to five years. The prevalence of severe cases of PCM . . . ranged up to 7·6 per cent. . . .

[There is] widespread incidence of PCM affecting one-quarter to one-third of the population in many developing countries.

The report admits that there are 300 to 500 million people in a starving or semi-starving state, but, like Clark, it shrinks from assessing the overall size of the malnutrition problem as distinct from that of actual hunger.

However, there are authoritative sources for wider estimates, and P. V. Sukhatme, Statistical Director of the FAO, estimated in 1966 that 'at least 20 per cent . . . in the LDCs are undernourished, one-third are protein malnourished and well over half are malnourished. . . . Some 60 per cent of the people in the LDCs suffer from undernutrition or malnutrition or both'.[11] Dumont and Rosier estimate that out of 60-odd million deaths a year, between 10 and 20 millions are caused by hunger or by disease exacerbated by malnutrition.[12]

Another way of looking at the problem is to ignore the statistics and use the evidence of your senses, as Arthur Hopcraft did after 45,000 miles of travel on behalf of the UK Freedom From Hunger Campaign: 'Hunger . . . at close quarters . . . is a dazzling sight. I do not mean only . . . the skeletal bodies and dead eyes of children . . . I mean also its more general evidence of withered land . . . shrivelled cattle and pervading human desolation.'[13]

Malnutrition has devastating consequences well beyond the immediate suffering caused to its victims. Protein deficiency in childhood causes malformation of the brain and central nervous system, and these in turn seriously impair intellectual potential and educational progress in later years and deplete the pool of human talent where it is very badly needed.

Finally, to give some slight idea what it *feels* like, I will quote from an essay written by a schoolgirl in Swaziland after the Save the Children Fund had introduced a simple lunch, a bowl of soup, into her school:

School feeding has come with a sort of civilisation into my body. When coming to school I walk freely without any pain in the body. Even if I run or jump it does not care. I usually run when coming to school. School feeding gives children strength and power, and their minds float about hunting for work to do.[14]

The population/food race

Table 15/1 shows the change in food production per head since pre-war days. The index of 100 equals average production between 1952 and 1957, so that numbers over one hundred imply an increase and those below a decrease. The 'world'

Table 15/1

*The population/food race. Average food production per head in selected regions Prewar–1971.** (1952–1957 average = 100)

Year	World	Western Europe	North America	Latin America	Africa	Far East
Prewar	88	98	87	104	101	103
1948–52	97	90	103	96	102	100
1952	98	95	103	99	99	94
1957	102	104	96	103	96	100
1962	107	116	99	100	97	106
1967	111	125	106	102	95	102
(1971)	113	134	111	99	95	106
1977						

*Based on FAO Production Yearbook.

column shows that average production per head has gone up slightly less than 1 per cent a year, very roughly, slowing down to about ½ per cent since 1967. However, the 'Western Europe' and 'North American' columns show that much of this increase is concentrated in those areas. The Far East is about 3 per cent up on the prewar figure, but Latin America—hardly touched by war—is 5 per cent down, while Africa is 6 per cent down on prewar and 7 per cent down on the 1948–52 average. Western Europe and North America are now overfed; but the Third World regions suffer severe under-feeding. In the case of Africa the index needs to leap from 95 to 135 or so, and the chances of this happening while populations continue to soar seem remote.

Boerma argues that the poverty of the poor countries is not so extreme as to be unassailable. Although the gap between their incomes and ours is widening rapidly, theirs are none the less increasing slightly and this means extra demand for food. Of the increased food needed by 1985, 71 per cent is needed because of the increase in numbers and 29 per cent because of increased per capita wealth. The official papers published in preparation for the World Food Conference show an even worse ratio, 80 per cent owing to increased numbers, and only 20 per cent because of increasing per capita demand. See UN E/Conf./65/Prep/6, 8 May 1974.

Figure 15/1.   Increasing food gap. World 1962–1985

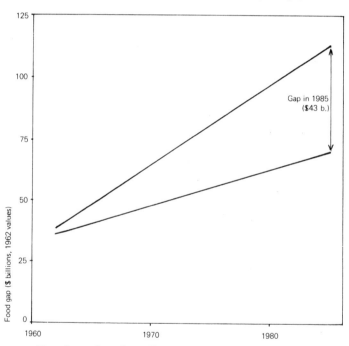

Based on data from Boerma A.H. (1970) op. cit.

Figure 15/1 shows the increasing gap between supply and demand which, of course, is one of the main causes of rising food prices. Boerma concludes that unless there is a huge improvement in food production in the poor countries there will by

1985 be a shortfall of 160 million tons in cereals alone, and 'demand for food will exceed supply by about $43 billion (1962 prices) . . . if it had to be filled by imports . . . although they had considerable difficulty in finding even 3 billions for food imports in 1962.[11]

Rate of increase of the malnourished
The best test of the theory that greater production will cure poverty and malnutrition without any limitation of numbers is to look at the historical record. Let us consider what has happened in the race between food and population since the scientific and industrial revolution began, taking 1650 as a convenient starting-point, over three centuries of what has been above all things a revolution of productivity. The great difficulty, however, lies in finding out just how much hunger there was in the past. We have seen that the Indian diet was better in the seventeenth century than in the twentieth, and this may well be true of other societies—especially since many of them used to control and optimise their populations. However, there seems little chance of finding reliable and systematic evidence, so we are reduced to making sets of assumptions and trying out their implications.

Rejecting Lord Boyd Orr's frequently quoted figure of two-thirds of the world population malnourished, the more tentative estimates of the Ehrlichs and others, and even the figure arrived at by the sober American President's Science Advisory Committee Panel on the World Food Supply—60 per cent hunger and malnutrition in the poor countries, equivalent to 40 per cent of the world population—I shall take the conservative figure of one-third underfed against two-thirds fed.

Table 15/2 shows the results of applying these proportions to the performance of the industrial revolution which by 1975 will have increased the numbers of the underfed eight times, from 167 millions to 1,333 millions, and fourteen times by 2000 if the trend continues. The rate of increase in the underfed is shown in the right-hand column as a percentage per century and this has risen geometrically. The proportion assumed is not critical. If we assume that only a quarter have been ill-fed throughout, then the number is still four times larger by 1975.

Table 15/2

Increase in the rate of increase of the malnourished.
World, 1650–2000 AD.

(Assuming that a constant proportion of
one-third is malnourished.)

Year	Pop. millions	Fed (millions)	Underfed (millions)	Rate of Increase in the unfed (% per century)*
1650	500	333	167	
1830	1,000	667	333	47%
1930	2,000	1,333	667	100%
1960	3,000	2,000	1,000	286%
1975	4,000	2,667	1,333	579%
2000	7,000?	4,667?	2,333?	838%?
Total increases since 1650	6,500	4,334	2,166**	

* Compound interest per century.
** 13 times greater in 350 yrs.

Similarly, if we assume four-fifths ill-fed then, and only one-fifth by 2000, the ratio of increase would have dropped only to three and a half. The argument still stands if we assume either of the two possible extreme positions:

(1) The whole population of the world was ill-fed in 1650. In this case the industrial revolution has, up to 1975, increased the number of the ill-fed by 833 millions, or 167 per cent.

(2) The whole population was well-fed in 1650. In this case by 1975 the ill-fed have increased by 1,333 millions, an infinite number when expressed as a proportion. If by 2000—a generation from now—the whole world was up to 1969 American standards (with about 13 per cent suffering from malnutrition), then the world total of the underfed would be over 900 millions, nearly double the world's total population when the production revolution started.

The mathematics of misery

If it is true that the proportion of the adequately fed is barely holding its own so that, as population rapidly increases, the absolute amount of malnutrition increases with it, what sort of judgement can we make about it. Can we quantify, can we say that if the *proportion* of human suffering is no greater, humanity as a whole is no worse off? Can we argue that a productive system generating, say, one extra well-fed person for every extra ill-fed person is level-pegging? Surely it is impossible to avoid the conclusion that a system producing ever larger absolute numbers of poverty-stricken, ill-fed, illiterate, and unemployed human beings should not be tolerated by rational and honourable people.

By any of the yardsticks mentioned above, productivity has failed miserably as a means of reducing total, and, possibly, even proportional human suffering, and it shows signs of doing worse rather than better in the immediate future.

The Green Revolution and the 'danger' of a breakthrough

There is a great danger that a major breakthrough in food productivity, such as the Green Revolution suggests, might tempt us to assume that the battle has been won. Yet even if productivity could be increased rapidly, by large amounts, and for a long time, it must fail in the long run if population is allowed to increase indefinitely. Let us examine a case of this scientific euphoria, in *Science Journal*, which put out a special issue called 'Feeding the World' in May 1968. The guest editorial by Lord Boyd-Orr started: 'There is a growing fear of an impending world food crisis. More than half the people in the world suffer from hunger or malnutrition, and the population is increasing faster than the food supply. . . .' But the issue as a whole took an optimistic line and made no attempt to come to terms with the problem of population growth.

For example, K. L. Blaxter wound up his article, 'The Animal Harvest'; 'There is no doubt in my mind that agricultural technology can meet this challenge of the immediate future and eradicate human hunger and . . . degradation. I am not willing to make projections . . . beyond the immediate future. . . . To predicate the reproductive performance of

THE TECHNOLOGICAL ARGUMENT

generations whose fathers and mothers are yet unborn, to derive fantasies of despair is not a rewarding occupation when
there is so much positive and useful work to be done in the
immediate tomorrow.'

The journal is filled with marvels achieved and greater
marvels still to come. For instance there is H. Boyko's article,
'Farming in the Desert', describing the 'desert garden' in
Israel, at Eilat on the Red Sea. This was planted in 1949 on
bare hills of sandy gravel and irrigated with highly saline
spring water. A more unpromising combination would be
hard to imagine. Nevertheless, crops are growing where nothing
but desert existed before. Boyko continues:

> The work . . . could solve two imminent problems of mankind . . .
> producing food for hundreds of millions . . . in 15–20 years time,
> and giving cheap and effective purification and re-use of danger-
> ously polluted water in densely populated industrial centres. . . .
> With . . . the help of the United Nations, the respective govern-
> ments and of the great humanitarian foundations . . . the most
> desolate parts of the earth, the sand deserts, might become the
> granaries of the future.

This is heartening news, and such work should be pressed
ahead with all possible vigour. None the less it will be a calamity
if progress of this kind so hypnotises us that we fail to see that
the earth is finite and that producing and consuming enough
food is not the be-all and end-all of human existence.

The green revolution—the expert view.
Let the last word on the fallacy of the 'technological' solution
rest with those acknowledged to be experts by Malthusians and
anti-Malthusians alike, those in the front line of the new
agricultural revolution. The opinion of W. M. Myers, Vice-
President of the Rockefeller Foundation, responsible for many
programmes for the development of more productive wheat
and rice strains, is: '*The battle will certainly be lost . . . if we do not
push ahead on both programmes . . . population control and food production* . . . with greatly increased resources from public and private
sectors, both of the developed and the developing countries.'[15]

And Norman Borlaug, Director of the International Maize and Wheat Improvement Centre in Mexico, writes:

> For the first time I am hopeful that modern agricultural technology can *temporarily* solve the world food production problems. *Perhaps through this development we can buy 25 to 30 years* of time. *During this period population growth* must be drastically slowed and brought into balance with food production and our ability to provide a better standard of education, housing, medical care for a rapidly exploding world population. *Unless there is a breakthrough in slowing population growth* on a world-wide basis, the world will disintegrate.

Conclusion

Roughly speaking, the hungry third of mankind is three times larger than the total population of the world at the beginning of the scientific and industrial revolution. If a Machiavelli bent on causing the greatest possible amount of suffering to mankind had been given a choice between killing us all off in 1650 or starting an Industrial Revolution, he would surely have chosen the latter.

However, though productivity has always failed so far to win the food and population race, the optimist can still argue that in future we can and must do better. Somehow production will be forced higher than the population growth-curve and held there, come what may. For this reason it is necessary to go a stage further and show that the really fundamental refutation of the productivity fallacy is not empirical, the record of all actual achievement, but logical, though the logic must be based upon the physical facts of existence, and of these the dominant aspect is the finiteness of the earth and all its resources.

CHAPTER 16

The Bounty of Nature argument: the fallacy of unlimited economic growth

'Nothing is given for the use of air and water . . . the indestructible powers of the soil . . . or for any other . . . gifts of nature which exist in boundless quantity . . . these natural aids are inexhaustible and at every man's disposal.' David Ricardo.[1]

'The productivity of the land can be increased *ad infinitum.*' Friedrich Engels.[2]

'Whatever man can decompose, man will be able to compound. . . . Thus wherever earth, and water, and the other original chemical substances may be found, there human art may hereafter produce nourishment; and thus we are presented with a real infinite series of increase in the means of subsistence, to match Mr Malthus' geometrical ratio for the multiplication of mankind.' William Godwin.[3]

'The resources which God in his goodness and wisdom has implanted in Nature are well-nigh inexhaustible . . . and . . . the progress of science and technology . . . opens up limitless horizons.' Pope John XXIII.[4]

'There is no reason to suppose that economic growth cannot continue for another 2,500 years.' Professor W. Beckerman.[5]

The 'Limits to Growth' debate
Since the publication in 1972 of the MIT study, *Limits To Growth*, carried out under the auspices of the Club of Rome, the air has been thick with accusations of 'hysteria', exaggeration and alarmism. The book itself is a very tentative and *un*hysterical, not to say humble, document, and the frenetic response to it appears to stem from a deeply rooted conviction that there are no limits to man's material achievements other than those in man himself and that these are of a kind which

221

can be overcome. This tradition is particularly strong in econ-omics, where some of the teachings of the founding fathers hold sway as if they were revealed truth.

Ricardo wrote about the 'gifts of nature which exist in boundless quantity'. However, even he did not fail to recognise some limits to man's demands on the environment: he was only too aware of the limitation of land, even in his day, when the population of Britain was less than a fifth of its 1973 level, and his theory of rent based on the increasing shortage of land was one of his main contributions to economic thought.

Once again the argument can be given a logical structure. First premise: Economic growth can be limited only by a shortage of material resources. Second premise: Potential material resources exist in boundless quantities. Conclusion: Economic growth will never be limited.

Both of these premises are not merely false but ludicrous. Yet virtually every day in politics and in the mass media the argument is defended passionately.

It is impossible to do justice to the MIT study—or even the condensed paperback report on it—here, and I shall simply indicate its general flavour and a few of the main points. The Foreword states that the purposes of the Club of Rome are: 'to foster understanding of the varied but interdependent compo-nents—economic, political, natural, and social—that make up the global system in which we all live; 'to bring that new understanding to the attention of policy-makers and the public'; and 'in this way to promote new policy initiatives and action'. The book grew out of Phase One of their Project on the Predi-cament of Mankind, and they say of it: 'We hope it will command critical attention and spark debate in all societies'.

The research team set out to examine 'the five basic factors that determine, and therefore ultimately limit, growth on this planet—population, agricultural production, natural resources, industrial production, and pollution'. They did this by means of computer simulations based on a mathematical model which they say at the outset is 'imperfect, oversimplified, and unfinished. We are well aware of its shortcomings but we believe it is important to publish the model and our findings now because decisions are being made every day—that will affect the physical, economic, and social conditions of the world system for decades to come and these cannot wait for perfect models and total understanding'.

With respect to the area in which they have been most criticised—for saying that the doom of mankind is at hand—they say: 'We emphasize . . . that none of these computer outputs is a prediction. We would not expect the real world to behave like the world model—especially in the collapse modes.'

The team tried out many different assumptions and got the computer to demonstrate the consequences if they were realised. Several of these showed that a very comfortable steady state sustainable far into the future is perfectly possible if appropriate decisions to control numbers, pollution, and non-renewable resource depletion are made and put into effect. Figure 16/1

Figure 16/1. Stabilized World Model 1

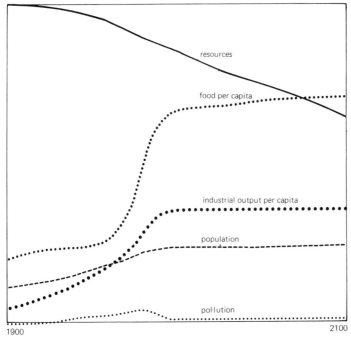

After Meadows, D. M., et al. (1972) The Limits to Growth (p. 165)

223

shows one of these possibilities, with a fairly large population enjoying a high life-expectancy plus twice as much food and three times as much wealth per head as the world's present average allows.

However, their main conclusion is pessimistic, tentative though it is, *in the absence of any corrective changes in the system:* 'Although we have many reservations about . . . the present world model, it has led us to one conclusion that appears to be justified under all the assumptions tested so far. *The basic behaviour mode of the world system is exponential growth of population and capital, followed by collapse.*'

The reason for this overshoot and collapse mode of behaviour is that, of the three imaginable outcomes 'unrestricted growth, a self-imposed . . . or a nature-imposed limitation', only the last two are possible. Of these two possibles the last was chosen and written into the computer programme—a critical decision

> because it is a basic part of the human value-system currently operational—that population and capital growth should be allowed to continue until they reach some 'natural' limit. . . . Whenever we incorporate this value—the result is that the system rises above its ultimate limit and then collapses—Given that first assumption we have not been able to find a set of policies that avoids the collapse mode.

If this unlimited growth value is not written in, then the whole thing changes but of course the 'limits' case is still made, this time by voluntary control

Their general conclusions are stated as follows:

> 1. If the present growth trends in world population etc. continue unchanged, the limits to growth on this planet will be reached sometime within the next one-hundred years. . . .
>
> 2. It is possible to alter these growth trends and establish a condition of ecological and economic stability, that is sustainable far into the future. . . .
>
> 3. If the world's people decide to strive for this second outcome rather than the first, the sooner they begin . . . the greater will be their chances of success.

The last point can be reinforced by one made earlier and very strongly: 'Under conditions of rapid growth . . ., the system is forced into new policies and actions long before the results of old policies, and actions can be properly assessed. The situation is even worse when the growth is exponential.' The disclaimer made by Boerma in the preceding section about the necessity, despite many misgivings, to take 'a calculated risk' on DDT in order to avert famine, is a good example of the operation of this pressure on moderate and responsible decision-makers.

The pro-growth school

In Britain among the best known individual spokesman for growth and against the 'Limits' study have been Beckerman, Bray, and Crosland.

Wilfred Beckerman's position is set forth in his much delayed inaugural lecture, *Economists, Scientists and Environmental Catastrophe* (1972) and in his book *In Defence of Economic Growth* (1974), and he has also argued it via the mass media. He dismisses with contempt the 'Limits' project and its parent body: 'It seemed to me . . . such a brazen, impudent piece of nonsense that nobody could possibly take it seriously . . . how silly do you have to be to be allowed to join . . .?' He goes on to conclude:

> Mankind will go bumbling along in much the same way as he has for centuries. There are certainly terrible problems . . . but most of them are age-old . . . if anything, economic growth has alleviated some of them. As for raw materials becoming exhausted it is most unlikely that this will cause any dislocation . . ., as for pollution this is really no problem at all. . . . So now you can all go home and sleep peacefully in your beds tonight, secure in the knowledge that in the sober and considered opinion of the latest occupant of the second oldest Chair in Political Economy in this country, if everything is not exactly all right on this Earth there is no reason to think that continued economic growth will make it any worse.'[5]

Jeremy Bray

This commentator is himself a member of the Club of Rome— 'rather inactive', he says—a scholar, a former Labour MP and a minister, and Deputy Chairman of Christian Aid. His rejection of the 'Limits' study is couched in more moderate terms than those of Professor Beckerman.[6]

Bray first argues that 'growth in world population is not exponential' (which is simply false[7]), and then denies that it will continue to grow exponentially, which so far as I am aware no one has ever asserted. Generally speaking, the more pessimistic the observer the more convinced he is that exponential growth of population cannot possibly continue much longer. Bray argues that world population is growing temporarily because of a 'large stepwise increase', and falls into the trap of the demographic transition, arguing that in the poor countries there will eventually be a 'decisive fertility decline towards the levels now prevailing in the more developed regions', apparently under the misapprehension that all our populations are stationary.

With respect to economic growth Bray argues that the concept of the GNP is a misleading indicator of growth because it 'includes pop festivals, sermons, visits to child welfare clinics, football, and Picasso'. Leaving aside the point that some of these activities have an obvious environmental impact, let us consider his next point, that because of the price mechanism, new technologies and the substitution of different materials, 'real output can go on increasing without limit'. This is false even if there is an infinite supply of raw materials and new technologies, because of the finiteness of the earth as a workshop for processing them all.

He does tone this conclusion down a bit later but concludes that if we think of technological 'migration', as we exhaust one raw material after another, 'of moving from one technology to the next, we have scarcely begun to conceive the possibilities'. He takes it for granted, without any discussion of the problem of radioactive wastes, that fission and fusion offer 'virtually unlimited sources of energy'.

On pollution Bray makes some unexceptionable points, that 'the polluter must pay' and so on, but concludes that 'other things being equal the tighter the control of pollution the more economic growth we shall need'.

On the 'Limits' model Bray's comments seem confused. On

the one hand he denies that either population or material outputs are growing exponentially—even approximately so—but
then argues that while 'Growth rates are unlikely to continue
. . . the idea of physical limits is misleading . . . as is the idea of
equilibrium'.

He also grants the central point that the likeliest mode of
world behaviour is overshoot and collapse, which 'is a common
feature of . . . dynamic systems . . . likely to be true of the world'.

He goes on to counter the argument that however bad the
'Limits' world model is, it is at least not so grossly oversimplified as the models at present used to manage the world,
the mental models in the heads of individual statesmen and
other leaders. Bray argues that the true comparison is between
the MIT computer model and

> the decision process . . . the interaction of Cabinet Committee . . .
> Government statements . . ., debates, press comments, trade . . .
> discussion, boardroom decisions, popular reaction, elections, re-
> search, and many other processes. . . . This vast 'computer model'
> . . . the process of decision making in human society is constantly
> interacting with the actual live course of events in real time . . .
> [its] adaptive capacity has enjoyed unparalleled success.

Bray concludes: 'There is no harm in the methods of For-
rester and Meadows provided they are recognised for what
they are—a means of articulating the intuitive judgements of
the model builder conditioned by his subjective preferences
for the future.'

In the case of our own country, Bray argues in favour of a
policy of sex education and free birth-control, while asserting
that 'there should not be any suggestion of population targets
because other policies should enable us to provide well for
whatever population we have'. He also supports pollution
control, massive research on environmental problems and
'continued growth of GNP'.

Anthony Crosland
Mr Crosland published his main contribution[8] to the
growth debate before the 'Limits' study came out. His main
points are as follows:

227

There is a genuine population-resources issue of some kind; he wants 'strict social control over the environment . . . to enable us to cope with our exploding problems'.

He is a socialist who wants the 'relief of poverty . . . a more equal distribution of wealth . . . and a wider ideal of social equality'.

These goals can be met only by 'continuous growth. . . . We cannot even approach our basic objectives with the present rate of growth . . . these require a redistribution of wealth and resources and . . . I assert dogmatically that in a democracy low or zero growth wholly excludes the possibility'.

A dogmatic assertion is a somewhat unpromising foundation for what purports to be a reasoned case, but Crosland seems to mean what he says, as his following pages demonstrate; I now call this argument the 'Crosland fallacy', which rests in part on a debunking of the environmental movement. True, he says he means only 'parts of the conservationist lobby', but he goes on to lambaste the whole movement whose 'approach is hostile to growth in principle and indifferent to the needs of ordinary people. It has a manifest class bias, and reflects a set of middle and upper class value judgements. Its champions are affluent and . . . want to kick the ladder down behind them'. Crosland goes on to argue that the conservationist approach is self-contradictory as well as morally repugnant:

> The anti-growth approach is not only unacceptable in terms of values; it is absurd in terms of the environment itself—the greater part of the environmental problem stems not from present or future growth, but from past growth. It is largely a backlog problem—and only rapid growth will give us any possibility . . . of finding the huge additional sums for coping with pollution.

The rest of the argument deals with Britain's past failure to grow fast enough, methods of stimulating growth, and more equitable ways of distributing the hoped-for increments of the future. Dogmatic assertions do not require evidence and there are no material facts throughout the entire document, except for a recapitulation of our growth rate, 2·2 per cent a year over the period 1965–70, and the rate of inflation, 7 per cent a year at that time. Nothing on population, raw materials, space, pollution, income distribution, or differential taxation.

As a fellow-socialist, I believe that the national cake should be equitably shared *whatever* its size. I think it escapist to post-pone the initiation of social and economic justice to some remote future period, and irresponsible in addition to avoid all reference to—let alone specification of—the point at which wealth would be sufficient to permit social justice, or of any progress to be made at intermediate states.

When Crosland wrote his pamphlet our GNP per head was $1,790, while in Kuwait it was $3,450. Would he expect twice as much social justice there? In the United States it was $3,980 a head, two and a quarter times ours. Could we expect to have eliminated poverty and exploitation if and when we reach that level? Have the Americans eliminated them? Would he expect about half the social justice in Eire at $980, and one quarter in Jamaica at $460? If not, why not? Some people think that poverty and injustice were long ago removed from Sweden, $2,620 per head in 1970, even from Denmark at $2,070 a year, about one sixth more than us.

Growth at 2 per cent a year, rather less than our recent per-formance, doubles our wealth every thirty-five years, which means an increase of 300 per cent between birth and death. At what point could we reasonably expect to attain social justice? After two lifespans and four doublings, our GNP per head would be over seven times greater than the present American figure: could we slow down or even stop growth at that point, or would we then need to continue for other reasons? It is hard to avoid the conclusion that above all things Crosland wants to avoid rocking the boat.

Two of the three 'Limits' goals seem to have been resound-ingly met—'to command critical attention and spark debate in all societies' and to 'encourage each reader to think through the consequences of continuing to equate growth with progress'. One of the team's most forceful critics, the Science Policy Research Unit at Sussex University, declares:

First . . . we are . . . in complete agreement with the MIT authors and their sponsors . . . that these . . . issues are urgent and of global concern. . . . Secondly . . . we agree that the social sciences can benefit from . . . computer model-building techniques and specifically from system dynamics. . . . Thirdly, we do not underestimate the positive importance of the MIT work as a courageous pioneering attempt.[9]

which the Meadows and their colleagues replied to in a postscript. Four things seem to emerge clearly from the controversy:
(1) That the world's socio-economic systems are of the utmost complexity and are accordingly interpreted and explained in such vastly different ways that no 'correct' or agreed analysis is possible at this stage.
(2) That notwithstanding (1) the earth is finite and it is impossible for population and/or consumption of material substances and energy to go on increasing indefinitely, or even for very long at present rates.
(3) That we ought to give a great deal more care, thought, and study to the way human societies interact with each other and their environment.
(4) Until we know more of the answers about raw materials, pollution, social possibilities, and other basic questions, we ought not to rush ahead quite so precipitately in the hope that a solution will be found to every one of our problems as it becomes critical. Most past civilisations have failed.

A third goal of the 'Limits' study has also very largely been met—the 'hope that it will lead thoughtful men and women in all fields of endeavour to consider the need for concerted action . . . to preserve the habitability of this planet'.

The Sussex critics agree that important changes in our way of doing things are necessary, and that the old carefree way of using up the fossil fuels must soon end, though 'it is difficult to see that real progress can be made except through a concerted *international* approach', one indication of the sort of radical change required. No fewer than six other academic teams across the world are already testing, criticising and developing the MIT model,[10] or working out new ones of their own, and many other bodies, including the World Bank and government departments, are analysing its assumptions, methodology, and findings.

Raw materials and energy

There do not as yet exist any final inventories of raw materials, partly because resources for the future may not be recognised as such, partly because some of those already recognised are hidden away and we haven't yet got the technology to find them (although survey satellites are now helping a lot), or because we haven't yet made the necessary effort. However there seems to be wide agreement that all the usable oil will be gone in less than a century and all the coal in less than a millennium; that atomic power stations could then supply our needs only with very high energy inputs for their construction, and at considerable risk from radio-active wastes. Even if fusion-energy comes along we shall soon run up against limits imposed by thermal pollution of the earth.

Weinberg and Hammond, the most optimistic of the experts, think the earth could sustain 10 thousand million people with an energy consumption per head double that of the present-day citizen of the United States before it heated up significantly ($\frac{1}{4}$°C).[11] This would give a human energy budget sixty times as great as the present one and a number of scientists think it much too high. Peter Chapman of the Open University thinks they have done their sums wrong and the effect will be three times greater than they allowed.[12] Another, Amory Lovins, has pointed out that 'without winds to disperse its manmade heat, Manhattan would fry', and argued that 'even a $\times 10$ jump from the present world average may be close to a reasonable thermal safety barrier.'[13] However, even if we reject these criticisms and accept the calculations of the optimists, there is a definite energy limit on the economic system, so that even if we could generate virtually indefinite amounts of energy more or less free, we could not permit ourselves to use it all.

There is still a thermal limit even if we use almost no energy for economic purposes. Professor Fremlin has calculated from elementary physical principles that if every difficulty of raw materials and manufacture can be overcome (including the abolition of all wild-life, of farming the whole of the sea, roofing in the oceans and completely covering the surface of the earth with a 2,000-storey block of flats—or, rather cubicles) the final limit to human expansion on earth would be reached in

600–800 years time when the heat generated by human bodies would be so great, even with the whole earth completely re-frigerated, that further growth would be *physically* impossible.[14]

We ought to work out all the possible physical limits to growth, and have the information at our fingertips. But, when we have, they will delineate for us only the boundaries beyond which we *cannot* go—they will tell us nothing whatever about how far we *ought* to go.

Let us now return to raw materials, and avoid the criticism of being too niggling about limitations to economic growth imposed by material shortages, by assuming that we can make anything out of anything. Fred Hoyle has pursued this train of thought to its logical conclusion.[15] Accepting the fact that we have filled up first the surface, then the interior of the earth with people, enabled them to live on pills and provided for all their other wants, he went on to say:

> At this stage, if not before, we must evidently leave the earth and undertake the job of populating the universe. . . . Again we can expect a new lease of life, but not for an indefinite time. . . . After a further six thousand years the mass of humanity will exceed the mass of the whole visible universe. . . . And here I refuse to follow the . . . optimists any further. Algae culture, yes; pill culture, yes; one person to the square yard, yes; refrigerate the earth, yes; populate the universe, yes; but exceed the universe, no.[16]

Many of the growth men accept that population will be controlled (some of them indeed, such as John Maddox, make the claim that to all intents and purposes it is controlled already), so they could attempt to wriggle out of Hoyle's cul de sac by saying numbers will soon cease to grow. However, if the mass of human flesh ceases to expand, the Hoyle argument still applies to the manufacturing through-put, and if growthmen try to talk their way out of this one by bringing in the idea of 'satura-tion'—i.e. that a limited world population simply couldn't get through more than a certain volume of raw materials, far short of the mass of the earth, let alone the universe—then they have ceased to be growthmen.

Saturation is itself a possible limit to growth which we can now tentatively explore.

The economic transition[17]

Virtually all the argumentation about growth, both pro and con, seems to take it for granted that if only resources and the economic system were inexhaustible there would be no problem, it is the finiteness of the world which creates our problems. The assumption is always made that man can absorb whatever wealth he can produce; but this also is false. If the optimists are right about resources we shall very rapidly come up against the limit imposed on the system by the wealth-absorbing capacity of individuals, rather than the limits imposed on the individual by the wealth-producing capacity of the system. We cannot all be millionaires unless we are very few in number and all goods and services are produced by machines.

Let us now return to the Beckerman argument. Beckerman claimed, as we have seen, that since economic growth has already gone on since 'the days of Pericles', there is no reason to suppose it cannot continue for another 2,500 years. Let us test this argument, first by looking at past economic growth to see how soundly it is based on historical evidence, and then look into the future and see how feasible millennia of further economic growth appear in the light of the evidence and of commonsense.

John Burnett's fascinating book, *A History of the Cost of Living*,[18] shows how difficult it is to compare prices and standards of living at very different historical periods, and hence to measure economic growth over time. But we can get a rough idea if we play the Beckerman record backwards, taking 1 per cent off each year to allow for the growth we have had already. We see in Table 16/2 that this fits reality very approximately for a few centuries and then tapers off into a never-never land, as it does in the 'future' table, to follow.

Five lifespans back, in 1620, the GNP per household would have been £1 7s 6d (£1·375) at 1970 values, probably a good deal less than the real value of the 6s a week the wage-earner actually got then. By 1270 it would be down to 10·3 old pence, almost exactly equal to the labourer's nominal wage; by Roman times it would be down to three ten thousandths of an old penny, and by the time of Pericles, Professor Beckerman's starting point, the income for the average household would be 1·5 ten millionths of one old penny.

Table 16/1

*Decrease in GNP per household at 1% a year over past
2,500 years. UK, 1970AD–550BC.*
(1970 prices)

Year AD/BC	No. of lifespans back	GNP per household per week.	Historical data
AD 1970		£44	
(−350)		÷32	
1620	5	£1 7 6	Average wage about 6/- a week.
(−350)		÷32	
1270	10	10.3d	Average labourers' wage about 1/- a week
(−350)		÷32	?
920	15	0·32d	?
(−350)		÷32	
570	20	0·01d	?
(−350)		÷32	
220	25	0·00031d	?
(−350)		÷32	
BC 130	30	0·00000975d	?
(−350)		÷32	
480	35	0·000000304d	?
(−70)		÷2	
550	36	0·000000152d	?

* Burnett (p. 71)
† Burnett (p. 10)

From this we see that even the modest sounding increase of
1 per cent a year in GNP per head has not gone on for very
long in past history and, by implication, cannot go on for very
long in the future. We are somewhere—probably near the
end—in what must be the very brief epoch in which economic
growth is the normal thing.

In his talk in the television programme 'Controversy'[19]
Beckerman extended his proposed 2,500 year growth period

to a million years; I want to explore the implications of this growth philosophy, taking the smaller of the two figures out of kindness. On neither occasion did he specify the rate of growth desired or possible, so I shall reject the 6 per cent a year of the TUC, the 5 per cent of the Government, (in 1973) the 2¼ per cent or so we have managed to average over the past few years, and take the extremely conservative figure of only 1 per cent a year.

At this rate the GNP doubles every lifespan (seventy years) so that on average we are twice as well off at death as at birth. In 1970 the GNP was £43 thousand million so that the average wealth per household (roughly 3 persons) was £2,310, and the GNP per person per week £14·77. To keep the figures more recognisably in focus I am going to take this a stage further and use the unorthodox concept of the GNP per person per working hour, assuming that everybody has a working year of 2000 hours (50 weeks × 40 hrs.). In 1970 this figure was 37 pence, and Table 16/2 shows how it would increase at 1 per cent a year compound, taking jumps of 350 years to simplify the presentation. (350 years equals five lifespans, giving five doublings, equal to a multiplier of 32). From this we see that after ten lifespans the family 'income' is over £45,000 a week or £379 per person per hour; after twenty lifespans it is over £46 millions a week; in thirty, over £47 millions a week; and after thirty-six lifespans—twenty years over Beckerman's deadline—it is £25 billions an hour for each person, over £3,000 billions a week for the household.

To put this in perspective, we can look at a small child's weekly pocket-money, allowing, say 0·5 per cent of the GNP per head, 7½ new pence in 1970 (1s 6d in old money.) At the same rate in 4490 the child would toddle down to the tuck-shop every week with a £5 billion pound note clutched in its fist. If we assume that by that time—the average salary still being about three-quarters of the GNP per household—the standard rate of income tax is 99·9 pence in the pound, we shall be left with £57 million a week take-home pay, and it will be necessary to work for only one and a half hours to earn a couple of millions or so to retire on.

It is obviously absurd to expect the average income in real

Table 16/2

Increase in GNP per working hour at 1% a year over 2,500 years. UK, 1970–4490 AD

(1970 prices)

Year AD	No. of lifespans ahead	GNP per household per week	GNP per person per 'working' hour
1970		£44	£0·37
(+350)		(×32)	(×32)
2320	5	£1,420	£11·83
(+350)		(×32)	(×32)
2670	10	£45,400	£379
(+350)		(×32)	(×32)
3020	15	£1·45m.	£12,100
(+350)		(×32)	(×32)
3370	20	£46·4m.	£388,000
(+350)		(×32)	(×32)
3720	25	£1·484b.	£12·4m.
(+350)		(×32)	(×32)
4070	30	£47·5b.	£397m.
(+350)		(×32)	(×32)
4420	35	£1,520b.	£12·7b.
(+70)		(×2)	(×2)
4490	36	£3,040b.	£25·4b.

terms to get anywhere near the higher levels just explored, and this presents a problem of both practicality and morality—where might and where should the line be drawn? A useful yardstick might be the level of consumption typical of the present-day millionaire. People might be satisfied with his standard of living at, say, £100,000 a year. This is fifty-five times the amount the average adult wage earner got in 1973, but a growth rate of only 1 per cent a year—giving an income doubling once every lifespan (seventy years)—would enable this goal to be reached in only six lifespans.

Figure 16/2 shows the time taken to hit the millionaire barrier at differing annual growth rates, making it obvious that from the perspective of a historian at any rate greater than

Figure 16/2. Number of lifespans required to reach the millionaire
barrier at different growth rates, UK from 1973

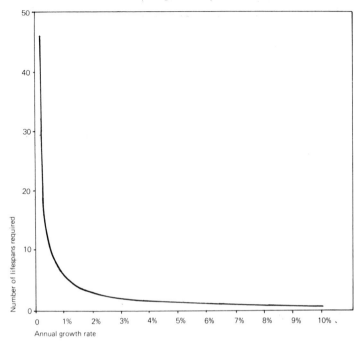

about a half of 1 per cent per annum the whole process must be
over in a flash. Of course the millionaire barrier is an arbitrary
concept, but the mechanics of exponential growth are such
that it makes little difference what barrier or saturation level
is postulated, or what rate of growth.

At the time of writing this part of the book, the UK growth
rate was announced—with fanfares—to be 5 per cent a year
(some euphoric commentators thought we may have been
'booming' along at 6 per cent) and, as many hoped at the time
that we could keep it up, we ought to take a brief look at what
it would mean in practice. The average take-home pay in
1973 was about £35 a week and at the lower figure of 5 per cent
a year increase this doubles every 14·2 years, giving five
doublings (equivalent to multiplying by 32) per lifespan of
seventy-one years. This means that one lifespan later the

237

average take-home pay would be just over £58,000 a year and that the millionaire's standard of living would be reached in less than one more doubling, by 2055, eighty years from 1975, when many tens of thousands then born will still be alive and well.

After one more lifespan at this rate, pay before tax would be £2 million a year, so that the average worker would be a millionaire after only six months. Could this be a reasonable goal of the trade unions, the parties, or the Government?

Man cannot live by bread alone
Virtually all discussion of economic growth and its possible limits takes place in strictly material terms: how much of raw material x is there, how fast are we using it up, how essential is it, with what can it be replaced when it is all gone, and so on? These questions are of great importance. But there are other and perhaps even more fundamental questions, concerning the quality of life.

Johan Huizinga argued in his book *Homo Ludens*[20] that man is above all things a creature of play (although he includes such things as mathematics under this heading) and that play generates most of our culture. The essence of play is freedom from restraint and this is especially important for play as it is most commonly understood: the enjoyment of recreation. The Russians have a word for this, 'otpusk', which means 'letting go', and it is just this which is becoming difficult.

Anthony Barber said at the Conservative Women's Conference in 1971: 'Without prosperity there is a limit to the time that the beauty of our countryside can withstand the pressure of a growing population.'[21] He didn't actually spell out the converse case that with prosperity there is *no* limit to the time that . . . but the implication was strong enough to hint at the fantasy world in which many of these speeches and policies are dreamed up. Pressure on resources is a reflection of demand, and demand is a function of numbers and individual spending power. A large population living in poverty would not be able to afford much mobility, let alone holidays, and therefore would not strain our communications system or recreational facilities, while a much smaller, wealthier and more leisured society could overtax them. A population increasing in size *and* prosperity doubly taxes them.

John Maddox is one of many who argue that we should use the price mechanism to regulate the use of scarce amenities: 'Is it not preferable to enjoy the . . . benefits of the invention of the motor car but to regulate the crowding of the beaches by other means?' We must 'decide what amenities are needed and then pay the cost of them either in taxes or higher prices.' Where 'visits . . . are restricted or . . . rationed it is . . . a powerful incentive to increase the acreage of national parks.'[22]

Needless to say, Maddox doesn't tell us where all the extra space is to come from, but this is in passing; the central point is that we are creating scarcity where none existed before— creating economic 'goods' out of non-goods and then working harder to enable us to pay more and more for less and less of what we used to enjoy free.

It is perfectly understandable and acceptable for a society in poverty to put considerable stress on economic growth, meaning by that attempts to produce and distribute enough wealth to remove hunger and deprivation. It is quite another when the sole aim of one (if not all) of the wealthiest countries in the world is to increase that wealth without limit into the future.

Societies need goals and some of these, such as independence and democracy, signify health. Others, such as racialism and militarism, indicate sickness. It does not follow that when a society has produced enough wealth to abolish poverty then extra growth should be absolutely taboo. Within reason, further economic growth arising spontaneously out of the pursuit of higher aims—such as a more just and neighbourly society, better health, a more sophisticated scientific understanding, higher educational standards, lasting peace, and so on—seems quite unexceptionable. However, when all or most of these higher goals are relegated to some remote future realm while, in the indefinitely protracted interim, as in Crosland-type socialism, the mind and sinews of the nation are bent to the task of raising the pile of loot ever higher, then something has gone badly wrong. There has been a 'displacement' of goals from a worthy means to an unworthy end. In people with an

239

already comfortable way of life it is a sign of actual or impending moral bankruptcy to be preoccupied with the quest for more money to get more material things.

Even if none of the previous objections or limitations were valid, if ever-increasing wealth is a healthy goal and there were no material limits to its pursuit there is yet another obstacle to its realisation, and this is that rapidly increasing wealth means rapid social change and change which is too great or too rapid is upsetting for many people. Increasing personal wealth is by no means an unmixed blessing and it can be argued that too much prosperity can be unsettling to a pathological degree. In his great work *Suicide*, Durkheim argued:

> If therefore industrial and financial crises increase suicides, this is not because they cause poverty, since crises of prosperity have the same result; it is because they are crises, that is disturbances of the collective order. Every disturbance of equilibrium, even though it achieves great comfort and a heightening of general vitality, is an impulse to voluntary death.

It is perhaps for reasons such as these that many people in our society now reject material prosperity as their life goal—the 'drop-outs' obviously, but many others who refuse overtime, piecework, promotion and ambition in order to live a quiet life—but in general we seem to have set ourselves an infinite goal, an ever-increasing standard of life for an ever-increasing number of people.

Durkheim raises another difficult question:

> How to determine the quantity of well-being, comfort, or luxury legitimately to be craved by a human being? Nothing appears in man's organic or psychological constitution which sets a limit to such tendencies. . . . Our capacity for feeling is an insatiable and bottomless abyss and if nothing external restrains this capacity it can only be a source of torment. . . . Unlimited desires are insatiable by definition and insatiability is rightly considered a sign of morbidity. . . .

All man's pleasure in acting, moving and exerting himself implies the sense that his efforts are not in vain and that by walking

240

he had advanced. However, *one does not advance when one walks towards no goal, or—which is the same thing—when one's goal is infinity.* (Italics added.)

We see from this that not only is it inevitable that economic growth must stop fairly soon but is it *desirable* that it should stop, or at least slow down a good deal, for most of those who are not in poverty.

There are other potential constraints on economic growth, or at least upon our enjoyment of its alleged fruits. Ivan Illich has argued in *Energy and Equity* (1974) that increments over and above a certain critical level of income both increase inequality and decrease individual liberty: 'Beyond a certain level of GNP, the cost of social control must rise faster than total output and become the major institutional activity within an economy. . . . Increased affluence requires increased control.'

It seems that we can be slaves to wealth in more senses than one.

The economic transition

Chapter 9 was about the demographic transition. I now want to raise the concept of the economic transition, something no less basic or inevitable, the transition from economic steady-state I to economic steady-state II.

Taking the fairly conservative figure of 100,000 years for true man's existence, and assuming that significant economic growth began with the invention of agriculture 10,000 years ago, a simple calculation shows that he has been in an economic steady-state for 90 per cent of his existence. In fact economic growth was almost negligible until less than 500 years ago, so that it has gone on, in any significant way, for only $\frac{1}{2}$ per cent of our time on earth. Man really is, and has to remain, an economic steady-state animal.

Figure 16/3 shows the essence of the form which the economic transition must take and an actual value it could conceivably have as it flattens out in steady-state II. Even taking the short base-line of 20,000 years—10,000 BC to AD 10,000—and a growth rate of only 2 per cent a year (far less than the 5 per cent

Figure 16/3. The economic transition. Steady-state I to steady-state II at 2% a year, 'UK' 1300 BC–AD 2250

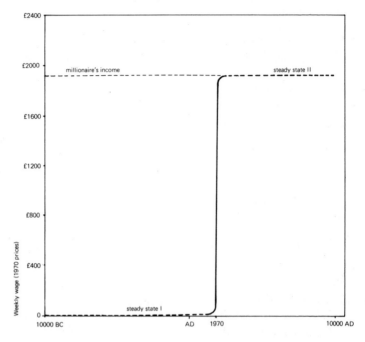

Government, the pundits, and the TUC wanted and less even than we have managed to average over the postwar years, up to the oil crisis), economic growth can continue for only four more lifespans. By 2250 it must have stopped, unless we can find ways of generating the torrent of goods and services demanded by a population of multi-millionaires, without anyone having to work, or persuade people to keep on working as they do now, however multi-multi-multi-millionaire they become.

Even India, starting from a GNP per head of $100 US in 1970 and normally thought of as a poverty-stricken country, would soon be suffering from an *embarras de richesses*. At 2 per cent a year increase, the GNP per household per year would exceed $1 million in less than six lifespans.

Conclusion

The evidence is conclusive that substantial economic growth has not been the normal state of affairs in human societies in the past and cannot be in the future. Mankind is engaged in a highly untypical scramble from steady-state I to steady-state II (in the absence of calamities), and the sooner we recognise this and develop a value system and appropriate behaviour patterns conducive to stability the better off we shall be.

Britain has in the past pioneered many useful moral values and social institutions, such as parliamentary government, religious tolerance, an abhorrence of slavery, and so forth, and we are well placed to calm the world's jagged economic nerves and gently lead the way into the next steady-state. The 'English Disease' which our Continental friends often point to, more in sorrow than in anger, our reluctance to scramble for profit and production with an ever more frenetic intensity, could in fact be the first stirrings of a new awareness, a loosening of the bonds of slavery to outdated economic shibboleths, the precursors of a new calmness and sanity.

Part V

CONCLUSIONS

CHAPTER 17

Summary and reflections

I have examined the main arguments used to justify ever-increasing population and/or economic growth, and tried to show that every one is fallacious in whole or in part, either logically or factually or both, and that even if they were all wholly true they could not justify ever-increasing numbers or consumption. The underlying fallacy is 'parochialism', or the short-term thinking that takes account of here and now but refuses to recognise the ultimate finiteness of the Earth.

I have argued that population growth is one of the greatest threats to individual liberty and that, paradoxically, beyond a certain point in growth population control is necessary in order to preserve liberty. If liberty resides in part in the expression of the will of the people, then the parties and the government should respect the overwhelming wave of public opinion in favour of recognition of the problem and the adoption of appropriate measures to deal with it.

'Commonsense' fallacies

In the section on 'commonsense' fallacies, I started with statistics and argued that these are essential to our large-scale and complicated societies, especially in the field of demography where the statistical evidence tends to be full and good, and that using the admitted weaknesses of statistics to discredit the whole edifice is irrational, self-indulgent and destructive.

The same is true of arguments rejecting our capacity to foretell the future. We are all aware that no one can do this with certainty, but on the whole the universe is a regular sort of place and we all understand the basic patterns well enough to regulate our personal lives and futures with some confidence. What we have to deal with in all walks of life is trends and probabilities, rather than certitude, and population is no exception.

245

My brief excursion into the military field was to show that population is only one of the factors in national power and that our security depends on internationalism, mutual aid and guarantees rather than on nationalism. Indeed, population pressure is one of the causes of militarism, violence, revolution and war.

With respect to the fallacy of migration I argued that this can of course help locally and in the short run, but, as a long-term measure, either on the earth or out into space, it is useless as a solution for the population problem. It would in any case raise insuperable problems of logistics, international politics, and morality.

On the benefits of the large family argument, while I agreed that there are a few things to be said for it from both individual and social points of view, the overwhelming mass of evidence is against. In height, weight, health, intelligence, academic success and virtually every other measurable sphere, the children of large families suffer.

'Scientific' fallacies

I don't think the 'scientific' fallacies are any more scientific than the 'commonsense' fallacies are commonsensical, but at least they sound rather technical. With respect to the growth-curve, I showed that though all populations tend to follow the S curve, this doesn't help us because in the absence of instinctive population control mechanisms of the kind to be found in most birds the 'natural' control process is onerous and unacceptable. There are only four reasonably possible outcomes for a human population explosion: a flattening of the growth-curve by means of 'spontaneous', 'social', 'biological', or 'physical' controls. If the spontaneous control should be the effective one, there is no guarantee that the outcome is an optimum population—though this would rarely be a serious matter in the short run. In any case, it is already much too late in Britain and we should opt for the social control curve. If we do, we can choose between a wide range of life-qualities and ought to do this by means of democratic decision-making processes, as well-informed and widespread as we know how to make them.

I dismissed the 'fallacy of the unattainable optimum' and recapitulated my concept of the 'quasi-optimum', a population size which is reasonably acceptable to a democratic society . . . etc., which could and probably must be defined and redefined as long as the species lasts.

On the demographic transition, I argued that, though it represents reality to an important degree, it is a rather loose concept based upon an almost non-existent theory, bandied around by people who have virtually no idea of population dynamics. Finally, if we do the appropriate sums we find that the demographic transition often takes a society from low population growth at high birth and death rates to high growth at low birth and death rates.

Economic fallacies

This section was split into two main parts, the first dealing with the economic 'macrofallacy', that economic growth depends on population growth. I showed the flaws in the arguments used by apologists and quoted evidence to show that, though the relations between population, technology, wealth, and culture are so complex that we may never sort them out, there is good evidence for the belief that too fast or too great a population growth hinders development, rather than encourages it, by increasing the burden of dependency and the demographic investment.

Looking at the three economic 'microfallacies', the 'labour-shortage', the 'burden of dependency', and 'economies of scale', I showed that the first two are almost complete nonsense from beginning to end and that, although the third argument is valid up to a point, scale of production is subject to the law of *decreasing* returns beyond the optimum size. However, once again, if all were wholly valid at all times we still have to learn to do with stationary populations sooner or later because of the finiteness of the earth.

Two more economic microfallacies are much weightier and were dealt with at greater length. The increasing production argument was stood on its head to show that, marvellous though increases in productivity have been, and fantastic though future developments may yet be, the sad fact is that

247

the scientific and industrial revolution has produced ever-increasing numbers of human beings suffering hunger and deprivation. Until numbers are controlled there seems no possibility of ever catching up.

Finally, I showed that there are definite physical limits to growth even if we develop a technology capable of making anything from anything, plus an infinite source of energy; and that the goal of indefinite economic growth is in any case a sign of social morbidity which tends to be coupled with individual psychological problems. An infinite goal is not a goal at all, and we must suffer the pangs of unrequitable ambition.

However, my main point here is that growthmen and environmentalists alike have got it wrong in assuming that the only limits are environmental constraints, actual or possible. These *may* limit growth, but if they don't do it in the very near future we shall come up against the limits of individual consumption. This led me to put forward the idea of the 'economic transition' which rests on the facts that for around 99 per cent of his existence man has been a steady-state animal, and that at 2 per cent a year economic growth—far less than the target we tend to set and less even than we have managed to achieve in recent years—the average wage and salary earner would be living at the millionaire's level in real terms in only four life-spans. The economic transition to steady-state II which should last (barring calamities) as long as the species, will have taken less than the time separating us from the Norman Conquest.

This demonstrates that the economic explosion is as 'un-natural' and temporary a phenomenon as the population explosion, and that we must spend the future, as we spent our past, in a steady-state with regard to quantity if not quality. Can we not, with profit, bend to the environmentalist's cause one of the less respectable aphorisms attributed to Confucius? 'Economic steady-state inevitable: Relax and enjoy!'

John Stuart Mill put forward what is still the best analysis of the obsession for growth as early as 1848:

> Towards what ultimate point is society tending by its industrial progress? When the programme ceases, in what condition . . . will it leave mankind . . . ? The increase of wealth is not boundless,

248

at the end of the progressive state lies the stationary state . . . and I am inclined to believe that it would be, on the whole a very considerable improvement on our present condition.

For the benefit of those who would describe this as a 'stagnant' society, with the implication that as few people want to live in one of these as want to bathe in a stagnant pool, Mill adds:

> It is scarcely necessary to remark that a stationary condition of capital and population implies no stationary state of human improvement. There would be as much scope as ever for all kinds of mental culture, and moral and social progress; as much room for improving the art of living, and much more' likelihood of its being improved, when minds ceased to be engrossed by the art of getting on.[1]

This surely should be the environmentalist's charter for the future. Somehow we have to develop a new ethic—or possibly return to the ethic of an earlier age—one recognising and stressing our absolute dependence on nature's bounty and our total incapacity to function above or outside the basic environmental mechanisms. Our quaint idea that modern science and technology can override these fundamental physical and biochemical chains was portrayed for what it is as early as the seventeenth century by the philosopher and pioneer of scientific method, Francis Bacon, in his aphorism: 'Man may command nature, but only by obeying her.'

As Lynn White[2] has argued, Christianity has played a big part in persuading us to adopt the sledgehammer approach to nature, at least in breaking down the earlier barriers in 'primitive' animalistic or pantheistic religions where every tree, plant, and stone, had its spirit or godly component which had to be respected before any environmental change could be wrought. Christianity took God out of things and made him transcendent, connecting with nature only sporadically by means of revelation, and leaving behind a despiritualised environment ripe for unlimited exploitation; bulldozers now rampage through the sacred groves.

Several attempts have been made to indicate a way towards a new morality, for instance Aldo Leopold has talked of a 'land

249

ethic', reflecting an 'ecological conscience', and even so hard-headed and unromantic a source as Soviet science has produced the concept of 'geohygiene'— the hygiene of the earth. The ecologist E. P. Odum[3] has tabulated the emphases in young and mature ecosystems as follows:

Young Ecosystem	Mature Ecosystem
Emphasis on:	Emphasis on:
Production	Protection
Growth	Stability
Quantity	Quality

In moving away from our obsession with material progress we shall find that we are creating something of a void in our hitherto crowded and hectic lives and Lewis Mumford has argued that we must try to change the emphasis from *homo faber*—man the maker of things—to *homo ludens*, playful man, the creature which develops its rich psychological, social, moral and spiritual potential and lives life to the full.

Postscript

On the food front the situation looks even bleaker, if that is possible, than it is painted in Chapter 15. The preparatory papers published by the UN for the World Food and World Population conferences show that food stocks are down to danger-ously low levels. The world reserve of cereals for instance, is down to a two-week supply, food prices are rocketing, both fertilisers and the energy required to make them are in short supply, so that their prices are rising very rapidly, and drastic efforts to increase production to meet the widening population food gap are causing so much environmental damage that food production in some critical regions is going down rather than up. One UN paper[4] has a whole chapter entitled 'Ecological Undermining of the World Food Economy' from which one example from the Sahel must suffice to show the nature and severity of the problem.

> Over the past 35 years, human and livestock populations along the sub-Saharan fringe have . . . in some areas nearly doubled. . . . The result is over-grazing, deforestation, and overall denudation of the land. As a result . . . the Sahara desert . . . is moving

southward at up to 30 miles per year . . . [and] human and live-stock populations retreat before it. The result is ever-greater pressure on the fringe area which in turn contributes to the de-nudation and deforestation, settting in process a self-reinforcing cycle. Failure to . . . alleviate the causes . . . means the Sahara may engulf much of central Africa in a matter of years, destroying a significant slice of the continents' food producing capacity.

It now seems virtually certain that massive famines will occur, and that the West must tighten its belt and get used to the idea of eating less, eating more simply, and paying more for it, in order that the world's increasing burden may be shared more equitably. 80 per cent of the annual increase in demand for food is caused by population increase, as we have seen, and a sad reflection on the preparation for the World Food Con-ference is that nowhere is there the slightest hint that numbers must be controlled. This issue is not even discussed, all the emphasis being on technological and economic 'fixes', which, by themselves, are bound to fail.

Finally, a word about the belief, which seems to be gaining a certain currency, that the continuing fall in the UK birth rate has somehow dished the population controllers, among whose ranks I wish to be counted. The first point to note here is that the views of those concerned about overpopulation in the world as a whole, and in Britain in particular, have gained a very wide acceptance over the past few years and undoubtedly now influence the behaviour of both governments and a minority at least of parents and potential parents. I have among my own acquaintances a number of individuals and couples who have refrained from reproducing themselves on grounds of conscience, at least in part, and/or rational self-interest vis-à-vis an overcrowded world. I know other couples who like children very much and want a large family who have switched from reproduction to adoption after having two or three children of their own.

A more fundamental point, however, concerns the wide-spread fallacy which rests on the identification of population control with the reduction of fertility *only*. In fact advocates of population control are concerned not only with the possibility of overtaxing environmental carrying capacity but with the quality of life as a whole. They wish not just to reduce births but to *balance* births against deaths, and numbers against resources. They would be just as concerned if numbers looked like declining towards too low a level—let alone extinction—as they are now with overpopulation. Measures to increase an undesirably low birth rate would be accepted on comparable grounds and just as readily as those advocated for dealing with the undesirably high birth-rates of the present time.

As I write my last few words it seems that we are in for a hard time, economically, socially, and politically. We are overcrowded, facing the energy shortage, inflation at a rate of 20 or 30 per cent a year, and what might amount to the beginnings of large cracks in the social structure. By the time this book appears my discussion of the economic transition may seem like ancient history. We are faced by so many imponderables that it is impossible to forecast even the immediate future with any confidence, but the possibility of a substantial decline in our living standards is obviously being taken seriously in a number of official and semi-official quarters. Sir William Haley, a former Director General of the BBC, has warned in a recent book that economic pressures may soon lead to a serious threat to the freedom of speech: 'The graver the situation becomes, the more persuasively will journalists be told that to reveal the whole truth will be dangerous'.[5]

Brigadier F. Kitson has gone further. As early as 1971 he published a book in which he argued that there is a danger of a fall in living standards so great that the ensuing civil unrest would be on a scale well beyond the capacity of the civil authorities to control; the Army must be ready and prepared to take over this function.[6]

It is greatly to be hoped that things never get to this pass, but if they do we must strive to re-establish an order based upon a realistic appraisal of the carrying capacity of our environment, good sense, and good values. If the great slump does come, the rallying cries could easily be: 'Back to economic growth!' and 'Larger populations mean more manpower and bigger markets!' Surely they ought to be based on attempts to steer us towards a quieter, saner, juster, more neighbourly, and more permanently viable way of life.

252

NOTES

Chapter 1

1. The Hague, June 1970.
2. 1968.
3. Scarborough, 1970.
4. Quoted Duggan, M. 'Birth Under Control', *Church Times*, 9th October 1970.
5. Testifying before the Parliamentary Select Committee. Population Report (1971) (p. 246).
6. The central theme of my earlier book, *Population Versus Liberty* (1971)
7. With two notable exceptions—The Conservation Society, and Friends of the Earth.
8. (a) (1972) *Population—The Liberals Reply* (pamphlet) Liberal Party Office;
   (b) 'Population Control, some facts and assumptions', in Holmes, N. J. (ed.) (1976) *Environment and the Industrial Society* (EUP).
9. Musson, C. (1972) *Population Survey* (Limited printing).
10. January 1973: For a brief summary see *New Society*, 18 January, 1973.
11. (1973) *Report of the Population Panel.*
12. (1971) *First Report from the Select Committee on Science and Technology. Population of the United Kingdom.*
13. There has been a small but significant step forward since these words were written. Addressing the World Population Conference at Bucharest in August 1974, Lord Shepherd, the Minister for Population, said of our falling birth rate that '. . . in so far as it represents an approach towards a stable population, we welcome it'.

Chapter 2

1. The lowest death rates are found in the poorer countries because it is there that medicine is having its greatest impact.
2. This is discussed in relation to the 'burden of dependency' in chapter 12.

253

3. The workings of the 'population flywheel', as it is sometimes called, are discussed in chapter 4, and in my chapter *op. cit.*, in Holmes, N. J. (ed.).

4. On paper there has been no increase because the official figures then were a little too high, 391,000 for England and Wales, as the 1971 Census showed.

5. I am indebted to the Office of Population Censuses and Surveys for the combined male/female death rate and some other figures in the table.

6. The death-rate is determined by life expectancy and, as this changes, so the level of the horizontal line in the graph would change. The method for calculating this is simple. Divide 1,000 by the average life-expectancy at birth to obtain the number of deaths per 1,000 per year. For a stationary population the birth rate must match this precisely (given zero migration, that is).

7. The Population Stabilisation Group has pointed to the probable connection between the arrival of the post-war bulge on the housing market and the unprecedented surge in prices. See their pamphlet, *Overpopulation, It's Costing Us the Earth* (1973).

8. 10 November 1973. Catholic Information Office of England and Wales.

Chapter 3

1. 20 July 1967.
2. (1961) *Mater et Magistra* (para. 188).
3. Quoted in Halbwachs, M. (1960) *Population and Society*.
4. (1865) *Alice's Adventures in Wonderland*.
5. HMSO (annual) *Planning Applications*.
6. Hansard, 1 July 1964, Col. 655ff.
7. BBC Radio 4, 7.30 p.m. 8 February 1972. (Figure kindly verified by the BBC Tapes and Transcription Unit.)
8. 1971 Census figures. See further details on immigration in chapter 11.
9. 'The Last Penalty'—leading article, 16 February 1956.
10. 'Still Time to Think Again on Hanging', *Sunday Telegraph* 3 January 1965.
11. Speaking at Rome, reported in the *Guardian*, 18 September 1969. The original passage went as follows:
'. . . Ci consola sapere che queste anime non hanno statistiche burocratiche . . .', *L'Osservatore Romano*, 18 September 1969.

This was translated as '. . . no screaming statistics. . . .' (sic) in the official English edition, 25 September 1969.

13. 'The Use and Abuse of Economic Statistics', in Marlow, B. (1968) *Charting the British Economy.*

Chapter 4

1. Letter to a Member of the National Assembly.
2. Burnt Norton, *Four Quartets.*
3. Reported by Dr. S. Bhagavantam, Scientific Adviser to the Indian Defence Ministry, to a conference of technologists, Madras, July 1969.
4. (a) Paddock and Paddock (1967) *Famine 1975! America's Decision: Who Will Survive?*
   (b) Borgstrom, G. (i) (1967) *The Hungry Planet,* and (ii) (1969) *Too Many: A Story of Earth's Biological Limitations.*
   (c) For a contrary view see Clark C. C. 'Too Much Food?', *Lloyds Bank Review,* January 1970.
5. 'Biological Backlash'—A series of three programmes by Gerald Leach, BBC, 7, 15 and 22 March 1967.
6. For a brief summary with diagrams see: *Population Versus Liberty,* ch. 11.
7. *Problems of the Human Environment* May 26, 1969.
8. *Op. cit.,*
9. See Johnson, C. G. (ed.) (1965) *The Biological Significance of Climatic Changes in Britain.*
10. For a very interesting fictional account by a distinguished scientist of an earth with disturbed temperature mechanisms read Hoyle, F. (1957), *The Black Cloud.* For another account see: Ballard, J. G. (1962) *The Drowned World.*
11. See, for example (1950–1972) *Worlds in Collision.*
12. Hansard July 7 1964, col. 655ff.
13. Thompson and Lewis (1965) *Population Problems* (p. 249).
14. (1971) HMSO. *Family Intentions* (chapter 6).
15. See Annual Report, 1971. For another study see Keyfitz, N. 'On the momentum of population growth', *Demography,* 8 (1971).
16. HMSO (1972) *Population Projections 1970–2010* (p. 1).

Chapter 5

1. (1966) *Population* (page 222).
2. As quoted in Inge, W. R. (1949) *The End of an Age* (page 242).
3. (1957) 'Of the True Greatness of Kingdoms and Estates'.

4. Wolf, E. R. 'On Peasant Rebellions' in Shanin, T. (ed.) (1971), *Peasants and Peasant Societies*.

Chapter 6
1. (1798) *Essay on the Principle of Population*, Vol. 2, p. 36.
2. *Nature, 181*, pages 1235–1236, 1965.
3. *New Statesman*, 14 May 1965.
4. Cumberland Lodge, Windsor, 19 January 1968.
5. (1970) *Population, Resources, Environment* (page 52).

Chapter 7
1. See p. 77 for details.
2. (1971) *Love Without Fear*.
3. 'Is Britain being threatened by overpopulation?' *The Listener*, 27 July 1967.
4. See *Population Versus Liberty*. Table 4/11 for a more detailed breakdown based on the 1961 census.
5. Details in *Population Versus Liberty* (page 335ff).
6. 'My Answer to Genocide', *Ebony*, October 1971.
7. Wedge, P. et. al. 'Weighing Children', *New Society*, 1 June 1972; cf. 'Health and Height in Children', *New Society*, 10 November 1970.
8. Based on McMahon, et. al. (1960) *Epidemiologic Methods*.
9. *New Statesman*, 20 May 1966.
10. Douglas and Blomfield (1958) *Children Under Five*.
11. McMahon, et. al. (1960) *Epidemiologic Methods* (p. 191).
12. OHE (1967) *Malnutrition in the 1960s*.
13. IPPF *Medical Bulletin* Vol. 2. Bo. 5, December 1968.
14. MacMahon, et. al. (1960) op. cit.
15. (1967) *Population Growth and Land Use* (p. 249).
16. (1957) *Essays on the Welfare State*.
17. (1959) *Social Science and Social Pathology*.
18. Private communication from W. R. McGregor, Principal Probation Officer, Dumbartonshire, 11 July 1969.

Chapter 8
1. BBC Home Service, 20 September 1965 (transcript kindly supplied by the BBC).
2. For those with mathematical leanings it expresses the equation
$$y = \frac{K}{(1 + e^{a+bx})}$$
Where y = population, x = time, and a, b, and K are constants.

3. (1928) *Contemporary Sociological Theories* (p. 376ff).
4. Wynne-Edwards, V.C (1962) *Animal Dispersion in Relation to Social Behaviour.*
5. Pearl, R. and Reed, L. J. (1920) *Proc. Natl. Acad. Sci.*, Vol. 6. Reported by Lotka, A. J. (1956) op. cit. (pp. 66-8).
6. Deevey, E. S. 'The Human Population', *Sc. Amer.* September 1960.
7. 'Land and Human Population', *The Listener*, 1 September 1966. Given a sufficiently rigorous policy and severe constraints on our diet, we could probably become self-sufficient in food even at the present level of population.
8. Is Britain being threatened by overpopulation? *The Listener*, 27 July 1967.
9. (1971) (para. 903). See my discussion in *Population Versus Liberty*.
10. (1973) (para. 33). *Report of the Population Panel.*
11. (1973) *Population policy: a modern delusion* (p. 12).
12. *Population Versus Liberty.* Appendix B.

Chapter 9

1. (1972) *The Closing Circle* (pp. 237 and 242).
2. John Maddox has boasted that he wrote *The Doomsday Syndrome* in three weeks.
3. (1949) *Human Society* (p. 600).
4. Duverger, M. (1966) *The Idea of Politics* (p. 35).
5. (1965) *Family Design: Marital Sexuality, Family Size and Contraception.*
6. Thomlinson, R. (1965) *Population Dynamics* (p. 18).
7. (1964) *The Politics of Population* (p. 166).
8. (1961) *The Human Species*, (p. 322). Barnett did not provide a diagram to illustrate his model, and we should note the italicised passages about 'approximate stability'.
9. Out of This Week. BBC 4, 25 July 1969.
10. (1955) (pp. 9-10).
11. (1955) op. cit.
12. (1964) op. cit. (p. 166ff).
13. 'The Problem', Chapter in Hutchinson, Sir J. (1969) *Population and Food Supply* (p. 6). Even the two sensible commentators, Peel and Potts, fall into the same trap in (1969) *Contraceptive Practice* (p. 19).
14. UN Preparatory Committee of the World Food Conference (April 1974). *Preliminary Assessment of the World Food Situation, Present and Future* (p. 49).

Chapter 10

1. (1897) *Progress and Poverty* (p. 141).
2. (1690) *Political Arithmetick*.
3. (9th impression 1970).
4. (Second edition 1971).
5. (1966).
6. Hoselitz, B. F. (1960) *Sociological Aspects of Economic Growth*.
7. Chapter in O'Brien, B. W., et al. (1951) *Readings in General Sociology* (p. 69).
8. From the *Monthly Labour Review*, December 1949.
9. (1966) *Invention and Economic Growth* (p. 196).
10. (1934) *Technics and Civilisation* (p. 53).
11. (1970).
12. (1974) *Technics and Civilisation*.
13. Op. cit., (p. 137).
14. Department of the Environment (1974). Production and Resources of Oil and Gas in the UK.
15. (1966) 'Population, Education and Economic Development'. One of several papers presented to the 11th Pacific Science Congress by members of the staff of the Institute of Population Problems, Ministry of Health and Welfare, Tokyo.
16. (1926) *Religion and the Rise of Capitalism* (pp. 210–211); the quotation within the quotation is from William Petty (1690) *Political Arithmetick*.
17. (1920) *History of Economic Thought* (p. 48).
18. (1961) *The Achieving Society* (p. 61).
19. (1945) *Mainsprings of Civilisation* (p. 204).
20. Op. cit., (p. 451).
21. (1945) op. cit., (p. 451).
22. Op. cit., (pp. 451–2).
23. (1962) *An Economic and Social History of Britain*, 1066–1939.
24. PEP (1955) *World Population and Resources* (pp. 171–2).
25. (1950) Department of External Affairs. *Irish Economic Development Since 1921*.
26. (1921) *Industrial and Commercial Revolutions in Great-Britain during the 19th Century* (p. 26).
27. (1968) *The Making of the English Working Class*. (p. 355–6).
28. See Thirlwell, A. P. 'The development "gap" ', *Nat. Westminster Bank Rev.* February 1970.
29. (1961) *Fertility and Survival* (p. 94ff)
30. See *Population Versus Liberty* for documentation (p. 112ff).
31. (1597) Essay XV. 'Of Seditions and Troubles'.

32. BBC Third Programme, 10 March 1969 (text kindly supplied by World Bank).
33. Quoted in 'People First' (British Humanist Association 1972) p.l.
34. (1957) *Social and Cultural Dynamics* (p. 636).
35. Toynbee, A. (1972) *A Study of History* (p. 86).
36. Spencer, H. (1893) *Principles of Sociology*, Volume III (Third Edition, p. 599).
37. Sorokin, P. (1928) *Contemporary Sociological Theories* (p. 408).

Chapter 11

1. (1947) *The Case For Conservatism* (p. 141).
2. Cmnd 7046 (1947) HMSO.
3. 'Is Britain being threatened by overpopulation?' *The Listener*, 27 July 1967.
4. Letter to Sir David Renton, one of a series of exchanges on Britain's population problems. Published by Sir David in pamphlet form (1967).
5. (1971) *Population of the United Kingdom* (HMSO para. 248).
6. Small, A. W. (1969) *The Cameralists: The Pioneers of German Social Policy.*
7. (1948) *The Ancient World* (pp. 323–4).
8. (1966) *The Agricultural Revolution 1750–1880.*
9. See Coulton, C. G. (1938) *Social Life in Britain From The Conquest to the Reformation* (p. 350ff).
10. 'The Use and Abuse of Economic Statistics'. Chapter in Marlow, B. (1968) *Charting the British Economy*, (pp. 11/12).
11. See Jones, K. and Smith, A. D. (1970) *The Economic Impact of Commonwealth Immigration.* The figure of 853,000 from the New Commonwealth includes a substantial number (possibly over 80,000) of European parentage. See Chapter 3 for 1971 Census figures.
12. (1962) *Economic Philosophy* (p. 102).
13. (1969) *Reformation to Industrial Revolution* (p. 257).
14. (1968) Op. cit., (p. 309).
15. (1968) Op. cit., (pp. 345–6).
16. (1921) Op. cit., (p. 65).
17. (1861) *Industrial Biography, Iron Workers and Tool Makers.* (p. 294).
18. PEP (1965) *Thrusters and Sleepers* (p. 265).
19. (1963) *Challenge to Affluence.*

20. 'Science and Society', *Science Journal*, Vol. 5A, No. 4 (October 1969).
21. *Guardian*, 23 March 1971.
22. *Guardian*, 3 May 1971.
23. (1972) Cmnd 5032.
24. 'Pathos of Development', *New Left Review* No. 36, 1966. Reprinted in Shanin, T. (ed.) (1971) *Peasants and Peasant Societies* (pp. 414/5).

Chapter 12
1. 'Is Britain being threatened by overpopulation?' *Listener*, 27 July 1967.
2. Letter. *The Lancet*, 17 April 1971.
3. 'Why fewer babies mean slower growth'. *Observer*, 23 May 1971.
4. Letter, *Guardian*, 24 January 1968.
5. (1959) *Demography*.
6. 'What is Profit' *The Accountant*, 22 July 1971.

Chapter 13
1. (1848) *Principles of Political Economy* (p. 100).
2. Anonymous reviewer of *Population Growth and Land Use*, 15 July 1967.
3. (1971) *The Population Explosion . . . an Interdisciplinary Approach* (p. 94).
4. Hunter, N. (1937) *Professor Branestawm's Treasure Hunt*.
5. Seldon and Pennance (1965) *Everyman's Dictionary of Economics*.
6. Seldon and Pennance, op. cit.
7. (1942) *What Happened in History* (p. 199).
8. (1776) *The Wealth of Nations* (Chapter 1).
9. Seldon and Pennance, op. cit.
10. Robinson, E. A. G. (ed.) (1963) *The Economic Consequences of the Size of Nations* (page xviii).

Chapter 14
1. Letter to Sir David Renton, published in pamphlet form in 1967.
2. (1798) *Principles*, Bk. 2, Ch. 1, Section 2.
3. (1844) *Critique of Political Economy*.
4. (1943) *Capitalism, Socialism, and Democracy* (p. 114).
5. (1965) op. cit.
6. (1920) *The Polish Peasant in Europe and America*.
7. (1949) *Social Theory and Social Structure*.

Chapter 15
1. (1952) *The Geography of Hunger* (p. 260).
2. (1961) *Mater et Magistra* (para. 189).
3. *New Statesman*, 14 May 1965.
4. Editorial, *Science Journal*, January 1965.
5. 'The Expansion of Scientific Knowledge'. Chapter in Albertson and Barnett (eds) (1972) *Managing the Planet* (p. 143).
6. Reported in the FAO review *Ceres*, Vol. 1 No. 5, September/October 1968 (p. 53).
7. (1970) Starvation or Plenty? (p. 53).
8. 'Too Much Food?' *Lloyds Bank Review* No. 95, January 1970.
9. Paddock (1967) *Famine—1975! America's Decision; Who Will Survive?;* Borgstrom (1967) *The Hungry Planet;* Ehrlich (1972) *Population Resources, Environment.*
10. A World Agricultural Plan, *Scientific American*, 223, No. 2, August 1970.
11. 'The World's Food Supplies', *J. Royal Statistical Society* 192, Pt. 2, 1966.
12. (1969) *The Hungry Future.*
13. (1968) *Born to Hunger* (p. 2–3).
14. Miriam Dludu, Goedgegun Central School. Quoted in *Oxfam News*, January 1966.
15. Reported in *Population Crisis*, the Washington Newsletter issued by the Population Crisis Committee, June 1968 (italics added).

Chapter 16
1. (1817) *The Principles of Political Economy and Taxation.*
2. (1848) *Critique of Political Economy.*
3. (1820) *Of Population.*
4. (1961) *Mater et Magistra.*
5. *Economists, Scientists, and Environmental Catastrophe.* Inaugural lecture, University College, London, 24 May 1972.
6. (1972) *The Politics of the environment.* Fabian pamphlet.
7. See Southwood, T. R. E. 'The Environmental Complaint . . . etc'. *Biologist,* 19, No. 2, May 1972.
8. (1971) *A social democratic Britain.* Fabian pamphlet.
9. Freeman, C. 'Malthus With a Computer'. Ch. 1 in *The Limits to Growth Controversy*, a special issue of *Futures*, 5, No. 1, February 1972. Published in book form later.
10. Meadows and Meadows have themselves made a further contribution to the debate. See their *Toward Global Equilibrium* (1973).

11. 'Global Effects of Increased Use of Energy'. Paper presented before the Fourth Conference on the Peaceful Uses of Atomic Energy, Geneva, 7 September 1971 (Copy kindly supplied by author).
12. 'No overdrafts on the energy economy'. *New Scientist 58* No. 846, 17 May 1973.
13. 'Thermal Limits to World Energy Use'. Mimeo, to be published in the *Bulletin of the Atomic Scientists* (Copy kindly supplied by authors).
14. 'How many people can the world support?' Reprinted Conservation Society Reprints. Vol. 1. October, 1968.
15. (1957) *Man and Materialism* (pp. 136–7).
16. Isaac Asimov, apparently unaware of Hoyle's earlier work, has recently redone this calculation for the present higher growth rate and his time is down to 4,860 years. It would take 470 years to convert earth's whole animal biomass to human flesh, and only 1,580 years to convert the total mass of the earth. 'The End', *Penthouse*, 5, No. 10, January 1971.
17. This theme is developed at greater length than there is space for here, in a monograph under the same name published by the Conservation Trust of the Conservation Society in 1975.
18. (1967).
19. BBC 2, 23 September 1972.
20. (1938/1970).
21. *Guardian*, 19 May 1971.
22. (1972) *The Doomsday Syndrome* (pp. 18–19 and 226).

Chapter 17
1. (1848) *Principles of Political Economy.*
2. 'The Historical Roots of Our Ecological Crisis', *Science 155*, 1205, 1967.
3. 'The Strategy of Ecosystem Development'. *Science*, 16, 1969.
4. World Population and Food Supplies. E/CONF 60/CBP/19, 22 March 1974.
5. (1974) *The Freedom of the Press.*
6. (1971) *Low Intensity Operations.*

Bibliography

Adler, J. H. 'Poverty Amidst Wealth'. BBC 3rd Programme, 10 March 1969.

American President's Science Advisory Cttee. Panel on World Food Supply.

Anon, Reviewer of Clark, C. (1967) op cit. *The Economist*, 15 July 1967.

Asimov, Isaac. 'The End'. *Penthouse*, 5, No. 10, January 1971.

Bacon, Sir Francis (i) (1597) Essay XXIX. 'Of the True Greatness of Kingdoms and Estates'. *Essays*.

    (ii) (1597) Essay XV. 'Of Seditions and Troubles'. *Essays*.

Ballard, J. G. (1962) *The Drowned World*.

Barber, Anthony. Reported *Guardian*, 19 May 1971.

Beckerman, W. (i) Economists, Scientists and Environmental Catastrophe. *Inaugural Lecture*, University College, London, 24 May 1972.

    (ii) (1974) *In Defence of Economic Growth*.

    (iii) 'Controversy'. BBC TV, 23 September 1972.

Benjamin, B. (1968) *Health and Vital Statistics*.

Blaxter, K. L. 'The Animal Harvest'. *Science Journal*, May 1968.

Boerma, A. H. (i) 'A World Agricultural Plan'. *Scientific American* 223, No, August 1970.

    (ii) Foreword. *FAO Annual Review. The State of Food and Agriculture 1972*.

Borlaug, Norman. Reported in *Population Crisis*, Washington Newsletter of the Population Crisis Committee, June 1968.

Borgstrom, G. (i) (1967) *The Hungry Planet*.

    (ii) (1969) *Too Many: A Story of the Earth's Biological Limitations*.

Bowen, I. (1966) *Population*.

Boyd-Orr, Lord. Guest Editorial. *Science Journal*, May 1968.

Boyko, H. 'Farming in the Desert'. *Science Journal*, May 1968.

Branestawm, Professor. See Hunter, N.

Bray, Jeremy. (1972) *The Politics of the Environment*.

British Humanist Association (1972) *People First*.

Burke, E. Letter to the National Assembly.

Cairncross, Frances. 'Why Fewer Babies mean Slower Growth'. *Observer*, 23 May 1971.

Carroll, Lewis. (1865) *Alice's Adventures in Wonderland.*

Chambers and Mingay. (1966) *The Agricultural Revolution 1750–1880.*

Chapman, Peter. 'No Overdrafts on the Energy Economy'. *New Scientist*, 58, No. 846, 17 May 1973.

Chesser, E. (1971) *Love without Fear.*

Childe, Gordon. (1948) *The Ancient World.*

Chinese Delegation, Stockholm Conference (1972).

Cicero. (106–43 BC) De officiis.

Clark, C. (i) (1951) *The Conditions of Economic Progress.*
      (ii) (1967) *Population Growth and Land Use.*
      (iii) 'Too Much Food?' *Lloyds Bank Review*, No. 95, January 1970.

Cole, H. S. D. (ed) (1973) *Thinking about the Future: A Critique of 'Limits to Growth'.*

Commoner, B. (1972) *The Closing Circle.*

Connell, K. H. (1950) *The Population of Ireland.*

Conservation Society, S. Bucks Branch. See Musson, C.

Cox, H. (1922) *The Problem of Population.*

Cox, P. R. (1959) *Demography.*

Crosland, Anthony. (1971) *A Social Democratic Britain.*

Coulton, C. G. (1938) *Social Life in Britain from the Conquest to the Reformation.*

Daily Mail. Survey. January 1972. See National Opinion Polls.

Davis, Kingsley. (1949) *Human Society.*

Deane, P. and Cole. (1964) *British Economic Growth, 1668–1959.*

Deevey, E. S. 'The Human Population'. *Sc. Amer.*, September 1960.

de Castro, J. (1952) *The Geography of Hunger.*

de Jouvenel, B. (1967) *Essay on the Art of Conjecture.*

de Solla Price, D. 'The Expansion of Scientific Knowledge'. In Albertson, P. and Barnett, M. (eds.) (1972) *Managing the Planet.*

Devlin, Polly. 'Happy Families'. *New Statesman*, 20 May 1966.

Dix, Arthur. See US. Committee on Public Information.

Dludu, Miriam. Save the Children Fund Essay on school lunches. Reported in *Oxfam News*, January 1966.

Douglas, J. W. B. (1964) *The Home and the School.*
    ,,   and Blomfield. (1958) *Children Under Five.*

Duggan, M. 'Birth Under Control'. *Church Times*, 9 October 1970.

Dumbartonshire Joint Probation Committee. Private communication.

Dumont and Rosier. (1969) *The Hungry Future.*

Durkheim, E. (1957) *Suicide*.
Duverger, M. (1966) *The Idea of Politics*.
Edward III. Statutes; 1349, 1350 and 1351.
Ehrlich, P. and A. (1970 and 1972) *Population, Resources, Environment*.
Eliot, T. S. (1944) Burnt Norton. In *The Four Quartets*.
Engels, F. (1844) *Critique of Political Economy*.
Eversley, D. E. C. 'Is Britain being threatened by over-population?' *The Listener*, 27 July 1967.
Everyman's. (1965) *Dictionary of Economics*.
Fairlie, H. 'Still time to think again on hanging'. *Sunday Telegraph*, 3 January 1965.
FAO. *Annual Review*.
    Production Yearbook (1972).
    Review, *Ceres*, Vol. 1, No. 5, September/October 1968.
Field, *et al*. See HMSO.
Flinn, M. W. (1962) *An Economic and Social History of Britain, 1066–1939*.
Freeman, C. 'Malthus with a Computer'. In 'The Limits to Growth Controversy'. *Futures*, 5, No. 1, February 1972. (Published in book form later.) See Cole, H. S. D.
Fremlin, J. H. 'How many people can the world support? *New Scientist*, 29 October 1964. Reprinted *Conservation Society Reprints*, Vol. 1, October 1968.
Gabor, D. (1963) *'Inventing the Future'*.
Geary, R. C. (1950) *Irish Economic Development Since 1921*.
George, Henry. (1897) *Progress and Poverty*.
Gittings, John. 'Mao's hand to land army'. *Guardian*, 3 May 1971.
Glenday, R. (1944) *The Future of Economic Society*.
Godwin, Wm. (1820) *Of Population*.
Gregory, Dick. 'My Answer to Genocide'. *Ebony*, October, 1971.
Halbwachs, M. (1960) *Population and Society*.
Hales-Took, Anne. The Neurotic Society. *Guardian*, 13 February, 1963.
Haley, Sir Wm. (1974) *The Freedom of the Press*.
Haney, L. H. (1920) *History of Economic Thought*.
Hawthorne, G. (1973) *Population Policy: a modern delusion*.
Hill, C. (1969) *Reformation to Industrial Revolution*.
Heenan, Cardinal. Speech, 10 November 1973. Catholic Information Office of England and Wales.
HMSO. *Annual Abstract of Statistics*.
HMSO. (1968) *Britain, an Official Handbook*.
HMSO. (1967) *Circumstances of Families*.

HMSO. Department of Employment Gazette.

HMSO. (1947) *Economic Survey.* Cmnd 7046.

HMSO. (1971) *Family Intentions.* See Woolf, Myra.

HMSO. Field, *et al.* (1971) *13 year-old Approved School Boys.*

HMSO. (1971) *First Report from the Select Committee on Science and Technology. Population of the UK.*

HMSO. (1963) Half Our Future, etc. The Newsom Report.

HMSO. Hansard. 1 July 1964.

HMSO. (Annual) *Planning Applications.*

HMSO. (1971) *Population of the United Kingdom.*

HMSO. (1972) *Population Projections 1970–2010.*

HMSO. (1973) *Report of the Population Panel.*

HMSO. (1949) *Report of the Royal Commission on Population.* Cmnd. 7695.

HMSO. (1971) *Robens Report.* Cmnd. 5032.

Hobbes, Thos. (1551) *Leviathan.*

Hogg, Q. (Lord Hailsham). (1947) *The Case for Conservatism.*

Hopcraft, Arthur. (1968) *Born to Hunger.*

Hoselitz, B. F. (1960) *Sociological Aspects of Economic Growth.*

Houghton, Douglas (Baron Houghton of Sowerby). Speech on large families. See Ch. 7 Note 4.

Hoyle, Fred. (i) (1957) *The Black Cloud.*
     (ii) (1957) *Man and Materialism.*

Hughes, D. R. Letter to *The Times,* 20 April 1964.

Huizinga, J. (1938/1970) *Homo Ludens.*

Hunter, N. (1937) *Professor Branestawm's Treasure Hunt.*

Huntingdon, E. (1945) *Mainsprings of Civilisation.*

Hutchinson, Sir J. (i) 'Land and Human Population'. *The Listener,* 1 September 1966.
     (ii) (ed.). (1969 *Population and Food Supply.*

Illich, Ivan. (1974) *Energy and Equity.*

Inge, W. R. (1949) *The End of an Age.*

Inner London Education Authority (ILEA). Research Committee. Private Communication.

International Conference on Economic Development. Cambridge, 1968. See Shanin, T.

International Economic Association. See Robinson, E. A. G.

International Encyclopaedia of Social Sciences. Section on Demography and Population Genetics for data on effective breeding communities.

International Planned Parenthood Federation (IPPF). Medical Bulletin 2.

Japanese Government. Bulletin before Pearl Harbour. Quoted by Bertrand Russell in Mudd, S. (1964) *The Population Crisis and the Use of World Resources.*

John, Pope, 23rd. (1961) *Mater et Magistra.*

Johnson, C. G. (ed.). (1965) *The Biological Significance of Climatic Changes in Britain.*

Johnson, Dr Saml. See Halbwachs.

Jones, K. and Smith, A. D. (1970) *The Economic Impact of Commonwealth Immigration.*

Jones, L. H. 'What is Profit?' *The Accountant*, 22 July 1971.

Keyfitz, N. 'On the momentum of population growth'. *Demography*, 8 (1971).

Kitson, Brig. F. (1971) *Low Intensity Operations.*

Knowles, L. C. A. (1921) *Industrial & Commercial Revolutions in Gt. Britain during the 19th Century.*

Kuznets, S. (1966) *Modern Economic Growth.*

Lamb, J. H. See Johnson, C. G. (ed.)

Larousse. (1966) *Encyclopaedia of Astronomy.*

Leach, Gerald. 'Biological Backlash'. A series of three programmes on the BBC. 7, 15, 22 March 1967.

Lewis, W. A. (9th impression 1970) *Theory of Economic Growth.*

Long, Walter. Local Government Board, Statement by. See Cox, H.

Lotka, A. J. (1956) *Elements of Mathematical Biology.*

Lovins, Amory. 'Thermal Limits to World Energy Use'. (See Ch. 13, Note 13.)

Maddox, J. (1972) *The Doomsday Syndrome.*

Malthus, T. R. (1798) *Essay on the Principle of Population.*

Marlow, B. (1968) *Charting the British Economy.*

Marshall, A. (1930) *Principles of Economics.*

Marx, Karl. (1867/1885) *Capital.*

McClelland, D. (1961) *The Achieving Society.*

McGregor, W. R. Private communication.

McMahon, *et al.* (1960) *Epidemiologic Methods.*

Meadows and Meadows (i) (1972) *Limits to Growth.*
                      (ii) (1973) *Toward Global Equilibrium.*

Merton, R. (1949) *Social Theory and Social Structure.*

Mill, J. S. (1848) *Principles of Political Economy.*

Millard, P. H. Letter to *The Lancet*, 17 April 1971.

Muggeridge, M. 'Backward Christian Soldiers'. *New Statesman*, 14 May 1965.

Mumford, L. (1934) *Technics and Civilisation.*

Munn, A. P. Letter to *The Times*, 13 April 1964.

Musson, C. (1972) Population Survey. Limited printing.

Myers, W. M. Reported in *Population Crisis*, the newsletter of the Population Crisis Committee, June 1968.

Myrdal, G. (1963) *Challenge to Affluence.*

National Opinion Polls (NOP) jointly with the *Daily Mail.* Surveys January 1972 and December 1972.

New Society. Survey report 18 January 1973.

Newsom Report. (1963) See HMSO. 'Half Our Future'. Report of the Central Advisory Council for Education (England).

New Statesman. Editorial. 29 April 1966.

O'Brien, B. W. *et al.* (1951) *Readings in General Sociology.*

Odum, E. P. 'The Strategy of Ecosystem Development'. *Science*, 164, pp. 262–270, 1969.

Office of Health Economics. (1967) *Malnutrition in the 1960s.*

Ogburn, W. F. See O'Brien, B. W. *et al.*

Okazaki, Y. (1966) *Population, Education and Economic Development.*

Open University. (1971) *The Population Explosion . . . an Interdisciplinary Approach.*

Paddock and Paddock. (1967) *Famine 1975! America's Decision: Who Will Survive?*

Parliamentary Select Cttee. on Science & Technology. See HMSO.

Parsons, Jack (i) Optimum Population. In Burton, J., (Intro.) 1971 *The Pollution of Our Environment.* Proc. Liberal Party Conference, London, 1970.

(ii) 'Population Policies'. *LASER*, No. 27, June 1971.

(iii) (1971) *Population Versus Liberty.*

(iv) (1972) *Population. The Liberals Reply.* Pamph.

(v) 'Population and Health'. *Health and Social Services Journal*, 10 March 1973.

(vi) 'Population and the Quality of Life. *J. Royal Society of Arts*, June 1974.

(vii) 'When breeding becomes a competitive weapon'. *The Times Special Report*, 19 August 1974.

(viii) Review. Beckerman, W. (1974) *In Defence of Economic Growth, New Humanist*, October 1974.

(ix) (1975) *The Economic Transition.* A monograph of the Conservation Trust.

(x) 'Population Control: Some Facts & Assumptions'. In Holmes, N. J. (ed.). (1976). *The Environment and the Industrial Society.*

(xi) 'Doctors and Demography'. In Elder, M. G. and Hawkins (in press) *Control of Fertility.*

268

Paul VI, Pope. Speech. Reported: (i) *Osservatore Romano*, and
(ii) *Guardian*, 18 September
1969.
Pearl, R. and Reed, L. J. *Proc. Natl. Acad. Sci.*, Vol. 6, 1920.
Reported by Lotka, q.v.
Peel, J. and Potts. (1969) *Contraceptive Practice*.
PEP. (i) (1955) *World Population and Resources*.
(ii) 1965) *Thrusters and Sleepers*.
Petersen, W. (1964) *The Politics of Population*.
Petty, Sir Wm. (1960) *Political Arithmetick*.
Polanyi, G. 'The Use & Abuse of Economic Statistics'. In Marlow,
B. (1968) *Charting the British Economy*.
Population Stabilization Group. (1973). *Over-population, It's Costing
Us the Earth*.
Population Reference Bureau. Washington DC. *Annual Population
Data Sheet*.
Pyke, Magnus. BBC talk. Home Service, 20 September 1965.
Rainwater, Lee. (1965) *Family Design: Marital Sexuality, Family Size
and Contraception*.
Ravenholt, Ray. 'World Epidemiology and Potential Fertility
Impact of Voluntary Sterilisation Services'. A paper presented
to the Third International Conference on Voluntary Sterilisa-
tion. Tunis. 2 February 1976.
Renton, Sir David. (1967) Exchange of letters with the Prime
Minister, Mr Harold Wilson.
Richardo, David. (1817) *On the Principles of Political Economy and
Taxation*.
Robens, Lord. See HMSO, Cmnd. 5032.
Robinson, E. A. G. (ed.). (1963) *The Economic Consequences of the Size
of Nations*.
Robinson, Joan. (1962) *Economic Philosophy*.
Robbins, Althea. Letter to *The Guardian*, 28 June 1967.
Roman Catholic Encyclopaedia. (1907).
Ross Panel. See HMSO.
Rostow, W. W. (i) (2nd edition 1971) *The Stages of Economic
Growth*.
(ii) (1971) *Politics and the Stages of Growth*.
Rousseau, J. J. (1762) *The Social Contract*.
Sauvy, A. (1961) *Fertility and Survival*.
Science Policy Research Unit, Sussex University. See Cole, H. S. D.
Schmookler, Jacob. (1966) *Invention and Economic Growth*.
Schumpeter, J. (1943) *Capitalism, Socialism and Democracy*.

Scott, Professor. Reported *The Guardian*, 23 March 1971.

Seldon, A. and Pennance. (1965) *Everyman's Dictionary of Economics.*

Shanin, T. (ed.). (1971) *Peasants and Peasant Societies.*

Shepherd, Lord. 253 (1974) Ministerial statement on UK Population at Bucharest.

Silver, S. 'Science & Society'. *Science Journal*, Vol. 5A, No. 4, October 1969.

Sklair, Leslie. (1970) *The Sociology of Progress.*

Small, Albion W. (1969) *The Cameralists: The Pioneers of German Social Policy.* B. Franklin reprint.

Smiles, Saml. (1863) *Industrial Biography, or Iron Workers and Tool Makers.*

Smith, Adam. (1776) *The Wealth of Nations.*

Smith, J. Maynard. In 'Biological Backlash'. BBC. See Leach, G.

Sorokin, P. A. (i)   (1928) *Contemporary Sociological Theories.*
              (ii)   (1957) *Social and Cultural Dynamics.*
              (iii) (1950) *A Study of American Good Neighbours and Christian Saints. Altruistic Love.*

Southwood, T. R. E. 'The Environmental Complaint'. *Biologist*, 19, No. 2 May 1972.

Spencer, H. (1893) *Principles of Sociology*, Vol. 3, 3rd edition (p. 599).

Spengler, O. (1929) *The Decline of the West.*

Stapledon, Olaf. (1930) *Last and First Men.*

St John Stevas, Norman. Radio Discussion. 'Out of this week'. BBC. 25 July 1969.

Sukhatme, P. V. 'The World's Food Supplies'. *Journal of the Royal Statistical Society*, 192, Pt. 2, 1966.

Tawney, R. H. (1926) *Religion and the Rise of Capitalism.*

Thoday, J. M. 'The Problem!' In Hutchinson, Sir J. (ed.) (1969) *Population and Food Supply.*

Thirlwell, A. P. 'The Development Gap'. *Nat. Westminster Bank Review*, February 1970.

Thomas, W. I. and Znaniecki, (1920) *The Polish Peasant in Europe and America.*

Thomlinson, R. (1965) *Population Dynamics.*

Thompson, E. P. (1968) *The Making of the English Working Class.*

Thompson and Lewis. (1965) *Population Problems.*

Titmus, R. (1957) *Essays on the Welfare State.*

Todd, Lord. Editorial. *Science Journal.* January 1965.

Toynbee, Arnold. (1972) *A Study of History.*

United Arab Republic (UAR). (1962) National Charter.

UNO. Ecological Undermining of the World Food Econ. In *World Population and Food Supplies*. E/conf/60/CBP/19, 22 March 2974.

UNO. E/Conf/65/Prep/6, 8 May 1974.

UNO. Preparatory Committee of the World Food Conf. *Preliminary Assessment of the World Food Situation. Present and Future.* April, 1974.

UNO. Secretary General. *Problems of the Human Environment.* 26 May 1969.

US Cttee. on Public Information, (1918) *Conquest and Kultur.*

U Thant. Statement as Secretary General of the UN. Reported in *People First*. British Humanist Association, 1972.

Velikovsky, I. (1950/1972) *Worlds in Collision.*

Verhulst, P. F. See Lotka, A. J.

Von Bernhardi. See US Committee on Public Information.

Von Loen. See Small, Albion W.

Walford, Cornelius. (1879/1970) *Famines of the World; Past and Present.*

Walley, Sir John. Letter to the *Guardian*, 24 January 1968.

Weber, Max. (1930) The Protestant Ethic and the Spirit of Capitalism.

Wedge, P. *et al.* 'Weighing Children'. *New Society*, 1 June 1972.

Weinberg, A. M. and Hammond, R. P. 'Global Effects of Increased Use of Energy'. See Ch. 16, Note 11.

White, Lynn. 'The Historical Roots of our Ecological Crisis'. *Science*, 155, 1205, 1967.

Wilson, (Sir) Harold. Letter to Sir David Renton (see Renton).

Wirth, Albrecht. See US Cttee. on Public Information.

Wolf, E. R. 'On Peasant Rebellions'. In Shanin, T. (ed.). (1971) *Peasants and Peasant Societies.*

Woolf, Myra. (1972) *Family Intentions.* (HMSO.)

Wootton, B. (1959) *Social Science and Social Pathology.*

Wynne-Edwards, V. C. (1962) *Animal Dispersion in Relation to Social Behaviour.*

Name Index

Subject Index

division of labour, 137, 158
  in British Army, 195
  and econs. of scale, 194
  in history, 194
  in pin-making, 195
'drive for maturity', the, 139
drop-outs, 176, 290
drought, 34
Dumbartonshire Joint Probation Committee, 94
dust bowls, 111

earth
  carrying capacity for population, 231
  escape velocity, 70
  fertility of, 30
  finiteness of, 60, 96, 100, 198, 207,
    219, 220, 226, 230, 245, 248
  infiniteness of, 100
  and space travel, 67
  stability of, 29, 32
ecology(ical)
  balance, 36
  conscience, 250
  imperatives in space
  of liberty, 62
economic(s)
  arguments summarised, *247–250*
  decline and social unrest, 252
  depression and falling birth rate, 15
  goods for non-goods, 239
  justice, 229
  as revealed truth, 222
  self-interest, 137
  survey, the, 160
  take-off, 139
  transition, the, *233–242*
  want v. demand, *199–202*
economic growth
  and anomie, *240–241*, 248
  'autonomous' v. 'induced', 141
  and the 'burden of dependency',
    184–187
  case for, *227–229*
  costs of, 149, 225, 228
  'disturbing factors' in, 139
  doublings, 229
  as explosion, 248
  five basic (MIT) limits to, 222
  implications of different rates, 229
  international comparison, 141, 149
  idea of limits misleading, 227

  limits on, 207, 227, *Ch. 16*
  and Marx, 138
  as morbid goal, *239–241*
  moral limits to, 235, 249
  need for caution, 230
  obsession with, 248
  opposition to, 227
  preconditions for, 139, 203
  and population growth (*Ch. 10*), 128,
    138
  a child's pocket money, 235
  as precondition for social justice, 228
  as rallying cry, 257
  saturation point, *232–240*
  and social change, 153
  stages of, 139
  targets for, 182
  theories of, *137–145*
  UK rates of, 228
  unlimited, 221, 222, 227
  without population growth, 136
economies
  eight basic types of, 141
  of scale and population size, 148,
    (*Ch. 13*)

families, large (*Ch. 7*)
  argument summarised, 246
  defined, 74
  and eugenics, 78, 79
  as irresponsible, 76
  and politics, 75, 76
  and productivity, 78
  and racialism, 77
  and religion, 77
  and social class, 77, 79
families, single parent, 91
family planning. See birth control.
family size
  completed. UK. *43–46*
  decline in, 92
  expected, UK, 45
  ideal, 45 and wealth, 45
  mean, 75
  need for Govt to reduce, 6, 79, 96
  replacement size, 118
  replacement size studies, *46–47*, 118
  and social class, 77, 87
  and social climate, 15, 118
  and suicide, 80
  unrelated to social need, 7
famine, 31, 146, 147, 163, 225, 251